Politics of Anxiety

Politics of Anxiety

Edited by
Emmy Eklundh, Andreja Zevnik and
Emmanuel-Pierre Guittet

ROWMAN &
LITTLEFIELD
─────INTERNATIONAL
London • New York

Published by Rowman & Littlefield International Ltd
Unit A, Whitacre Mews, 26–34 Stannary Street, London SE11 4AB
www.rowmaninternational.com

Rowman & Littlefield International Ltd. is an affiliate of Rowman & Littlefield

4501 Forbes Boulevard, Suite 200, Lanham, Maryland 20706, USA
With additional offices in Boulder, New York, Toronto (Canada), and Plymouth (UK)
www.rowman.com

Selection and editorial matter © 2017 Emmy Eklundh, Andreja Zevnik and Emmanuel-Pierre Guittet

Copyright in individual chapters is held by the respective chapter authors.

All rights reserved. No part of this book may be reproduced in any form or by any electronic or mechanical means, including information storage and retrieval systems, without written permission from the publisher, except by a reviewer who may quote passages in a review.

British Library Cataloguing-in-Publication Data
A catalogue record for this book is available from the British Library

ISBN: HB 978-1-7834-8990-9

Library of Congress Cataloging-in-Publication Data Is Available

ISBN: 978-1-78348-990-9 (cloth : alk. paper)
ISBN: 978-1-78348-992-3 (electronic)

∞™ The paper used in this publication meets the minimum requirements of American National Standard for Information Sciences—Permanence of Paper for Printed Library Materials, ANSI/NISO Z39.48–1992.

Printed in the United States of America

Contents

Acknowledgements — vii

1 Introduction: The Politics of Anxiety — 1
Emmy Eklundh, Emmanuel-Pierre Guittet and Andreja Zevnik

PART I: POLITICISING ANXIETY — 15

2 For Want of Not: Lacan's Conception of Anxiety — 17
J. Peter Burgess

3 When Does Repression Become Political? The Use of the Language of Trauma in the Context of Violence and Anxiety — 37
Henrique Tavares Furtado

PART II: SECURITY: CONTROL — 59

4 Anxiety: Trauma: Resilience — 61
Mark Neocleous

5 The New Age of Suspicion — 79
Emmanuel-Pierre Guittet and Fabienne Brion

6 The Effects of Uncertainty: Anxiety and Crisis Preparedness — 101
Carsten Baran

PART III: RESISTANCE: RECLAIMING 121

7 The Politics of Anxiety and the Rise of Far-Right
  Parties in Europe 123
  Norma Rossi

8 Indignation as Resistance: Beyond the Anxiety of No Future
  Alternatives 141
  Paolo Cossarini

9 Neurotic Neoliberalism and the Economics of Anxiety 165
  Japhy Wilson

PART IV: EPILOGUE 189

10 Sovereign Anxiety and Baroque Politics 191
   Michael Dillon

Index 221

Author Biographies 231

Acknowledgements

Anxiety seems to feature more and more strongly in current political and social debates. No longer being only a private experience of the individual, anxiety permeates populations, societies, states and global orders. Social and political practices aim to limit the impact of anxiety on our everyday lives as well as embrace and prolong this anxious state. This volume tackles through its contributions a variety of ways in which anxiety is understood and practiced.

This volume is a result of the research project entitled *Politics in Times of Anxiety* that was led by Andreja Zevnik, Emmanuel-Pierre Guittet and Emmy Eklundh at the University of Manchester. We were also very lucky to have the support of the *Critical Global Politics Cluster* in the Politics department throughout the project.

The volume has benefitted from the input, support and comments of many people and institutions, and it is a pleasure to acknowledge our debts to them. The University of Manchester provided invaluable support in many regards, without which this volume would not have been possible. The initial project *Politics in Times of Anxiety* received financial support of the University of Manchester's *Faculty of Humanities Strategic Fund* and from the logistical support of the University of Manchester's Politics Discipline Area. When the idea for this book emerged, we were all active members of this department and its vibrant and lively atmosphere. Special thanks go to the members of the *Critical Global Politics Research Cluster*: Aoileann Ni Mhurchu, Elena Barabantseva, Henrique Tavares Furtado, Rachel Massey, Cristina Masters, Laura McLeod, Peter Lawler, Will Palmer, Veronique Pin-Fat, Thom Tyerman and Maja Zehfuss. We also gratefully acknowledge our colleagues at the Politics Discipline Area for support, advice and sometimes a much-needed sense of direction: Greig Charnock, Carl Death, Andrew Russell,

Stuart Shields, Nick Turnbull and Japhy Wilson. We would like to thank the Department of European and International Studies at King's College London, as well as the Politics Department at the Université Saint-Louis (Belgium) for their support and intellectual inspiration. They both welcomed the book project with enthusiasm and provided time and support to complete it.

The majority of the contributions were presented at the project conference[1] in July 2014, where the idea for this volume also emerged. For very provoking, invigorating and entertaining discussions held during these three days and subsequent comments, criticisms and suggestions, we would like to thank Zygmunt Bauman, Didier Bigo, Michael Dillon, Costas Douzinas and Elena Loizidou. Many of our colleagues read parts or all of this work, and our appreciation goes to them for the many conversations, comments and feedback.

We have been privileged to work with this group of contributing authors who have all generously given their time to produce these chapters, and have shown patience and enthusiasm throughout the production of the volume. Their encouragements and remarkable skills to keep to the deadline are greatly appreciated.

There are many others who played an important, yet not all that visible, role in the preparation of this book or who have angered us enough to begin thinking about this project. We are also exceptionally lucky to be part of some truly special relationships and share our everyday life with amazing individuals who never cease to surprise and inspire. Neither of us could do without them. We acknowledge the debt to our partners and families for having to put up with us while we focused all too much attention on this work.

For the invaluable help and support we would also like to thank Anna Reeve (who has now left the publishers), and Dhara Patel and Michel Watson at Rowman and Littlefield International. They were a pleasure to work with as they helped us travel the distance from a manuscript to a book.

Finally, this volume is more than just an exposition of anxiety in the field of politics. Hopefully it will also serve as a provocative statement as to how we need and should think anew about contemporary politics. We hope this intervention will incite and foster further debate. The book is offered with this in mind.

NOTE

1. Please see the project website for more information: https://politicalhorizons.wordpress.com/politics-in-times-of-anxiety/.

Chapter 1

Introduction: The Politics of Anxiety

Emmy Eklundh,
Emmanuel-Pierre Guittet and
Andreja Zevnik

Over the past few years, anxiety has become central for the understanding of socio-political phenomena and community life. Ignited and reinforced, but not caused, by the financial crisis of 2008, our world seems more uncertain, more insecure and, indeed, more anxious than before. At least this is how we seem to perceive it. Several phenomena bear witness of this surge of uncertainty. Young people are now the first generation in a long time which will not gain better living standards than their parents. Across Europe and other continents, youth unemployment is rife, and access to basic living needs, such as housing or a stable income, is for many but a dream. Similarly, conflict and violence are constant in our environment, with serious intra- and inter-state conflicts in the Middle East, increased tensions in the EU's Eastern neighbourhood and several high-profile terrorist attacks on the European soil in the past years. All of this suffices to establish that many feel anxious about the world and about its future. Politics as we know it, with relative peace in Europe, with increased welfare provisions and with a stable party system, is increasingly challenged. The last few years have also seen the establishment of innumerous anti-establishment parties. Ranging from Front Nacional in France, UK Independence Party in Great Britain, Alternative fur Deutschland in Germany, Syriza in Greece and Podemos in Spain, these parties tell a story of discontent and frustration among the electorate, to the same degree as more favourably viewed left-wing political endeavours for a different politics.

As such, it can be concluded empirically that we live in anxious times, if anxious means an uncertainty about the future, and a present discomfort caused by this uncertainty. However, such a statement carries our focus into questions such as, what does anxiety mean, and how is it different from other accounts of political uncertainty?

These two questions summarise the main focus of this volume. It intends to explain to its reader, by referring to a range of empirical and contemporary examples, how what we refer to as a *logic of anxiety* can help us analytically disentangle the web of explanations available to assess contemporary political challenges. In doing so, it sketches a trail of politics which is not reliant on two of our more common narratives: the recurrence of cyclical capitalist crises, or the inevitability of increased control trying to secure the population.

IS IT ALL ABOUT CLASS?
MATERIALITY AND IMMATERIALITY

When taking stock on discussions which try to explain why our world has become more anxious, one often finds oneself choosing between two sides of political studies: the economic or the political. On the one side, structural economic explanations of discontent and anxiety are represented by critical theories of political economy, which have become very much in vogue since the 2008 financial crisis. Thinkers such as Guy Standing or David Harvey put forward a clear explanation as to why it is that we are facing this uncertainty: the presence of capitalist crises.[1] Anyone familiar with Marxist theory will recognise in contemporary times how capitalism eventually drives itself to its own ruin and that the process will indeed be painful but necessary.

Indeed, many are the merits and benefits of such a perspective. It is true that economic inequality is increasing and that the capitalist class seems to be getting richer and richer. Standing's account of a new political class, the precariat, aptly describes how the working class has shifted in its composition over the years. With the arrival of increasingly uncertain working conditions, such as being an Uber driver or a Deliveroo employee, many have found themselves belonging to a class of the working poor, where there is employment, but this employment cannot by any means cover the cost of living.

Although anti-capitalist approaches provide a clear analytical path for the analysis of contemporary unrest, one must question the possible limits or shortcomings of such a perspective. The contributions to this volume, although largely sympathetic to the explanatory power of Marxism, also recognise that alternative explanations are needed for a further understanding of the topic. Based on a post-material or post-Marxist ground, the contributions of this volume acknowledge the power of affect and emotions to explain social behaviour. Some would say that capitalism produces anxiety, but this volume describes how capitalism and anxiety revel in an intricate relationship which is neigh-on impossible to separate and, therefore, crucial to study.

As such, contrary to the material component of capitalism, this volume also recognises the ideational and less material aspect of anxiety. Importantly, the volume does not abide by a strong division between material and immaterial, discursive and non-discursive, as seen in the recent material turn of political studies.[2] Rather, the volume seeks to point to the ever-present interfaces and interjections between theory and practice, and material and immaterial.

This is highly relevant when it comes to anxiety. Some would argue that anxiety, as an emotion, can and should be controlled, or that it is not a driving force of social relations, merely a consequence thereof. This volume begs to differ with this statement. It does not recognise that material conditions are the sole drivers of social interactions, but that the social and political is constantly constituted and reconstituted through both material and immaterial planes. As such, the volume recognises that material conditions can indeed cause anxiety, but the relationship is mutually constitutive rather than a one-way street.

Recent works within the emotional and affective turns within international relations and social and cultural theory bear witness to this blurring of distinctions. No longer is the affective and the emotional supposed to be seen as negative components of political life (as argued by early theories of crowds, such as Canetti or Le Bon),[3] but they are in fact vital to all aspects of politics. Following on from the emotional turn in sociology in the early 1990s,[4] the affective turn has afterwards argued that both emotions – as a cognitivised version of our inner selves – and the very bodily sensations which are our daily experience are important to politics.[5] The sensation of anger, joy or discomfort is political, due to its direct connection and intrinsic relationship with anything we as political subjects say or do. As such, the relation between the corporeal (the material) and the cognitive (the immaterial) is if not reversed then at least muddled. Ruth Leys elegantly argues that previous literature within cultural and social theory has operated 'at once with a highly intellectualist or rationalist concept of meaning and an unexamined assumption that everything that is not "meaning" in this limited sense belongs to the body'.[6] Contrary to this perspective, this volume contends that anxiety – as a sensation, an emotion and a thought – prevails through all stages of being and must therefore be central for any political analysis. And with the understanding of anxiety as a logic conditioning the very existence of the political subject of modern politics further opens a new vista of research. That is one which studies anxiety as a co-constitutive element of who 'we' as political subjects are and in turn 'embraces' or aims to understand its effects rather than aims to overturn or overcome its effects. In other words, anxiety is here to stay.

At the centre of this reasoning lies a reconsideration of political subjectivity. As will be demonstrated in this volume, political subjects are indeed not only confined by structural constraints, such as security concerns or economic prudence, nor are they 'free' in the sense of complete autonomy. This volume rather tries to depict not only the constant compromise which anxiety imposes on political subjectivity but also the space for action which can be created through anxious states.

IS IT ALL ABOUT RISK? CHANGING TEMPORALITIES OF SECURITY

As we aim to show in this volume, the significance of anxiety stems from its operational and ordering logics. What exactly does this mean?

Since World War II, modern societies have progressively come closer to a perfectly countable and scientifically governed society whose future can be foreseen by eliminating knowable or predictable threats. This so-called risk society was based around the identification of danger, which when quantified as 'risk' was assigned ways by which it can be eliminated. In doing so, the 'risk society' not only eliminated danger but also took control of the individual's experience of fear. Ulrich Beck and Antony Giddens speak about risk society as a distinct practice of social order and governance.[7] In their account, the expert and scientific knowledge took over the social field, by quantifying every possible social situation – from the individuals' everyday lifestyle to community actions, state behaviour and risks imposed by external phenomena such as natural disasters and the environment. By knowing the risks, the individual and the community could make a number of informed choices, which, in turn, shaped, moulded and transformed their social and political everyday life in ways which would eliminate or considerably lower the risk. Such risk society was, on the one hand, an answer to individual and societal fears, while, on the other hand, it produced fear of things that were previously not regarded as threats. The logic of risk was, in a sense, omnipresent as it governed the subject's most intimate and private spheres, as well as grand strategies of national and international security. Such future-oriented logics of governance were, at its origins, conservative; instead of progress, the risk society relied on the maintenance of the status quo. The fear of violence and death was in the very centre of risk society and worked as a deterrent against any radical action. The status quo was, on the one hand, comforting and reassuring; on the other hand, it left little space for urges and desires for political change.

Similarly, the quantification of risk also incited fear and suspicion in the population. The threat from terrorism with a government's sanctioned degrees of the existing terror threat seems to be at the forefront of these calculations. After 9/11 the United States and the United Kingdom, for example, were known for their colour-coded terror alerts. Ranging from green to red, the colours were to represent the level of threat or the likelihood of a terror attack. The peculiarity of the scale was that it was consistently elevated at amber (one below red), thus denoting that a risk of a terror attack is high and very likely. Such daily assessment of danger had an effect on the society and its population. On the one end, society learnt to live by being constantly alert to the possibility of a terrorist attack, while on the other end, such an elevated state of risk became an everyday normal. The individual learnt how to cope with it or how to pay little to no attention to it, yet, with the help of daily reminders of 'report if you see anything suspicious', vigilant and suspicious. One could argue that such a management of a security threat paralysed the population into accepting the status quo and learning to live with (at least a perceived) greater threat to their everyday security, while, on the other end, also pushed the 'old' risk-focused governing practices towards those which not only aim to manage, but also trigger, anxieties.

The present times of anxiety – as contributions in this book aim to show – have changed this logic of operation. As seen on the example of a terror alert, it is important to note that while the logic of anxiety is not a break, but a logical continuation of societal logics of fear and risk, there are also several important differences between the two. If the risk society mainly aimed at addressing fear with a hope to maintain the status quo and a continuation of life as it was, anxiety offers no such reassurance. In other words, in times of anxiety, the quantifying logic of risk no longer holds. Here, the object of danger or fear is either absent/non-identifiable, or in such a proximity that no reassurance can be offered. Such a destabilising moment opens up a new political space, which is governed by different political strategies and subject to different mobilising forces. In its extreme form, anxiety is thus a response to the realisation that the government, the state, security agencies and insurance companies, despite their claims, do not know how to provide for the well-being of its communities, secure the everyday, and respond to the arising internal and external threats.

As such, the logic of anxiety replaces the future-oriented, yet status-quo driven, politics of the risk society. Instead, it offers a different political temporality, one which, while indeterminate, unpredictable and insecure, offers a return to politics par excellence, as opposed to politics as a technocratic procedural practice. What we mean by it is that while more terrifying and at times no doubt more exposed to authoritarian practices, the logic of anxiety can also lead to a positive change precisely because its politics is not one of the future but that of present. In a risk society, the individual had to become immunised against all possible social risks, dangers, diseases and even everyday processes. These posed dangers to the individual's ability to make rational and informed decisions, or to their emotional well-being, and therefore had to be subject to control. For example, this logic reached as far as one's love life, where dating sites or agencies actively promoted a safe way of 'falling in love'. That is, you 'fall in love' without the 'fall' (the fall being too disturbing for the everyday productivity of the individual). While perhaps banal, such practices of risk reduction aimed to immunise society from external dangers and unnecessary risk-takings. Such governing practices gave individuals and societies a sense of continuity, history and future, and it also bereaved that same future of the possibility of change. In the society governed by anxiety, those practices persist but the guarantee of their ever-delivering 'a sense of security', continuity or history diminished. Despite knowing the risks, being presented with the solutions, there is little guarantee that those solutions will deliver the expected outcome. This uncertainty is very much visible in the mainstream political discourse today – just think of campaigns for Brexit or the US presidential election of 2016. The discourse of apocalypse on the one end is juxtaposed to the discourse of experience and the ability to manage unpredictable situations. Yet the politics driven by data, evidence, facts or technocratic practices of governance is absent from both ends. Technocratic politics no longer appeals to voters and the general public; instead, this politics has been replaced by a character, emotion, a sense of belonging or unsubstantiated promises of a better, different world.

In addition, two major shifts in contemporary political reality have incited a change of perspective from risk to anxiety: for example, the Arab Spring and the revelations concerning mass surveillance and the abrogation of human rights and political freedoms in the name of the war on terror. The aftermath and the consequences of these two events began to chart a different political reality. Drawing from the two aforementioned political shifts the logic of anxiety works in two different, yet interconnected, logics.

THE TWO LOGICS OF ANXIETY: SECURITY AND RESISTANCE

The first logic aims to paralyse the subject, by exposing it to great, unknown, unpredictable dangers, which in turn makes them more prone to guidance and control. Joanna Bourke speaks of anxiety as a form of anaesthesia that penetrates into all pores of social and political life, with an aim to displace time.[8] That is, it fixates the existence of the subject in the present moment, while dismantling any dreams or illusions of a different/better future. In anxiety, existence is reduced to its bare form fighting for a survival in a present moment. Anxiety as a governing practice cancels political futures as seen in the society of fear. Instead of reassurance, it is panic or apocalyptic scenarios, driven by the proximity of the overwhelming fear, which face society.

The second logic is a mobilising force, which departs from a linear conception of time and breaks with the status quo – ordered and – negotiated future. While indeed paralysing in the moment of encounter with a particularly displacing event or danger, in time the individual or society finds a different imaginary with which they respond to the growing instability, danger or injustice. Instead of politics as a technocratic procedural practice, the new temporality draws on a hive of possibilities, multiplicity of choices, and actions influencing, shaping and producing the socio-political every day. While indeed lacking in 'assurance', anxiety liberates society from the present political institutions and technocratic governing practices, and returns the individual to the driving seat of politics.

The perception of time and space becomes displaced by the modes in which anxiety operates and changes the socio-political landscape. This also incites questions such as, is anxiety tied to a particular temporal framework, and is it a phenomenon of a modern/present world? Is it something everyone to a degree share, or does anxiety impact social classes differently and expose certain parts of society to greater vulnerability? As such, anxiety can be seen as the underlying logic for both phenomena; anxiety spurs both economic and political insecurities, but is not intrinsically bound to either of them. Anxiety feeds off any situation where there is uncertainty, and can be utilised for many different purposes.

As a governing strategy of security, anxiety can be seen as the extreme end of the risk society where subjects give away their personal freedoms, civil and political rights and human rights, for the promise of a better life in the future. Yet, is there a limit to the rights and privileges subjects are asked to give away? Are they seeing the coming of a better, more prosperous and secure future?

ANXIETY AND SECURITY – THE EXCESSIVE PRESENT

Anxiety represents a shift in the thinking about security and securitisation. If the object or the source of security (fear, risk or danger) was previously known, the anxious times incite a type of security which aims to police, deter or surveil the unknown, either through means of technology or through social capital. The unknown unknowns thus become a central practice of securitisation programmes. It is not *fear* which enables increased security measures, surveillance or practices of policing, but *anxiety* about the unknown threat. 'Abandon hope all ye who enter here', to paraphrase Dante, is a social condition distinct to politics of anxiety as a governing practice of security. That is, instead of perceiving a tangible threat, the anxious security practice works without knowing exactly what it is looking for. By controlling, surveilling, profiling and policing the socio-political sphere, it also constructs suspicious patterns, which it in turn pursues. Anxious security practices thus operate on the logics of milieus, algorithms, the sharing of data and the confiscation of individual's private information for the purposes of public security. They also justify their actions by the threat of a possible apocalypse that is no longer only a scenario, but a looming reality that is to come. Such highly instable, precarious and allegedly insecure times escalate public anxieties. Mechanisms of control, security or other governing practices channel these general senses of anxiety into particular threats, such as migration, radicalisation, war on terror, austerity and environment. For example, anxiety breaks with cosmopolitan culture and brings out, highlights and radicalises divisions between race, religion, ethnicity and nationality. The illusive idea of a foreigner becomes the ultimate product of anxiety, a political scapegoat and a driving force for nationalist political ends. In other words, anxious security practices aim to create a sense of safety by policing every pore of socio-political life, from national and international security, to risk, insurance, health, environment and so on. As such, the temporality of security shifts from securing the future, to focus solely on the insecure present, from tangible threats to an excess of possible insecure outcomes.

ANXIETY AND RESISTANCE – A LACK OF FUTURE

However, at a point when conditions of life hit a low, anxiety can transform from a paralysing to a mobilising force, from a controlling security practice to a practice of resistance. Mobilisation can take place at the back of the realisation that the Other, in the form of state authority, is flawed (the king is naked). When stripped of its knowledge, state authority and political institutions become delegitimised and are thus left bare. In response, political formations backed by an array of different social movements and civil actions can begin to counter the governing narratives, demanding and creating a change. Examples of such politics could be the recent upheavals in the Arab world or in southern Europe. Here, anxiety is a resistance practice: the anxious state is taken on and consciously – if not strategically – turned into resistance against governing structures. As such, anxiety as resistance signifies a double move. First, it rejects the previously mentioned governing or policing modes, which tried to create anxious states among the population. Second, it takes on this sense of anxiety in order to use that very motion to work against these oppressive structures, and to incite protest.

The most recent political embodiments of such anxious movements could be the *Indignados* in Spain and Greece, various occupation movements in Italy or in the United States or the hunger strikes of *sans papiers* throughout Europe. Furthermore, one can look at the protests, walkouts or die-ins, which have emanated at the back of police violence in the United States and which call for a return to the questions of race, ethnicity and class. In these upheavals the two sites of anxiety clash: the governing strategy aims to seek more radical reasons or threats which would deter individuals from action, whereas individuals grasp for more radical (but also innovative) actions.

Resistance as a response to anxiety of the moment delegitimises the political elites, while it often remains silent on the desired futures. In moments when individuals recognise that they count, and that there is another way, a sense of time is recovered. The lack of the future is what makes the resistance practice of the anxious moment powerful and what enabled existence of different political imaginaries.

OUTLINE OF VOLUME

The task of this volume is perfectly described by Peter Burgess. In his contribution to this volume he writes, 'The shift in our time from an experience of security threats as exogenous to our nation-state reality complex, toward a more reflexive, indigenous experience of danger mirrors the rise of a new age of anxiety.' To take on this task and explore 'the new age of anxiety', the volume is divided into three sections, each speaking to a particular angle of the 'logic of anxiety'. The first section engages with the theoretical premise of anxiety and offers ways in which we can or should understand anxiety in the socio-political realm, while the remaining two sections mirror the aforementioned dual logics of anxiety.

The volume opens with a theoretical and a methodological exposition of anxiety. The two contributions – Burgess's and Furtado's – could be read in three different ways: as an invitation to understand what anxiety actually is, what is at stake when speaking about it and how it functions in the socio-political sphere. Drawing on psychoanalysis and thinkers such as Jacques Lacan and Sigmund Freud, the Burgess chapter draws out a crucial parallel between the perception of an external threat and the subjective domain of insecurity which is, as Burgess describes, aligned with the so-called anxiety's threat to the ego. Anxiety interrupts an understanding of the self as a political subject, disturbs the subject's political mandate and in turn realigns and changes the subject's own experiences and comprehensions of what is security and what constitutes the insecurity. Through a meticulous reading of Lacan's and Freud's notion of anxiety, Burgess exposes the problem of the absent object of fear. Unlike in fear (or in the society of risk) the subject or the societies knew of what they were afraid. In contrast in the logic of anxiety, the object of fear is somewhat more illusive (object a) which in turn poses a threat to the ego and to the ideas of wholeness of the society as well as the subject. Burgess concludes by outlining what would be at stake when thinking about security on the level of anxiety, and the problem that the 'absent' object of fear poses. In contrast, Furtado's contribution outlines how the concept of trauma and the assumption that some experiences are unspeakable affect current representations of violence. Drawing on both Freud and Derrida, Furtado contends that while some acts of violence are seen as incomprehensible ruptures, representations are by nature violent practices. As argued by Derrida, Freud's theory of the dream as a suppression of certain experiences can be utilised as a theory for representation at large, where omissions and oppressions of certain facts are inevitable. Furtado thus turns against much of contemporary literature on trauma, and argues that by categorising certain acts of violence as 'unspeakable' one individualises the violent experience and thus makes structural forms of violence less 'speakable'. Furtado's chapter thus helps us understand how anxiety is by nature political, and why defining some acts of violence as 'unrepresentable' contributes to depoliticisation rather than recognising the inherent political and exclusionary nature of representation.

In the second section, we investigate how anxiety is a measure of control, and how this control expresses and sediments itself in contemporary politics. While focusing specifically on the realm of security and security measures, the chapters engage with a range of issues and practices that set and sustain anxious control in contemporary politics. The section opens with Mark Neocleous's contribution which interrogates the central claim of this volume; that is, anxiety is everywhere, both in political life and in contemporary literature. Neocleous, however, wants to draw this conclusion to its limits, and contends that anxiety is not only central as a figure of mental well-being, but is also inextricably linked to the age of neoliberal authoritarianism in which we currently reside. As such, like other contributors in this volume, such as Furtado and Rossi, Neocleous sees neoliberalism as in need of the anxious subject, and current security practices are all centred on the channelling of anxious thoughts. Neocleous thus describes how, because the current liberal state is reliant on anxious subject, we are constantly searching for the resilient subject and the resilient state in order to overcome and avoid new traumatic experiences. The first logic of anxiety is crucial to this conclusion, and Neocleous demonstrates how trauma and resilience are also tightly knit with the anxious state. Further, Emmanuel-Pierre Guittet and Fabienne Brion investigate and continue Neocleous's thread and position anxiety in line with suspicion, and further explore the interactions and connections between the two. They contend that, due to an increased presence of suspicion in modern liberal societies, the logic of anxiety becomes highly accentuated. In an anxious situation, the outlet of suspicion becomes a risk-mitigating tool, a channel through which the fear of the future can be canalised. By looking at current security practices in Belgium and the United Kingdom, Brion and Guittet conclude that suspicion is a new technique of governance, which by using the first logic of anxiety produces new forms of trust, truth and normality. Finally, Carsten Baran exposes the different ways in which a logic of anxiety works between state and private actors. By referring to the case of pandemics in Germany, such as the recent bird and swine flu outbreaks, Baran demonstrates how a logic of anxiety contributes to risk-mitigating responses in a different way for a private company. Arguing that there has been a transfer of responsibility from the state to the private sector, his contribution points out how these companies suffer from several problems in defining and responding to national health crises such as pandemics, and how, ultimately, their main concern is a loss of profit rather than ensuring the health of the citizens. Anxiety, in this case, leads to an increased search for routines which can ensure the resilience of the organisation, but whose ultimate goal is profit accumulation. Here we can see an interplay of the controlling mechanisms of anxiety and the risks and consequences of these consequences beyond the realm of the public sector.

If the second section was concerned with anxiety as a logic of control, the third section turns to anxiety as a force for a socio-political change. Ranging from cultural imaginaries (e.g. zombies), to far Right and the 15M movement in Spain, the contributions in this section explore the 'openings' in society that anxiety can foster.

Norma Rossi, in the opening chapter of this section, explains how anxiety interacts with the far Right in the context of the Italian state's attitude towards the Sicilian mafia. By describing how the far Right and neoliberal politics work in a co-constitutive manner, Rossi manages to carefully point out how the far Right, instead of being a resistance or insurgency to neoliberal narratives of contemporary Italian politics, in fact enables and develops neoliberal politics of the 'state of exception', which has enabled militarised responses to the Sicilian mafia. Due to the logics of anxiety, the mainstream parties can simply adopt very controversial policies of the far Right, in order to mitigate an increased power position for the extremes of the political spectrum. Rossi's chapter thus offers valuable insights on the (im)possibilities of resistance, and how anxiety can, even when it poses as a break with the mainstream politics – which the far Right represents – lead to increased depoliticisation. This contribution thus offers a perspective on both logics of anxiety – how the first logic seeks to control and tie down the uncertainty of the present – and how the possibility for a different future is made even more difficult when depoliticisation covers and increases part of the political spectrum. In contrast to Rossi's discussion of right-wing politics, Paolo Cossarini offers an insight into the working of anxiety on the left of the political spectrum. Cossarini discusses how, in the wake of the financial crisis in Spain, politics of austerity has had a significant impact on the daily lives of the population. While some would argue that the resistance which has since erupted, such as the 15M movement and Podemos, are simply grown out of worsened material conditions, Cossarini points to the very central role of emotions within these movements. By looking closely at the movements against austerity and evictions, Cossarini highlights the increased importance of emotions for the sustenance and success of these movements. The second logic of anxiety is very evident here, and Cossarini's contribution states that anxiety in this case is indeed a case of a mobilising force rather than a paralysing experience.

And, finally, Japhy Wilson in his contribution speaks about the role of anxiety in the neoliberal order by returning to already-mentioned Lacanian and Žižekian understandings on anxiety. The starting premise of Wilson's chapter is the ongoing economic crisis which, despite its well-documented failures, still seems to present itself as the only solution to the problem it started. The chapter offers a reconceptualisation neoliberalism which Wilson in line with Lacan and Žižek read as an anxious social fantasy that structures reality against the traumatic proximity of the Real of Capital. He argues that the resilience and transformability of neoliberalism can be explained as a form of obsessional neurosis, in which the neoliberal engages in frenetic activity to prevent anything Real from happening. This argument is developed through an analysis of the career of the influential development economist Jeffrey Sachs. From shock therapy to the salvation of 'Africa', Sachs's peculiar trajectory betrays the classic traits of the neoliberal neurosis.

Finally, this volume is brought to a close with a contribution provocatively entitled 'Sovereign Anxiety and Baroque Politics'. If previous contributors dealt with the effects of anxiety on the population and/or the governing of anxiety, Michael Dillon draws our attention to anxieties that govern the sovereigns, making it perfectly clear that anxiety is not 'only' experienced by the populations, citizens or political individuals, but is also very much experienced at the level of the state. It asks a very pertinent question of how, as Dillon himself describes it, 'modern sovereignty, seeking escape from the aporetic anxiety and terror posed by the prospect of sovereign decision, and through the ever more baroque and militarised architecture of modern power relations, mourns the catastrophic outcomes of its decision-making in equally baroque self-justifications'. This is not an entirely new phenomenon: it has existed, as Dillon shows through the study of Foucault's and Derrida's works, in the past and through transformation those past practices of governance are still present today. Dillon focuses in particular on the transformation of the politics of truth and on the technologies, which produce, uphold and disprove political truths. Focusing in particular on the relationship between the truth and knowing, Dillon exposes the sovereign anxieties when they are confronted with the *aporia* (or the impossibility) of truth, and the realisation that the sovereign will never know enough. The danger arises precisely from this 'double realisation': on the one end, the sovereign's realisation about their lack of knowledge, and on the other end the people's realisation that the sovereign does not know. It is this provocative statement on knowledge and the impossibility of security or knowing that this volume is brought to a close.

NOTES

1. Harvey, David, *The Enigma of Capital and the Crises of Capitalism* (London: Profile Books, 2010); Standing, Guy, *The Precariat: The New Dangerous Class* (London: Bloomsbury, 2011).
2. Connolly, William, *Neuropolitics: Thinking, Culture, Speed* (Minneapolis: University of Minnesota Press 2002); and 'The "New Materialism" and the Fragility of Things', *Millennium: Journal of International Studies*, 41 no. 3 (2013): 399–412; Bennett, Jane, *Vibrant Matter: A Political Ecology of Things* (Durham, NC: Duke University Press, 2010); Coole, Diana and Samantha Frost, eds., *New Materialism: Ontology, Agency, and Politics* (Durham, NC: Duke University Press, 2010).
3. Le Bon, Gustave, *The Crowd* (New York: Viking Press 1960 [1895]); Canetti, Elias, *Crowds and Power* (London: Penguin Books Ltd, 1960).
4. Goodwin, Jeff, James M. Jasper and Francesca Polletta, 'The Return of the Repressed: The Fall and Rise of Emotions in Social Movement Theory', *Mobilization*, 5 no. 1 (2000): 65–83; Goodwin, Jeff, James M. Jasper and Francesca Polletta, eds., *Passionate Politics* (Chicago: University of Chicago Press, 2001).
5. Massumi, Brian, 'The Autonomy of Affect', *Cultural Critique*, 31 no. 2 (1995): 83–109.
6. Leys, Ruth, 'The Turn to Affect: A Critique', *Critical Inquiry*, 37 no. 3 (2011): 458.
7. Beck, Ulrich, *Risk Society: Towards a New Modernity* (London: SAGE Publications, 1992); Giddens, Anthony, *The Consequences of Modernity* (London: Polity Press, 1991); *Turbulent and Mighty Continental: What Future for Europe* (London: Polity Press, 2013).
8. Bourke, Joanna, *Fear: A Cultural History* (Emeryville, CA: Shoemaker & Hoard, 2006).

BIBLIOGRAPHY

Beck, Ulrich, *Risk Society: Towards a New Modernity* (London: SAGE Publications, 1992).
Bennett, Jane, *Vibrant Matter: A Political Ecology of Things* (Durham, NC: Duke University Press, 2010).
Bourke, Joanna, *Fear: A Cultural History* (Emeryville, CA: Shoemaker & Hoard, 2006).
Canetti, Elias, *Crowds and Power* (London: Penguin Books Ltd, 1960).
Connolly, William, *Neuropolitics: Thinking, Culture, Speed* (Minneapolis: University of Minnesota Press, 2002).
Connolly, William, 'The "New Materialism" and the Fragility of Things', *Millennium: Journal of International Studies*, 41 no. 3 (2013): 399–412.

Coole, Diana and Samantha Frost, eds., *New Materialism: Ontology, Agency, and Politics* (Durham, NC: Duke University Press, 2010).

Giddens, Anthony, *The Consequences of Modernity* (London: Polity Press, 1991); *Turbulent and Mighty Continental: What Future for Europe* (London: Polity Press, 2013).

Goodwin, Jeff, James M. Jasper and Francesca Polletta, eds., *Passionate Politics* (Chicago: University of Chicago Press, 2001).

Goodwin, Jeff, James M. Jasper and Francesca Polletta, 'The Return of the Repressed: The Fall and Rise of Emotions in Social Movement Theory', *Mobilization*, 5 no. 1 (2000): 65–83.

Harvey, David, *The Enigma of Capital and the Crises of Capitalism* (London: Profile Books, 2010).

Le Bon, Gustave, *The Crowd* (New York: Viking Press 1960 [1895]).

Leys, Ruth, 'The Turn to Affect: A Critique', *Critical Inquiry*, 37 no. 3 (2011): 434–472.

Massumi, Brian, 'The Autonomy of Affect', *Cultural Critique*, 31 no. 2 (1995): 83–109.

Standing, Guy, *The Precariat: The New Dangerous Class* (London: Bloomsbury, 2011).

Part I

POLITICISING ANXIETY

Chapter 2

For Want of Not: Lacan's Conception of Anxiety

J. Peter Burgess

The early history of psychoanalysis, both in theory and in practice, maps compellingly onto a number of concrete historic-political correlations. Shifting class structures in Europe, rapidly changing social institutions, transformed state powers, sharply weakening religious culture, the rise of modern experimental science converge distinctly at the turn of the European twentieth century at a time when psychoanalytic explanations attain a certain legitimacy and psychotherapeutic practices obtain a certain credibility.[1] The first generation of psychoanalytic theory and practice also finds its relatively distinct origins in the life and work of Freud, where we will start our story.[2]

The emergence of psychoanalysis at around the turn of the twentieth century takes place as a unique clash of science, political power and subjectivity. The sequence of events surrounding its first appearance in the 1890s in Freud's early writings, through its challenge to the hegemony of hysteria studies and to its spawning of schools and disciplines, thrusts it into a landscape of social tensions, political intrigues and cultural and countercultural clashes. The extraordinary transition in the arts and sciences, both exposing the uncharted depths of subjectivity and clearing the path for the cultural battles looming on the horizon, was the scene of the therapeutic concept of anxiety. The stakes of the cultural-political conflict are exemplified by the famous blood feud between the Mann brothers – Thomas and Heinrich – in the first years of the twentieth century, with Heinrich arguing for a 'civilisational' vision for human progress, instrumental, rational, republican, and Thomas insisting on an organic, cultural, somatic; indeed, sensual understanding of the sense and promise of European modernity cries out the anxiety that lies in an irreducible complexity in the painful transition to European modernity.[3]

The key terms of a general politics of anxiety – security and insecurity, defence, resistance, vulnerability, aggresivity, affect, etc. – are all present from the beginning of the story of psychoanalysis. Indeed the violence of psychic life is perhaps the red thread of psychoanalysis, its reason to be and the force of its evolution. Psychic disorders, emotional suffering and mental illness are from the outset determined, defined, diagnosed and treated through politics of psychic life, a struggle, both public and private, over what illness is, who is ill, what dangers illness implies for society and what means can be deployed to protect the individual, family and society.

The shift in our time from an experience of security threats as exogenous to our nation-state reality complex towards a more reflexive, indigenous experience of danger mirrors the rise of a new age of anxiety. The perceived or imagined dangers of our everyday lives, from terrorism, computer viruses, climate change, pandemic disease, quality of food and water, etc., reflect not only the ubiquity of threat in the everyday but also its inseparability from who or what we are. Danger is perceived all around us, but to the degree that our security imaginaries are complicit in our insecurity. Our obsessive insecurity – no place better reflected than in the populist turn in national politics in the Europe and the United States – reveals not only that threat is immanent, but that we, through our psychic lives, are a danger unto ourselves. This is the horizon of the new anxiety, where the increasingly reflexive character of our own insecurities alters the traditional equation of danger and protection that gives form and legitimacy to our social, political, economic and cultural institutions in the intimate, collective, national and international arenas. It interrupts a deep understanding of the self as the subject of politics and reconfigures the ideas of security and insecurity in relation to the material borders of the body.[4]

'Anxiety' plays a particularly important role in this constellation of ideas and tendencies, and this is reflected sharply in Freud's vision of cultural and psychic life. It is an everyday term, which at the same time takes on great valence in philosophy, theology, social studies, political science, psychology and, eventually, in psychoanalytic theory.[5] Yet even in the course of Freud's career, as we will underscore later, the use of the term mutates quite considerably from a question of repression of psychic desires to a more anthropological, or even physical notion, of danger.

However it is Lacan's revisiting of the notion of 'anxiety' in his 1962–1963 seminar by the same name, and the peripheral texts that inform it, that will be the main focus of this chapter. We will try to show the Laconian conceptualisation of anxiety, while maintaining attention to the Freudian characterisation of anxiety as a certain relation to a certain object of danger or insecurity, and will relocate anxiety as a question of being itself, of the being of the fear and danger, and of the dialectical assumption of the politics of therapy that their finality lies in fulfilling desire or eliminating the object of desire.

IMMINENT INSECURITY: FREUD, ANXIETY AND THE THREAT TO THE EGO

Anxiety is a core theme for Freud, and its re-interpretation a central challenge for Lacan. Freud's understanding of, and therapeutic approach to, anxiety famously has two quite distinct phases. It first emerges as a component in his earliest formulations of psychoanalytic theory.

The second of Freud's early 'Three Essays on the Theory of Sexuality',[6] entitled 'Infantile Sexuality', presents the now-somewhat-derided theory of 'castration anxiety', associated with male children between the ages of three and five, which describes the fear – both symbolical and actual – of loss of or damage to the penis. Freud's approach to anxiety is couched in the fear of castration, in an imagined danger of castration, of losing connection to the symbolic object, originally conceived as part of the self, which is the phallus, or in being denied access to it as a symbolic object. Freud claims that anxiety is a repressed reaction to the fear of being cut off from this symbolic object. It is an imagined – and feared – separation from the core part of oneself. What that core part actually is that it evolves over the course of a child's life.

The fear is interpreted as the result of guilt, or actual or possible punishment for sexual feelings for the mother. The counterpart for female children, according to Freud, is the 'penis envy', according to which the sanction has symbolically already been exercised.[7] The theory has been widely criticised or discredited, in part by Freud himself in later writings. Important for us, however, is the transformation of the concept of anxiety in Freud's later writing, and Lacan's reaction to this later concept. In 1923, with the publication of *The Ego and the Id*, Freud expanded his understanding of anxiety as part of an economy of psychic force, whereby repression could be observed as both a cause of anxiety and the result of it. In this text, anxiety is understood as the expression of the release of this tension. Finally reflecting elements from his earlier 1916 lecture entitled 'Anxiety', and then more definitively in the 1926 essay 'Inhibitions, Symptoms and Anxiety', Freud moves his point of view in a new direction, more oriented towards the role of repressive mechanisms.[8] Voluminous scholarly debate has focused on the question of whether the anxiety of the early theory expresses the release of physical tension, which is the cause of the 'anxiety neurosis', or whether anxiety and its dissipation are conceived in its first version as psychic functions.[9] Strachey, Freud's original English-language editor, attributes Freud's understanding of anxiety as a need for resolution of sexual energy as the result of his dependence, as a young medical doctor, on the vocabulary of physiology.[10] As we will see, this argument is relevant for Lacan's re-casting of anxiety as a symbolic, not 'natural', bodily or somatic, function, and will reveal itself as an unresolvable material and eventually political dimension of anxiety understood as a psychic disorder. But the core difference between the first and the second Freud for us in this short chapter is the question of a threat – psychic, cultural, social, political or otherwise – posed to the ego, what this means for Freud and how it flows into the Lacan's theory of anxiety, threat and danger.

A core question in understanding the notion of a threat to the ego is one that haunts political theory today, namely the reality of danger. The first question in the Freudian approach to perceptions of danger is whether there is any objective reality in such threats. This is in part the index/measurement of the wellness of the patient. Someone suffering from one form or another of neurosis will nurture this suffering on perceived dangers. In classical – and early Freudian – psychoanalytic theory, these dangers are interpreted as symptoms of a psychic disorder (on the assumption that a dysfunctional psychic constitution can nonetheless communicate through a fully functioning mechanism of symbolisation). By contrast, a different patient may perceive different dangers and yet these are understood to be firmly planted in 'reality'. In short, the dangers that may be menacing a given subject are factual, real, though perceived, integrated and resolved differently by different subjects. In his 1926 article, 'Inhibitions, Symptoms and Anxiety', he explains:

> Anxiety has an unmistakable relation to expectation: it is anxiety about something. It has a quality of indefiniteness and lack of object. In precise speech we use the word 'fear' rather than 'anxiety' if it has found an object. Moreover, in addition to its relation to danger, anxiety has a relation to neurosis which we have long been trying to elucidate. The question arises: why are not all reactions of anxiety neurotic—why do we accept so many of them as normal? And finally, the problem of the difference between realistic anxiety and neurotic anxiety awaits a thorough examination.
> . . .
> Real danger is a danger that is known, and realistic anxiety is anxiety about a known danger of this sort. Neurotic anxiety is anxiety about an unknown danger. Neurotic danger is thus a danger that has still to be discovered. Analysis has shown the it is an instinctual danger. By bring this danger which is not known to the ego into consciousness, the analysis makes neurotic anxiety no different from realistic anxiety, so that it can be dealt with in the same way.[11]

In the previous passage, Freud advances a realism that forms the basis for an ongoing distinction between two types of reaction to 'real danger'. The danger is real, but the impulse to address it varies. On the one hand there is 'affective reaction', that is, anxiety. On the other hand, there is actual 'protective action'. The political springs out of the affective, not as some kind of superficial reflex, but from the core of the emotional experience. In other words, the politics of anxiety is not some kind of symptom, not a reaction to something else more profound, more fundamentally ill, more damaged or more dangerous. It is, rather, the very force and meaning of anxiety: Anxiety is the political. Anxiety is the fundamental antagonism of underlying forces, cast together in an unresolved economy of struggle. Without seeking to open a new debate about the nature of violence, we can safely say that it is the core of violence, the meaning of violence.

This is a first cut, but nonetheless critical starting point for an understanding of Lacan's notion of anxiety, his politics of anxiety and, most importantly, his theory of the subject. All three emerge out of a situation of danger, a perception and affective experience of danger, yes, but more importantly a general structure of danger, danger as a structuring moment, and indeed the very structuring moment of subjectivity itself. They are not merely symptoms of danger or symbols of some platonic notion of danger. 'They are not merely symptoms of some more immanent danger nor symbols of some transcendental notion of danger. They form a phenomenology of danger itself. They represent the pressure of dread itself, governed through a moral economy of retribution, itself situated on the horizon of some actual physical disruption, pain or suffering, or even a sign of the end of life.' Anxiety, even in this pre-Lacanian iteration, does not mean anything, does not motivate or respond or distance itself from anything that is not its cause. It is its own damage.

Subjectivity, as we hope to show, is not a position from which danger and threat are empirically perceived or experienced, and thus not a position from which political claims can be made about how best to address challenges to give security to this or that object from this or that position of stability and viability of the autonomous subject. Rather, danger, threat and insecurity are constitutive of the subject. The subject emerges from danger, and carries its trace within it. Danger is not understood as a threat to others, but as a threat to itself; the constant risk that makes the subject what it is, let's call it subjectivity, is at any moment at risk of collapse, dispersion, erosion. The being of the subject is the politics of risk.

The political moment is thus not one where the autonomous ('sovereign') subject decides. Rather, it is the moment where danger becomes subjectivity, the moment where the mode of existence of the subject reveals itself as carrying within itself the horizon of danger.

ANXIETY AND AFFECT

It is no secret that Lacan regards his own project as in many ways a revisiting and revision of Freud's theory. He is both recognisant of Freud's contributions in the various phases of his work and keen to underscore what he regards as the advances on it. Some of these advances can be traced to the general innovations in the Lacanian system of thought, for example, the discovery and development of the notion of the *objet a*. Others related to the specific critique of Freud's theory of anxiety.

In Lacan's own view, the theory of anxiety, as presented in the seminar Anxiety of 1962–63, is a turning point for his relation to Freud and his earlier interpretations of Freud, a kind of convergence of the work done until then. As he assures his audience on the first day of the seminar on 14 November 1962:

> Anxiety is very precisely the meeting point where everything from my previous disquisition is lying wait for you. You're going to see how a certain number of terms, which until now may not have appeared adequately linked to one another, can now be connected up. You're going to see, I think, how in being knotted together more tightly on the ground of anxiety each one will fall into place even better.[12]

Like Freud, Lacan takes anxiety to be an 'affect'.[13] It is a physical expression or symptom, not one which points the way to any truth or direct insight about what a given anxiety is or should be, not even what causes or could resolve anxiety. A full conceptualisation of anxiety in Lacan's optic requires several additional theoretical components. Most prominently, but also generally, is the notion of desire. For Lacan, anxiety is a key figure, an orientation for understanding the nature of desire, the forces at work in its economy and the immensely powerful and consequential results it can have. It is not an object, not even a signifier of an object, but, rather, the situation or state of being that permits us to approach the signifier.

This is perhaps the key importance of the notion of the 'affect'. Affect is neither a stimulus nor the emotion it provokes. Rather, it is the name of the interaction between the body and the meaning it seeks to facilitate. Affect is the junction point between body and meaning, between that which is desiring and the body through which desire is channelled and will ultimately be rewarded.[14] In concrete terms, when a subject is under analysis, his/her conscious dialogue with the analyst or the response is not exclusively a discursive one. The analysand cannot say why anxiety is present, but can identify the affect reaction as part of charting the territory around it.[15]

Lacan notes the key role that anxiety plays in the new existentialist philosophies, starting above all with Kierkegaard, but including also Marcel, Chostov, Berdiaev and, of course, Sartre and Heidegger.[16] In addition to the philosophical interpretations of anxiety that have become fashionable in recent years, Lacan notes three more: The first is a pathological interpretation of anxiety, according to which it refers to psychic force that manifests itself in the body or on the body through material symptoms; second, a certain notion of anxiety refers to the day-to-day experience of neurotics; and thirdly, it is used to refer to the more extreme behaviour of psychosis or acute psychic disturbance.

What makes catalogues like this quite seductive, according to Lacan, is that they build on a certainty kind of continuity or 'homogeneity', in the sense that they all structurally presuppose a unified experience of a subject, having a certain experience, more or less acute, more or less comprehensible, of something finite, totalisable and treatable called 'anxiety'. In short, anxiety, in Lacan's reading of his contemporaries amounts to nothing more, nothing less than these conceptualisations regarded as an object, something that is produced or provoked at the end of a chain of psychic (or cultural, social, even political) casualty,[17] and which responds to the logical of causality when it comes to its governance and regulation.

Lacan's point of departure is inherently sceptical to this vision. Instead of situating anxiety in a linear flow of events and responses, he understands 'anxiety' as part and parcel of the ebb and flow, the push and pull, the force and resistance of a multilayered psychic economy. Indeed, he is not looking to ask what anxiety is, what object the word, or even a given set of symptoms, is referring to. For Lacan, anxiety is a way of opening the question of what one's relation to desire is when one is in a state of anxiety. Anxiety is an affect, not an object. It is an affect, it is a state of being oneself whose existence – not its sense or meaning – stems from the relationship to the desire that it facilitates.[18] 'Desire' and its relation to the 'Other' is, however, an important matter in Lacan's theory, and merits a parenthesis.

VULNERABILITY THROUGH DESIRE

An approach to Lacan's notion of desire begins with a reminder of the degradation of the term's ordinary meaning in common discourse. It is enough, says Lacan, to reflect upon the relationship between 'desire' and 'need' in common language in order to see the ambiguity or opening that Lacan seeks to seize. Both 'desire' and 'need' describe a relation to something other, which, when acquired or assimilated should theoretically play a fulfilling or completing role for the subject of the desire or need. Both these terms are negative in the sense that they designate a lack, a deficiency, scarcity, deficit or inadequacy. Both terms express, in different ways, the presence of an absence, an absence that in concrete terms can be closed or made obsolete. Yet beyond this similarity, the 'desire' and 'need' are different in an essential way. In effect, while a need can be satisfied, a desire cannot. Even when the need is not (yet) satisfied, it cannot be a source of frustration, resentment or disappointment. There is no investment in a need, only the closed 'natural' economy of solicitation and satisfaction. Desire, on the other hand, knows no finite satisfaction. This assertion is stable throughout Lacan's work. 'There is no object that can satisfy a desire', he insists, evoking Socrates, in Book 14 of the *Seminar, The Logic of Fantasy*, 'even when the object is the cause of desire'.[19] We will return to this strange logic of the 'cause of desire' shortly. Whereas need is regarded as natural, imbedded in a closed economy of demand and satisfaction, desire is understood as exogenous to the psychic economy.

Indeed, according to Lacan, lack of satisfaction, frustrated satisfaction is at the very heart of desire, making it what it is. In this regard it is also inseparable from some form of pain or suffering.[20] Desire is desire because of its eccentricity, because of the frustration it holds in wait. For this reason, Lacan underscores that desire is not 'natural', not a function of naturally occurring beings as a virtue of the being naturally occurring. It is rather a core component of human subjectivity, both a mark or sign of the subject and a kind of built-in disappointment in that it becomes a kind of ambient awareness that the subject will never be completed or constituted, precisely because its desire cannot ever be filled. The subject is this un-closable opening towards a perennially longed-for satisfaction.

Desire in Lacan's thought – Freud advances a similar, if less radical, conception – thus functions to some extent like the *objet a* (to which we return later): Its existence is a marker or expression of its impossibility. There is nothing 'in' it, nothing which could be concretised into an object that can be fully grasped, or enjoyed, something that could quench the desire, or even be fully understood or even observed, or fully assimilated. As negative as this feature of human consciousness may seem, it contributes a tenacious quality of resilience to both human life and consciousness. Ironically, since desire can never be satisfied, it can also never be destroyed. It can also never be pulverised, diluted or divided by the object it is fixed upon. It represents a kind of stability or security, even a resistance against what would existentially threaten the man being. The guarantee of life, the force of life is desire. Yet this tenacity or resistance opens up a wide field of issues, several of which become apparent in Lacan's treatment of anxiety.

The most frequently evoked moment in the logic of desire – and the final step before turning back to the concept of anxiety – springs from one of Lacan's most celebrated formula:

Man's desire is the desire of the Other.[21]

Less an assertion than a clinical observation; this axiom adds to the tenacity of desire towards the object of desire – never satisfied – an intersubjective dimension. The double genitive form expressed in the 'of the Other' wraps desire into a complex of desires in relation to the abstract Other explained previously. On the one hand, it refers to the desire that takes the Other as its object – the abstract other that transcends and envelopes experience in the world – people, institutions, language, law, etc. On the other hand, it is the desire of what the Other desires, the desire to appropriate the object of desire of the other, an object, it must be said, which is equally unobtainable for the Other.

Lacan tries to clarify this notion of 'desire for desire' by comparing it to the concept of desire, well known and well regarded in the academic discourses of post-war Paris – developed by Hegel and interpreted by Alexander Kojève, and reproduced in his influential *Introduction to the Reading of Hegel*,[22] otherness and desire are linked by the subject's need for recognition, for being seen and ascribed being. Being is triggered through recognition. Once the subject understands itself as having been seen, its being and subjectivity are established in a higher order of self-hood. Lacan contrasts this dialectical conception of desire to his own 'analytical' conception[23] ('analytic', here, should not be understood in terms of a notion of analytic philosophy but, rather, as a subset of Lacanian psychoanalytic theory). According to Lacan's enchanting slogan ('Man's desire is the desire of the Other'), it is the desire of the other's desire, not the other's recognition, which counts. The primordial search for the desire of desire implies both a will to be desired – which is indeed analogous to the will to recognition in the Hegelian, dialectical logic – and a drive to a kind of pulsing towards mimicry, of affirmation of the self by desiring what the other desires.

[T]he Other is there as an un-conscious that is constituted as such. The Other concerns my desire to the extent of what he lacks and what he does not know. It's at the level of what he lacks, and at the level of him not knowing. It is at the level of what he lacks that I'm concerned in the most prominent way because there is no other path for me to find what I lack as object of my desire.[24]

This structure, the structure of the Other in Lacanian terms, is utterly primordial. In the child's establishment of subjectivity it is both the trigger and the structuring force. The Other precedes the self, precedes subjectivity. It is the primordial affect. There is not utterly logical subject. The subject is always affected by desire, always a desiring subject.[25] In some sense, this principle, a fundament of Lacan's theory from the 1960s and on, is a kind of guarantee that the subject of psychoanalysis should remain irreducible to any fixed opposite or structure, a kind of anti-structuralist guarantee of the sovereignty of the subject, a built-in security measure against instrumentalisation and assimilation to the machinery or simple instrumental rationality. On the other hand, this is the object of our reflection; it is the path which reveals anxiety as a fundamental component of the constitution of the subject.

Whereas in contrast to a Hegelian schema of desire, which would have the structure, I love you even if you don't want me to – that is, the recognition of the desire is enough to establish, on the part of the one who desires, of the subjective experience of it, the Lacanian logic of the unconscious Other goes much further. It not only affirms that I desire what I desire even though I don't know what it is I desire but also goes further by suggesting that the subject that desires is constituted and structured through the search to know the object of its desire. The object of desire – soon to be identified as the *objet a* – will reveal itself as the original cornerstone of subjectivity in Lacan's thought.

ANXIETY AND THE OTHER

In order to advance in our argumentation, it is necessary to introduce some rudimentary elements of the highly idiosyncratic Lacanian vocabulary. By far the most important is the Other (Autre), in particular in distinction from the other (autre). The distinction, set out already in the Seminar II in 1953,[26] does not lie far from what is often used in the philosophical discourse. The 'other' with a small 'o' designates an empirically occurring other, the thing that is not me, not this, not something, that is also empirically identifiable and discrete. The 'Other' with a capital 'O' is far more complex. It designates a function of otherness, a role, a situation, an institution, code, supreme fiction, transcendence, that which cannot be reduced or frozen as an empirically granted object. In short, it does not exist in any empirical sense and yet it plays a crucial role in setting the horizon for thought and action, for opening and making meaningful alterity or otherness in general. It is what makes contact and intelligibility with others at all possible.[27] In this sense the Other implies a system of governance, a regulating force, an institution of law, a disciplining, normative force, parents, siblings, cohorts, colleagues, friends, desired others, detested others. It can be language, with all the constraints implied by linguistic structure. It is a structure that offers promise, sets conditions, makes demands and, as we will see later, generates and governs desire.

In Lacan's analysis of anxiety, the Other is a signpost, a necessary navigation point along the way. Against the background of Lacan's studies of infant development, the mirror stage, the Other plays the role of a reference that has existed prior to all others. Anxiety is the notion that pushes it to a new and higher level.

THE *OBJET A*

To these two 'others', a third 'other' must be added, crucial to Lacan's account of anxiety. It is the '*objet a*' – the 'object little a' – which Lacan gave instructions not to translate. In any subject's experience of the world, as an experience of the Other, the transcendental horizon, the general and universal 'out-there' which facilitates meaning (but which is not meaning) there is what can be called a blind spot. Take the example of the most immediate experience of ourselves in the world, our image in a mirror, say, through the lens of a smartphone, that we have seen many times; it is the very aperture of the camera:

> 'a' results from an operation of logical structure, it took effect not in vivo, not even upon the living being, not properly speaking in the confused sense that the term 'body' holds, it's not necessarily the pound of flesh, even if it could be, and that, after all, when it is, it doesn't help matters much. But indeed it appears that in this entity of the body so little apprehended, there is something that lends itself to this operation of logical structure which remains for us to determine. It is the care, the scyballe, the regard, the voice: these detachable pieces are however deeply linked to the body, and this is what is concerned in the *objet a*, to make the 'a', let us therefore limit ourselves because we are obligated to some rigour of logic, to signal that indebtedness is needed to provide it.[28]

Everything in the field of the gaze can be represented and understood except for that one tiny black spot, which is opening to something very strange, horrifying, if at all conceivable. It is the *objet a*. It is present in our experience not just of ourselves in a mirror – the most immediate self-perception – but in all experiences of the world. If the visual field is the Other, the horizon that makes meaning possible – Lacan calls it in a different vocabulary, the Symbolic – then the point of the aperture of our camera, that blind spot, which is present in any 'selfie', is somehow outside of the image, while at the same time being within it. It gives no image, reflects no light; it is an empty space, emptiness itself. We can in principle see and take in absolutely anything in our field of vision except the very aperture of the eyeball that is doing the seeing. This spot is utterly un-representable. Not only can we not observe into that hole, this absolute inaccessibility shapes and structures the rest of what we do indeed see and take in. In Lacan's terminology, this spot is the 'Real'. It is outside of language, outside of symbolisation, beyond conceivability.

This visual, the 'specular', must now be generalised to all forms and fields of perception, understanding and experience of the empirical world at large. The point from which the subject's experience of the world emanates can never be an object of experience. It is always, by ontological necessity, excluded from experience, from symbolisation, communication, etc. By extension, the aperture of the selfie-camera is a metaphor for the point of the intellectual, which is not always placed spatial at the point of origin of the subject. Rather, it is itself projected. In everyday, conscious life, my experience is not an object of my experience. I do not see the lens of the selfie-camera; I only see and smell, and taste and perceive what is presented as the world. This does not prevent us from glimpsing and even grasping discrete moments where the radical otherness of the black spot which is the place from which we experience the world, this strange vanish point becomes present in it. This is the moment of anxiety.

In order to bring the Lacanian schema and the question of anxiety together, we require one more element, the notion of 'desire'.

Like Freud, Lacan also has two phases in his understanding of 'anxiety'. The first dates to his direct reinterpretation of Freud's concept of 'castration anxiety' in his pre-war writings, where he uses the notion of the 'mirror stage' to explain anxiety as fear of bodily fragmentation.[29] Anxiety takes a more complete and complex form in the writings and seminars that build upon the three-part schema Symbolic-Imaginary-Real, launched in 1953 in a lecture by the same title,[30] and shortly thereafter, and more famously, in the 'The Function and Field of Speech and Language in Psychoanalysis', also known as the 'Discourse of Rome'.[31] The category of the 'real' is the key to opening Lacan's original approach to anxiety – with the help of the concept of the *objet a*. The 'real' is the precisely that which, in the psychic universe, is exterior to symbolisation, cannot be symbolised and resists signification of any kind. In this sense it has a purely negative relation to the 'symbolic' in the Lacanian schema. It does, however, hold a relationship with the 'imaginary' since this radical inaccessibility is the product of some traumatic experience – also exterior to symbolisation, though its traumatic origin and valence give it an expression as affect.

Affect is the link to Lacan's understanding of anxiety. Anxiety is an affect – not an emotion – built around the notion of the *objet a* briefly presented previously.[32] We have already underscored the role that desire plays both in constituting the subject and in laying it open to the world as insecure. The relation between the subject and the object of the subject's desire is a multilevel relation to the Other, to the desires of the Other and the desire for the Other. This relationship is captured by the term 'affect', by the special way in which the subject both emerges and sustains itself not by any ordinary relation to a foundation or referent, but rather by a constellation of affects that support and sustain it. There are, of course, any number of affects, and Freud, as we say, seized upon them for his late theory of anxiety.

In a nutshell, anxiety stems from the situation whereby the subject pursues what it takes to be the object of its desire. The experience of anxiety is the confrontation with the inaccessible character of the object of desire. The subject, in pursuit of the realisation of its desire, is not simply thwarted or frustrated by the inability to capture, possess or realise its desire. Anxiety is far more the very experience of this inaccessibility. Anxiety is bound to the *objet a*. It is the presence of the *objet a*, this impossible conduit to the unthinkable, that is the generator of anxiety. We all – psychically healthy subjects – experience the *objet a* – the mysterious, disquieting, unattainable – and, above all, disquieting-because-unattainable – object.

The *objet a* is thus the cause of desire without it being assimilable to. It is something which has escaped desire, its own cause gone astray, 'fallen' away from it, but is still associated with it. It leaves a gap, an absence. It is a hole, a dark fleck or a passage to another space.

Anxiety is not the experience of what is feared lost, or what has been lost and is feared irrecoverable. It is an expression of the need to have in place the absence of the absent thing. This figure or trope is particular meaning by virtue of the 'negative' valence of common security logic. Security, it is commonly said, represents the absence of threat or danger. Where we are aware that there is 'nothing', we find ourselves secure, pacified, 'without care (sine cura)'. A dialectically oriented deconstruction of the concept of security would point out the presence of the danger or threat to security in the thought or being of its absence. The Hegelian theory of negativity shows that the negative only supports the positive: The thought of security guarantees the dialectical inexorability of our insecurity on a higher order, as the foundation of our security.

Lacan, however, sees in anxiety a detour, or perhaps a subversion of the dialectical approach to desire. Anxiety, for Lacan, is not, as for Freud, a problem of satisfaction of non-satisfaction of a need, set into a general economy of drives. It is not a frustrated desire for what is absent. It is an affective reaction to the absence of the desire that should be there.

> But what does experience teach us here about anxiety in its relation to the object of desire, if not simply that prohibition is temptation? Anxiety isn't about the loss of the object, but its presence. The objects aren't missing. Let's move up to the next level, that of the superego's love, with everything this is deemed to entail on what is said to be the path to failure. What does that mean, if not that what is feared is success? Once more, there's no lack.[33]

Anxiety is not a yearning for the re-establishment of the empty hole in the subject. It is rather the need for stabilisation of the subject in its desire. Anxiety is a response to a need to desire, a need to keep desire open. It reflects a sense that the insecurity subject is not the exception, but rather the datum, the orientation, or perhaps mode of existence, that constitutes subjectivity. There is, in short, a fundamental vulnerability, openness, threatened-ness and danger at the heart of subjectivity.

THE CHEATING SUBJECT: THE 'DESIRE TO KNOW'

This interpretation of anxiety has consequences for questions of the subject's being and for its ontological security. However, Lacan is attentive to anxiety as an epistemological matter. This is the case, on basic level, because the practice of psychoanalysis is charged with knowing and, above all, understanding things, and for some, with teaching or transmitting things. Yet Lacan is sceptical to this kind of Cartesian rationality of the knowledge, drawn from clinical experience, transmitted to students of analysis and re-applied to clinical patients. For this linear life cycle of knowledge rests entirely on an understanding of what is said in the course of analysis, on the content of the consciousness and on the non-verbal expressions of affect, in short, on everything that is or should be understandable. However, this, for Lacan, is missing the point: 'From this perspective, it is preferable to warn people that they aren't to believe too much of what they may comprehend'.[34]

Indeed the self-consciousness, which Lacan at times incredulously calls 'the subject-supposed-to-know', is precisely an attempt to get at the fact that analysts – and we theoreticians as analysts of analysts – must at times work not with knowledge, but rather placeholders of knowledge, replacements or step-ins: 'That the Selbstbewußtsein, considered to be constitutive of the cognising subject, is an illusion.'[35]

Worse, the mechanisms of the psyche seem in many cases to function – naturally and normally – as cheats, seeking by their very make-up to mislead conscious analysis, and the work of analysis. Anxiety is a notorious example.

> Anxiety has a different sort of object from the object whose perception is prepared and structured. By what? But the model of the cut, of the furrow, of the nunnery trait, of the *there it is*, which in operating always remain tight-lipped— the tight lip or lips of the cut—which become a closed book on the subject, unopened letters sending him off again under closed seal to further traces.[36]

The crucial insight – for both analysts and those who seek to relate to the character and manifestations of anxiety – is that elusive, or evasive, meaning is the key to meaning. In closing his last lecture of 1962, Lacan admonishes his listeners:

> Don't let yourselves be taken in by appearances. Just because anxiety's link to doubt, to hesitation, to the obsessional's so-called ambivalent game, may strike you as clinically tangible, this doesn't mean that they are the same thing. Anxiety is not doubt, anxiety is the cause of doubt.[37]

Anxiety is thus the cause of doubt not because it some has the facts right, whereas doubt has an ambivalent relation to the facts. Rather anxiety is the cause of doubt because it destabilises or precedes causality. Psychic 'causality'. The failure of doubt to overcome anxiety – and this failure is manifestly structural – becomes a form of certainty, 'dreadful certainty', as Lacan calls it; in the discourse of anxiety, the insight that the instability or non-linear knowledge that fuels anxiety is the moment of certainty we can know: 'The effort that doubt expense is exerted merely to combat anxiety, and precisely through lures, to the extent that what it strives to avoid is what hold firm in anxiety with dreadful certainty.'[38] The function of doubt is to combat (vainly) anxiety to apply Cartesian rationality to the mode of existence and a means of signifying that never sought to adopt them in the first place.

It goes nearly without saying, though Lacan does not hesitate to repeat it through his career, that psychoanalysis, in theory and practice, is intimately wrapped up with the desire to know. If desire and knowledge are the key references to the psychoanalytic cure – self-knowledge and knowledge of the other, knowledge of the other's knowledge, etc. – then psychoanalysis – like political analysis – must also be under scrutiny. For it also desires to know.

CONCLUSION: THE POLITICS OF ANXIETY

Anxiety is a name for several kinds of failures in the subject's attempt to understand and navigate in the world. All of these failures flow from a kind of psychic hubris, a desire to know, have control, and singular type of affect that responds to such failures. Lacan begins with a critique psychologising 'causality', a collapse of causality in all its forms. First and foremost it is the failure in terms of 'reading' the political meaning of political events. Second, it is a misunderstanding of the place of anxiety outside of the machinery of the causality, most often in the analytic setting, as a pre-emptory moment, determining the meaning and cause of our desires before they themselves become a reality.

Despite first appearances, Freud and Lacan share a number of fundamental principles. The most forceful is dissatisfaction with any simple linking between anxiety and the ego. Even if we could zoom in on what it would mean to say, in the Freudian schema, that ego is under threat – exposed to danger, to which anxiety is somehow a response – the ego to which we refer would not simply precede the anxiety. It is rather co-constituted by the danger, by the threat to a substantial self which cannot pre-exist, but which is somehow generated by the presence of the threat. According to Shepherdson, there are also two versions of Lacan in play, both different from Freud's, the first of which understands the threat that provokes anxiety as a threat to a kind of sovereignty of the imaginary body (in contrast to Freud's vision as a threat to the imaginary ego).

Ironically, it is Freud, not Lacan, who regards himself as unable to concretise the fear that both take as the primary axis of anxiety. For Freud, there is a contingent reality, which is not possible to identify; for Lacan it is the status of fear as constituent of the imaginary that grants it its reality, a reality more pregnant than the lost reality of the fear that Freudian psychoanalysis seeks to recover through the psychoanalytic therapy. The 'castration anxiety' that the Freudian approach seeks to demystify for the benefit of the patient remains, in the Lacanian perspective, essential to the very structure of the imaginary. The subject is constantly in danger of the imaginary castration; this is what makes it a subject. Anxiety is therefore not a natural or adaptive phenomenon but rather the correlate of the imaginary structure of the ego, a structure that supplements and re-organises organic life, and is unique to the human being, so that it should not be misconstrued in terms of the adaptive functioning of the animal in relation to reality.[39]

Lacan's reading of anxiety signals a new form of danger to the ego.[40] In *The Ego and the Id* he remarks that 'what it is that the ego fears cannot be specified; we know that the fear is of being overwhelmed or annihilated; but it cannot be grasped analytically'.[41] For Lacan, the danger is readily interpretable in terms of an explanation of the unity of the ego that is lacking in Freud, a unity that goes beyond, or most likely before, the closed, finite character of causality itself, the imagined support of by and large all insecurity. Bringing the analysis of security to a higher, Lacanian level will mean searching for security in the imaginary, and understanding the misleading dangers lying in fact.

NOTES

1. Cf. Zaretsky, Eli, *Secrets of the Soul: A Social and Cultural History of Psychoanalysis*. 1st ed. New York: Alfred A. Knopf, 2004.

2. Gay, Peter, *Freud: A Life for Our Time*. New York: Norton, 2006; Gelfand, Toby, and John Kerr, *Freud and the History of Psychoanalysis*. Hillsdale, NJ: Analytic Press; Gay, Peter, *A Godless Jew: Freud, Atheism, and the Making of Psychoanalysis*. New Haven, CT; Cincinnati, OH: Yale University Press; Hebrew Union College Press, 1987.

3. Kesting, H., *Heinrich Mann und Thomas Mann: Ein deutscher Bruderzwist*. Göttingen: Wallstein, 2003.

4. Burgess, J. Peter, 'An Ethics of Security'. In *Transformations of Security Studies: Dialogues, Diversity and Discipline*, edited by Gabi Schlag, Julian Junk and Christopher Daase, 94–108. London: Routledge, 2015, 99.

5. Cf., for example, May, R., *The Meaning of Anxiety*. New York: Norton, 1977.

6. Freud, S., 'Three Essays on the Theory of Sexuality'. In *Complete Psychological Works of Sigmund Freud, Volume 7*, edited by James Strachey, 125–243. London: Vintage Classics, 2001 [1905].

7. Ibid.

8. Freud, Sigmund, 'Introductory Lectures on Psycho-Analysis, Part Iii, General Neuroses'. In *Complete Psychological Works of Sigmund Freud, Volume 16*, edited by James Strachey. London: Vintage Classics, 2001 [1916–17]. Freud, Sigmund, 'Inhibitions, Symptoms and Anxiety'. In *Complete Psychological Works of Sigmund Freud, Volume 20*, edited by James Strachey, 125–243. London: Vintage Classics, 2001 [1926].

9. Summarised in Shepherdson, Charles, 'Foreword'. In *Lacan's Seminar on 'Anxiety': An Introduction*, edited by Roberto Harari, ix–lxii. New York: Other Press, 2001, xxxvi–xlv.

10. Strachey, James, 'Editor's Introduction'. In *Complete Psychological Works of Sigmund Freud, Volume 20, Inhibitions, Symptoms and Anxiety*, edited by James Strachey, xxv–xxxvii. London: Vintage Classics, 2001 [1959].

11. Freud, Sigmund, 'Inhibitions, Symptoms and Anxiety'. In *Complete Psychological Works of Sigmund Freud, Volume 20*, edited by James Strachey. London: Vintage Classics, 2001, 100–101.

12. Lacan, Jacques, *The Seminar of Jacques Lacan, Book X, Anxiety*. Translated by A.R. Price. Cambridge: Polity, 2014, 3.

13. Ibid., 14.

14. Seigworth, Gregory J., and Melissa Gregg, 'An Inventory of Shimmers'. In *The Affect Reader*, edited by Gregory J. Seigworth and Melissa Gregg, 1–25. Durham, NC: Duke University Press, 2010.

15. Soler, Colette, *Les Affects Lacaniens*. Paris: Presses Universitaires de Frances, 2011, 5.

16. Lacan, *The Seminar Book X*, 7–8.

17. Ibid., 18.

18. Lacan, *The Seminar Book X*, 22.

19. Lacan, Jacques,'Le Séminaire. Livre XIV, .La Logique du Fantasme, 1966–1967, 16 November 1966'. "https://emea01.safelinks.protection.outlook.com/?url=http%3A%2F%2Fgaogoa.free.fr%2FSeminaires_HTML%2F14-LF%2FLF16111966&data=01%7C01%7Cemmy.eklundh%40kcl.ac.uk%7C518c0e1437a14267ea8408d44a913bbf%7C8370cf1416f34c16b83c724071654356%7C0&sdata=kkN%2BYqX6O35uyJhEF34ZSBIN1szEEuG%2F7H6UqpnQBGw%3D&reserved=0" http://gaogoa.free.fr/Seminaires_HTML/14-LF/LF16111966. htm, 208.

20. Lacan, Jacques, *The Seminar of Jacques Lacan, Book Xi. The Four Fundamental Concepts of Psycho-Analysis*. New York/London: W.W. Norton, 1998, 23.

21. Lacan, Jacques, *The Seminar of Jacques Lacan, Book Xi: The Four Fundamental Concepts of Psycho-Analysis*. New York/London: W.W. Norton, 1998, 235.

22. Kojève, A., *Introduction to the Reading of Hegel*. Ithaca, NY: Cornell University Press, 1980.

23. Lacan, *The Seminar Book X*, 24–25.

24. Lacan, *The Seminar Book X*, 23.

25. Cf. Deleuze, Gilles, and Félix Guattari, *Anti-Oedipus: Capitalism and Schizophrenia*. Penguin Classics. New York: Penguin, 2009, 325.

26. Lacan, J., *Freud's Papers on Technique, 1953–1954*. New York: W.W. Norton, 1988, 235–246.

27. Cf. Cléro, J.-P., *Dictionnaire Lacan*. Paris: Ellipses, 2008, 41–42.
28. Lacan, J., 'Le séminaire. Livre XIV. La logique du fantasme -1966–1967, 16 November, 1966'. 1967, gaogoa, from http://gaogoa.free.fr/Seminaires_HTML/14-LF/LF16111966.htm.
29. Lacan, J., *Les complexes familiaux dans la formation de l'individu: essai d'analayse d'une fonction en psychologie*. Paris: Navarin, 1984, 44.
30. Lacan, J., *On the Names-of-the-Father*. Cambridge: Polity, 2013.
31. Lacan, J., *The Function and Field of Speech and Language in Psychoanalysis*. Écrits. New York: W.W. Norton & Co., 2006, 197–268.
32. Lacan, *On the Names-of-the-Father*, 57–58.
33. Lacan, *The Seminar Book X*, 54.
34. Lacan, *The Seminar Book X*, 54.
35. Ibid., 59.
36. Ibid., 76.
37. Ibid.
38. Lacan, *The Seminar Book X*, 77.
39. Shepherdson, 'Foreword', liii–liv.
40. Boothby, R., *Death and Desire: Psychoanalytic Theory in Lacan's Return to Freud*. New York: Routledge, 1991, 143; Boothby: 1991, 143.
41. Freud, Sigmund, *The Ego and the Id: The Standard Edition of the Complete Psychological Works of Sigmund Freud*. New York, Volume 19, Vintage, 1999. 57.

BIBLIOGRAPHY

Boothby, R. *Death and Desire: Psychoanalytic Theory in Lacan's Return to Freud*. New York: Routledge, 1991.
Burgess, J. Peter. 'An Ethics of Security'. In *Transformations of Security Studies: Dialogues, Diversity and Discipline*, edited by Gabi Schlag, Julian Junk and Christopher Daase, 94–108. London: Routledge, 2015.
Cléro, J.-P. *Dictionnaire Lacan*. Paris: Ellipses, 2018.
Deleuze, Gilles, and Félix Guattari. *Anti-Oedipus: Capitalism and Schizophrenia*. Penguin Classics. New York: Penguin, 2009.
Freud, Sigmund. 'Inhibitions, Symptoms and Anxiety'. In *Complete Psychological Works of Sigmund Freud, Volume 20*, edited by James Strachey, 125–243. London: Vintage Classics, 2001 [1926].
Freud, Sigmund. 'Inhibitions, Symptoms and Anxiety'. In *Complete Psychological Works of Sigmund Freud, Volume 20*, edited by James Strachey. London: Vintage Classics, 2001.
Freud, Sigmund. 'Introductory Lectures on Psycho-Analysis, Part Iii, General Neuroses'. In *Complete Psychological Works of Sigmund Freud, Volume 16*, edited by James Strachey. London: Vintage Classics, 2001 [1916–1917].
Freud, Sigmund. 'Three Essays on the Theory of Sexuality'. In *Complete Psychological Works of Sigmund Freud, Volume 7*, edited by James Strachey, 125–243. London: Vintage Classics, 2001 [1905].

Gay, Peter. *A Godless Jew: Freud, Atheism, and the Making of Psychoanalysis*. New Haven, CT; Cincinnati, OH: Yale University Press: Hebrew Union College Press, 1987.
Gay, Peter. *Freud: A Life for Our Time*. New York: Norton, 2006.
Gelfand, Toby, and John Kerr. *Freud and the History of Psychoanalysis*. Hillsdale, NJ: Analytic Press, 1992.
Kesting, H. *Heinrich Mann and Thomas Mann: A German Fraternal Dispute*. Göttingen: Wallstein, 2003.
Kojève, A. *Introduction to the Reading of Hegel*. Ithaca, NY: Cornell University Press, 1980.
Lacan, Jacques. *Freud's Papers on Technique, 1953–1954*. New York: W. W. Norton, 1988.
Lacan, Jacques. *The Function and Field of Speech and Language in Psychoanalysis*. Écrits, 197–268. New York: W. W. Norton & Co., 2006.
Lacan, Jacques. 'La Logique Du Fantasme'. http://staferla.free.fr/S14/S14%20 LOGIQUE.pdf.
Lacan, Jacques. *Familial Complexes in the formation of the individual: Attempt at the analysis of a function in psychology*. Paris: Navarin, 1984.
Lacan, Jacques. 'Le Séminaire. Livre Xiv. La Logique Du Fantasme-1966–1967, 16 November 1966'. http://gaogoa.free.fr/Seminaires_HTML/14-LF/LF16111966.htm.
Lacan, Jacques. *On the Names-of-the-Father*. Cambridge: Polity, 2013.
Lacan, Jacques. *The Seminar of Jacques Lacan, Book X, Anxiety*. Translated by A. R. Price. Cambridge: Polity, 2014.
Lacan, Jacques. *The Seminar of Jacques Lacan, Book Xi: The Four Fundamental Concepts of Psycho-Analysis*. New York/London: W. W. Norton, 1998.
Lacan, Jacques. 'The Symbolic, the Imaginary and the Real'. In *On the Names-of-the-Father*, edited by Jacques-Alain Miller and Judith Miller, 1–52. Cambridge: Polity, 2013.
May, R. *The Meaning of Anxiety*. New York: Norton, 1977.
Seigworth, Gregory J., and Melissa Gregg. 'An Inventory of Shimmers'. In *The Affect Reader*, edited by Gregory J. Seigworth and Melissa Gregg, 1–25. Durham, NC: Duke University Press, 2010.
Shepherdson, Charles. 'Foreword'. In *Lacan's Seminar on 'Anxiety': An Introduction*, edited by Roberto Harari, ix–lxii. New York: Other Press, 2001.
Soler, Colette. *Les Affects Lacaniens*. Paris: Presses Universitaires de Frances, 2011.
Strachey, James. 'Editor's Introduction'. In *Complete Psychological Works of Sigmund Freud, Volume 20, Inhibitions, Symptoms and Anxiety*, edited by James Strachey, xxv–xxxvii. London: Vintage Classics, 2001 [1959].
Zaretsky, Eli. *Secrets of the Soul: A Social and Cultural History of Psychoanalysis*. 1st ed. New York: Alfred A. Knopf, 2004.

Chapter 3

When Does Repression Become Political? The Use of the Language of Trauma in the Context of Violence and Anxiety

Henrique Tavares Furtado
University of the West of England

In the history of psychoanalytical thought, anxiety is described as a form of fear that lacks an object of reference.[1] Anxious individuals live in a condition of free-floating danger, always acting as though their actions could trigger apocalyptic scenarios, but never capable of describing the source of their affliction. Anxiety is fear that cannot be pinned down, an all-pervasive and all-encompassing fear that has removed itself so far away from any specific object (see introduction) to the point of becoming unfathomable. As a general condition of indiscriminate fear, anxiety leaves people breathing heavily and experiencing palpitations without any apparent danger, paralyses them by the sight of different patterns on the pavement,[2] makes them afraid of walking into shops.[3] In the post-11 September world, where individuals are supposed 'to say something if they see something'[4] this condition of free-floating fear has been turned on its head, challenged against the signs of anxiety themselves: we start to breathe heavily and experience palpitations by the sight of others breathing heavily and experiencing palpitations, although no objective event or reason has triggered this 'hysterical' cycle. For Freud, such incomprehensible phobias were associated to a link between a *traumatic origin* and a *process of unconscious repression*. Be it a pre-puberty sexual encounter[5] or a 'severe mechanical shock',[6] there was a point in time where the stability of someone's mind was crushed by the violence of an unexpected or incomprehensible event (the terrorist attack that inaugurated the 2000s being the obvious reference here). The anxious behaviour – that is, the all-encompassing fear that we cannot understand – is what follows from the mental suppression of this original violence (the sexual abuse or the shock).

It is not hard to understand why the anxiety metaphor has a strong appeal to students and researches of global politics, especially in the fields of human rights and security studies. For a discipline that struggles to explain the seemingly incomprehensible, almost pathological repetition of wanton violence that haunted the last two centuries (e.g., wars, insurgencies, terror, crimes against humanity), a return to the psychoanalytical language provides an interesting solution. If offers an explanation in which trauma, violence and finally political repression are all inextricably connected by the dynamics of the human psyche. Violence thus becomes a question of subjective processes. The suggestion being that *political repression* – understood as the suppression or obliteration of social and political dissent – is, after all, *not unlike unconscious repression*, understood as the psychological suppression of a reality that is too painful or incomprehensible for the mind. All these complex political events just described become symptoms [*sic*] of repressed traumas (previous instances of violence – the shocks – or libidinal drives – the desires) re-enacted time and time again. Žižek's analysis of the terrorist attack to the World Trade Center and the Oklahoma City bombings through the logics of 'resentment' provides a clear explanation of this approach. According to Žižek, these instances of terrorism can be read as a direct consequence of envy, of the terrorists' own feeling of inferiority towards those being terrorised (their western victims). Incapable of experiencing the same pleasures offered by a hedonistic, materialistic western life, the terrorist then desires to destroy the Other's capacity for enjoyment. In this abstract and superficial logic – Žižek does not provide a single empirical example of the cases mentioned – political violence is nothing but the translation of a symptom, of 'hatred pure and simple'.[7] Only by 'working through' this traumatic hatred, that is, by finding their source, ascribing them meaning and remembering the past in a coherent narrative, we can overcome their heritage of pathological violence.

As appealing as they might be, both the anxiety metaphor and the language of trauma that accompanies it have consequences for social scientific research. My objective in this chapter is to present an initial enquiry into theses consequences, opening a pathway for critique that questions the assumptions and the positionality of analyses of violence in terms of the relationship between trauma and anxiety. In other words, this is a first attempt at investigating the position from which the anxiety metaphor emanates; who is behind it and who does it serve as a scientific discourse. In the following pages I present a clear and concise explanation of what I define as the language of trauma, or trauma talk: this psychoanalytically inclined theorisation of *political violence* in terms of a Freudian theory of *unconscious repression* and a Derridean theory of *representation*. Most specifically, I am interested in how trauma talk situates the problematic of experiencing violent events, such as wars, terrorist attacks, genocides and gross violations of human rights, in relation to plethora of different forms of violence. And my tentative conclusion for future research points to the problems of this approach and the focus on the difficulties of *bearing witness*. More specifically, I suggest that posing violence as an *essentially incomprehensible occurrence* - as the language of trauma often does - speaks more of the analyst's position in relation to violence than of the phenomenon itself.

In the first section, I trace the concept of trauma back to its origins in the medical literature and describe its development into a socio-political category of analysis throughout the twentieth century. Primarily, I centre on the most widely recognisable exponent of the language of trauma, Cathy Caruth, the literary theorist commonly referenced by trauma theorists in global studies. I then move on to describe Caruth's conceptualisation of the traumatic as a moment that evades comprehension, and the second and third sections investigate the Freudian and Derridean bases of her work. Frist, I explain how violence enters the discursive space of trauma talk in between the functions of unconscious repression and the dynamics of representation, and how, through a Derridean-Freudian reading, violence is understood as emanating from the processes of exclusion intrinsic in the way human beings make sense of their surroundings. Then, I follow on to explain how this psychoanalytical-philosophical definition of violence connects the idea of political repression with the subjective dynamics of unconscious repression, and what conclusions it could lead to in the study of violent events. Finally, I present a series of questions addressed to researchers who wish to adopt this appealing, but nonetheless problematic, approach, based on the extrapolation of the language of trauma to its extreme logic, whereby every single individual is a possible perpetrator.

THE LANGUAGE OF TRAUMA

The concept of trauma originally refers to the medical literature. It is supposed to mean a rupture produced on the body (a wound) by an external factor (a shock),[8] like a concussion capable of breaking the bones or tearing the flesh of human beings. Over the years, the concept was progressively relocated into more abstract meanings applicable to the most diverse fields (ranging from social psychology and literary criticism to transitional justice[9] and, finally, security studies[10]). This process began in the early stages of psychoanalytical thought – when Pierre Janet, and later, Freud[11] analysed trauma as an abstract wound that ruptured the stability of the mind – and was intensified in the late twentieth century. From the 1980s onwards, and especially after the political mobilisation of veterans of the Vietnam War,[12] trauma became one of the trendiest concepts within the humanities and the social sciences. The traumatic became virtually applicable to any form of experience and capable of explaining any form of violence or violation.

In this long transition to the social context, and via a metaphorical transposition of its medicalised meaning, trauma became associated with the *breakdown of the faculty of understanding*. The one responsible for theorising and disseminating a wider idea of trauma in the 1990s was Cathy Caruth, a literary theorist based at Yale University. Caruth's writings were not exactly extensive – her main works consisted of one book and two introductory articles in an edited volume – but they presented a powerful idea. Through a Freudian and Derridean analysis of the unconscious and cognitive/representational practices, Caruth defined 'trauma', or the 'traumatic' as 'the confrontation with an event that, in its unexpectedness or horror, cannot be placed within the schemes of prior knowledge—that cannot . . . become a matter of 'intelligence'.[13] She defined trauma as the outcome of an experience of ultimate loss of control imposed on the mind – or consciousness – by an untamed reality that disturbs it; that is, that refuses to fit into any previous frames of knowledge. The rupture caused by Caruth's trauma is not a rupture of the flesh, but of the process via which subjects attribute meaning to the reality they experience. It presents a loss of control over how reality is understood, severing the fundamental distinctions used by individuals to make sense of their surroundings.

This idea of trauma, and its relation with the notion of incomprehensibility, are well expressed in Van der Kolk and Van der Hart's analyses of Irène, a famous patient of Pierre Janet's who suffered from a post-traumatic disorder. Irène's malady was caused by the loss of her mother, a victim of tuberculosis. With an absent and alcoholic father, twenty-three-year-old Irène had had to practically take care of her moribund mother by herself, working hard to sustain her family living in that delicate and precarious situation. When death finally came, she was totally exhausted, having 'hardly slept for sixty consecutive nights',[14] which led to a complete breakdown. Instead of making the proper funeral arrangements, a traumatised Irène treated the corpse as though it were still 'alive'. She normally spoke with the cadaver, kept medicating it and struggled to put the lifeless mass back in place again whenever it was knocked over. Irène was finally admitted to Janet's workplace, the Pitié-Salpêtrière Hospital in Paris, after a close aunt, who was unaware of her sister's death, became suspicious of her niece's behaviour.[15]

Irène's disorder was explained by Janet as the result of the denial of her mother's death,[16] which Van der Kolk and Van der Hart take as the direct fruit of her inability to comprehend the situation. Although the event seems perfectly understandable to any outsider – a terminal death from tuberculosis in the early twentieth century is not exactly unintelligible – the traumatic always departs from the subjective level of experience. It must be understood from the perspective of the individual to which a situation appears as incomprehensible, and hence, acquires a traumatic nature. In this sense Janet's patient perfectly fits into Caruth's description of trauma. By the time her mother died, a young, exhausted and impotent 'Irène was unable to grasp the reality of this event.'[17]

The idea of incomprehensibility has been a recurrent trope during the twentieth century, always associated with naturally induced, or artificially created, traumatic events. In fact, Caruth's concept of social or cultural trauma reproduces the themes underlying classic responses to the violent tragedies of our age. For instance, the Nazi programme for the extermination of the European Jewry (the Holocaust or *Shoah*) was and continues to be described by the likes of Arendt,[18] Adorno[19] and, more recently, Agamben[20] as an utterly incomprehensible occurrence and a testimony to the unbridgeable contradictions of human existence. This perspective was synthesised by French filmmaker Claude Lanzmann in a very clear point. For Lanzmann, it is enough to ask the question 'why have the Jews been killed? – for the question to reveal right away its obscenity'.[21] In his perspective, there remains an inevitable gap between any attempt to logically explain the outcome of the Holocaust, be it economic, psychological or structural causes, and its dreadful result, the physical destruction of six million human beings. It is not surprising that such an incomprehensible event was imprinted on the global 'western' imaginary[22] as 'the epoch's inaugural historical trauma'.[23]

Survivors and witnesses of other tragedies often refer to this loss of control, this difficulty in understanding the reasons for, or the causes of, the violence they experienced as constitutive of their own trauma. Testimonies of victims of state terror – the systematic practices of arbitrary detentions and torture – regularly express a difficulty in describing the violations they endured in a way that does justice to their suffering.[24] In the immediate aftermath of 9/11, Judith Barnes, a reporter from the *New York Times*, transcribed the testimony of those who were close by the Twin Towers the very moment they sunk down. If anything, those reports corroborate Caruth's description of the incomprehensible traumatic event, and its dimension of the unspeakable:

> I was walking by the Winter Garden, and then there was this huge noise. Then there was all this paper falling around me. The building just sank down on itself, and tilted over. Then it all turned black; the smoke was all around me, you couldn't see at all.
>
> I thought it was an earthquake or a bomb. We were all panicking; we didn't know what to do.[25]

More recently, columnist Natalie Nougayrède clearly expressed the sense of awe with which French and global audiences were struck after the coordinated terror attacks in Paris on 15 November 2015: 'How could this happen?'[26] A huge noise, paper everywhere, a dark smoke that engulfs the observer, a big question mark. The immediate reaction is to look for something that at least minimally resembles the ongoing experience. But the exercise is futile; previous knowledge fails the observer the moment they are struck by the traumatic. With the lack of knowledge, the incapacity of attributing meaning (a bomb, an earthquake) to what the subject experiences, comes the mind's loss of control and the terror of being left without guidance. They panic, because for not knowing what is happening they are left guideless, with no control over what to do. According to Caruth, a traumatic experience casts a particularly perverse curse on survivors: the burden of bearing witness to something they could not, and never will, fully understand. In more literal terms, the burden of not having understood the experience that they, as survivors, are supposed and expected to recount.

Luckhurst explains this transition from a medicalised idea of trauma to a social understanding in which the traumatic represents a failure of comprehension as a symptom of modernity. It is in the age defined by the contraction of space and time (the invention of the railway system) and the contradictions of development and horror that the widespread production of anxiety and uncertainty pushes trauma to the forefront of social and political life. Incomprehensibility appears as the main product of a time when 'all that is solid melts into air',[27] when the breathtaking achievements of the Industrial Revolution are followed by the dreadful consequences of capitalist exploitation and the rule of 'reason' coexists with the horrendous 'final solution'. It is easy to see how Caruth's definition provides an appealing theoretical framework with which to read the heritage from the violent events of the twentieth and twenty-first centuries. The horror of trauma – or, as it were, its inherent violence – refers to the fact that it exposes the volatility and precariousness of existence, piecing through a fictitious façade of security, quietude and wholesomeness.[28] As modern subjects, always relying on the illusion of rational control over the world, this open and crude precariousness appears as ultimately horrific. And this dynamic operates from the most individualised atomistic level of experience to the grand collective events. In Irène's case, the traumatic accounted for her passivity and inability to react to her mother's death and to interfere with fate. In the collective tragedies of the Holocaust, the 'Dirty Wars' of the Global South and the terrorist attacks in the Global North, the 'traumatic' exposed a series of unbearable truths usually concealed by the veil of normalcy: the barbarism in the heartland of civilisation,[29] the terror of inexplicable disappearances and the fragility of the World's safest places.

VIOLENCE BETWEEN REPRESENTATION AND REPRESSION

The transposition of Caruth's idea of the traumatic as an event that evades comprehension into the realm of political violence, and most specifically political repression, might seem as an appealing move. In fact, several scholars in the human rights and security studies literature have already taken the idea on board, producing an incipient body of knowledge about the effects of trauma and insecurity (see notes 2 and 3). Notwithstanding, speaking of violence via the tropes associated to the traumatic – such as incomprehensibility, the unspeakable and, most of all, the mechanism of repression – has serious and seriously overlooked consequences. To understand these consequences, it is worthwhile returning to Caruth's main theoretical influences: Derrida's account on representation and the Freudian theory of dreams.

Derrida reads the tradition of 'western' philosophy and most specifically of 'western' metaphysics as a mode of reasoning based on a logocentric premise – from the Greek word λόγος (logos) meaning, among other things, both 'reason' and 'speech'. Very succinctly, the term 'logocentrism' refers to the essential privilege of *presence* over *absence*, which from Plato to Husserl has been produced and re-produced by western philosophers.[30] Such a hierarchy, described in the easily identifiable formula presence/absence and all its derivative dichotomies, defines the central core of philosophical reasoning. It is the core of the 'metaphysics of presence'; thereby human beings make sense of the world surrounding them.

Derrida's idea of metaphysics of presence is easily understood vis-a-vis one common instance of logocentrism: the favouring of the *act of speech* over *the act of writing*, also known as the tradition of phonocentrism.[31] It is proper to common sense to see the act of speaking as a much more efficient way of controlling the outcomes of communication. Anyone would acknowledge a face-to-face interaction as the best possible means of dialogue, especially when it comes to explaining the meaning of statements to an addressee in a regular conversation. Partaking in a face-to-face interaction means that the speaker – the one conveying information – is *present*, and hence capable of amending minor misunderstandings about the message he or she intends to pass on. On the other hand, for the phonocentric tradition, the lonely act of reading constitutes the extreme opposite of a face-to-face interaction. Done in the *absence* of the writer, reading presents a dangerous form of representation, prone to error and misappropriations.

This apparently obvious reasoning relies on a theory of representation for which the representational act (in this case writing) is seen as the reproduction of an original presence (in this case the intended message of the writer). For the logocentric logic based on a metaphysics of presence, representation works, in fact, as a reproduction: the re-presentation of a pure and clearly identifiable intention, that is, what the conveyer of information 'wanted to say'[32] through their spoken or written words. Based on this assumed function of representational practices, this rationale creates a hierarchy between different modes of representation ranked as to how 'perfectly' they reproduce an individual's 'wanting to say'. For instance, writing comes last. It is a dangerous form of representation because written words merely reproduce the presence – the meaning – of spoken ones and, as such, they can be easily misunderstood. As mentioned, speaking is a reasonably good form of communication, because the speaker is present during the interaction and can correct their addressee whenever deemed necessary. They can explain the right meaning of what they said. But, in an ideal world, some form of telepathy or paranormal exchange would be the optimum form of communication. Obviously, stressing the logocentric logic to the maximum, the best way to ensure comprehension is to be granted direct access to each other's minds. This way we can all see, crystal-clear and without any mediation, what we all really want to say.

As a matter of fact, Derrida argues, the logocentric logic must assume that individuals are fully aware of their intentions, that they have a translucent relationship with their own minds. This is to say that 'western' philosophy only sees representation as a possibility because it presupposes that the speaker, any speaker, know exactly what they 'want to say'. The metaphysical logic presupposes that, deep within our minds, in soliloquy (when we speak to ourselves) the meaning of an idea is immediately present. And by doing so, metaphysics poses *consciousness as the ultimate source of truth and meaning*. According to this rationale, representation (or re-presentation) is a straightforward possible, albeit imperfect, action. It might not be as good as telepathy, but it still delivers the job.

It is in this sense that the traumatic is conceptualised as 'a crisis of representation, of history and truth'.[33] For the abstract idea of trauma as a blow to the mind and a rupture of the faculty of understanding, traumatic events are situations that interrupt one's mind's immediacy towards oneself. The traumatic event occurs when the re-presentation of a 'wanting to say', the purity of an original description of a violent event, completely breaks down. In other words, the violence of trauma refers to a movement of separation, a blow whereby the subject is separated from itself. This is where both Derrida's and Caruth's works heavily draw on Freud and his equally powerful suggestion that, contrary to common sense, one does not always know what one 'wants to say'.

In his later years, Freud elaborated at length a scientific theory of dreams' interpretation known for its deep description of the structure of the unconscious.[34] His commendable effort was based on a threefold hypothesis. First, Freud envisioned that the fantasies that constitute dreams could indeed be interpreted, a fact latter emphasised by Lacan's return to Freud and his description of the unconscious as a book. He believed there was a hidden meaning behind multiple oneiric imaginations. Second, departing from traditional accounts that saw dreams as omens foretelling the future, Freud's science assumed that the object of dreaming had an inextricable relationship with the past, more specifically with his patients' past experiences. Finally, and following his clinical observations, Freud believed that dreams possessed, or were caused by, an unconscious mechanism defined by its wish-fulfilling functions.

Freudian theory elucidates the idea of a subject that is, for every practical purpose, separated from itself. It interests us here because it poses a counterpart to the logocentric idea of subjective immediacy. In the course of his clinical practice, Freud encountered a recurrent problem. His patients, including Freud himself, were often not automatically aware of the meaning of a given dream. Instead of presenting themselves automatically to the consciousness of the dreamer, dreams were never clear, but were rather fantastically distorted, hiding what Freud believed was the raison d'être of the dream itself. Hence, he presented the work of the interpreter as an indirect excavation, as an attempt to try to get access to the hidden meaning behind the misleading oneiric deliria. Moreover, it is this process of self-concealing that Freud identifies as one of the primary mechanisms of repression: the full meaning of dreams – that is, what the fantasies 'wanted to say' – was effectively concealed from the dreamer due to a process of unconscious repression. In an effort to preserve the healthy structure of the mind from excessive external stimuli, the unconscious repressed ones' 'undesired ideas'[35]: wishes that were too painful, too shameful and too traumatic to immediately appear to oneself. It is worthwhile looking at one of Freud's examples:

> A father had been watching day and night beside the sickbed of his child. After the child died, he retired to rest in an adjoining room, but left the door ajar so that he could look from his room into the next, where the child's body lay surrounded by tall candles. An old man, who had been installed as a watcher, sat beside the body, murmuring prayers. After sleeping for a few hours the father dreamed that the child was standing by his bed, clasping his arm and crying reproachfully: 'Father, don't you see that I am burning?' The father woke up and noticed a bright light coming from the adjoining room. Rushing in, he found that the old man had fallen asleep, and the sheets and one arm of the beloved body were burnt by a fallen candle.[36]

This dream – the 'burning child' – is used by Freud as an extreme case of the wish-fulfilling theory. What is interesting about the dream is the interplay between the father's wish, the violent reality and the function of unconscious repression. Freud reckons that the dream of the burning child is incited by the gloom of light that comes from a candle in the adjoining room where his child's cadaver lays. But the sensory stimulus that would have made an anxiously caring father wake up immediately to protect his boy instead triggers a dream, prolonging the father's sleep. The wish, that here appears through the fantasy of a walking and talking child, is nothing more than the father's wish that his boy was still alive. The postponement of waking and the continuation of sleep serve the wish-fulfilling purpose to 'elaborate the external sensory stimulus [the candle light] . . . they weave it into a dream in order to rob it of any claims it might make as a reminder of the outer world'.[37]

Here lies the most powerfully political suggestion of Freud's work. To explain this self-act of repression – in which case it is an uncomfortable and painful reality that becomes repressed – he resorted to the metaphor of *political censorship*. Freud sees in the unconscious processes that create the dream work and break with the immediacy of the mind a dynamic much similar to that of the 'Russian censorship . . . which allows only those foreign journals which have had certain passages blacked out to fall into the hands of the readers to be protected'.[38] He considered it fruitful to explain *psychological repression at the level of the individual* through a metaphorical analysis of *political repression at the level of the state*. According to his view, anxious individuals are capable of repressing undesirable realities in a much similar way as authoritarian states were capable of repressing undesirable truths.[39] This simple and apparently harmless comparison is very illustrative of the problems inherent in current uses of the language of trauma in the realm of political affairs.

THE 'DICTATOR' INSIDE OUR MINDS?

The appropriation of the language of trauma to describe past experiences of violence has long been criticised for medicalising acts of political resistance, arriving at a simplistic account of 'traumatic' events and for creating the conditions for the management and control of populations by the state apparatus, as is argued elsewhere in this volume.[40] But there is yet another dimension to 'trauma talk': a dimension that in its specific conjunction of Freudian, Derridean and Caruthian insights leads to an analysis of violence based on an *individualised* and rather abstract idea of *political repression* that is both caused and reinforced by existential anxieties.

Freud's understanding of a shattered subject, always capable of carrying out acts of unconscious repression that alienate themselves from their 'own intentions', is at the basis of Derrida's deconstruction of the logocentric order. Derrida uses the Freudian description of the unconscious to illustrate how the *logocentric privilege of presence over absence is arbitrary* and how the notion of a 'wanting to say', which conditions the possibility of re-presentation as such, is deceptive. The dream distortions analysed by Freud have no place whatsoever in the logocentric order that claims the mind as the source of meaning and truth. Instead, they seem to point out exactly the opposite; the division between mechanisms of wish-fulfilment and repression within a subject's mind are testimony to the fallacy of logocentrism. In much the same way that an individual's wish is obscured by the almost unintelligible hallucinations of the dream work, every instance of representation – the reproduction of an original 'wanting to say' via speaking, writing, etc. – is based on a *fundamental act of repression*. In clearer terms, Derrida uses Freud to argue that the recounting of an event, the describing of an intention or the recollection of the past never actually recovers an original presence ('wanting to say'). Instead, these instances of representation are repressive-like moments that serve the purpose of concealing the uncomfortable and 'traumatic' *absence of any possible origin*.

Much in the same way as the Freudian mind, the Derridean theory of the 'event' defines that the meaning of an event is never immediate to itself. It is rather the case that, in its overwhelming immediacy, an event eludes the dynamics of signification and evades the mind's capacity to make sense of its surroundings. This happens because in Derridean thought, meaning is understood as a function of iterability, or repetition and *différance* (difference in both time and space). It possesses a backwards temporality, meaning that the mind can only understand and make sense of something insofar as this something is the expression of a *genre already previously acknowledged*.

The implications of 'trauma talk' become particularly clear when it is the violent events themselves that must be represented in their original incomprehensibility. When individuals are called to recount 'the memory of the horrors'[41] they bore witness to, their acts of truth-telling are also expected to respect the logics of logocentrism. They are supposed to infuse their stories of pain and sorrow with an original 'wanting to say', much in the same way as 'writing' does, that puts forth a sense of morale, an objective and truthful account of the past.[42]

When discussing 9/11, Derrida points out that this dynamic is precisely what a violent event lacks. Using a very similar trope to Caruth's he argues that events are experiences that come 'to surprise and to suspend comprehension: the event is first of all that which I do not . . . comprehend'.[43] In this sense, an event – a presence in the past – has no intrinsic truth or meaning. On the contrary, to constitute an 'event' proper, the occurrence must be defined by the traumatic: the absence of meaning that characterises its pure unintelligibility. And the language of trauma uses these instances when violence is recounted, remembered and commemorated – in other words, represented – as testimonies to the inner limitations of representation and the very problem of bearing witness. This brings us back to the first section: how is it possible to remember or recount an event that evades comprehension and defies the faculties of the mind? Does that not lead witnesses and the survivors to a mere unarticulated repetition of the event itself? Does it not restrict their lives to an acting-out that risks re-traumatising a fragile and already traumatised mind like Irène's?

This understanding of the 'traumatic event', as it were, brings us to a fundamental point. Because an event has no original meaning and because it discloses no 'wanting to say', its original and truthful presence can never be reproduced by representational practices, but only artificially produced *through them* and in hindsight. This belated exercise of signification – the *nachträglich* involved in any attempt to produce meaning[44] – is what connects the *experience of violence* with the drive towards a *psychoanalytical interpretation of repression*. Because the event has no origin and no meaning, its immediacy translated as pure potentiality 'calls for a movement of appropriation'.[45] Just like in the dream of the burning child, the absence represented by the child's death calls for the father's dream.

This movement of appropriation seeks, first and foremost, to repress the traumatic in the event. It poses an attempt to attribute meaning, that is, to comprehend and explain an incomprehensible or undesirable situation so as to create an artificial 'wanting to say' and to appease the anxiety generated by the complete loss of control. The useless violence of Nazi officials is 'explained' as an instance of dehumanisation,[46] the disappearances in Argentina are blamed on the victims themselves,[47] the terrorist is described as mentally unstable.[48] These moments of appropriation trigger a series of dispute over the meaning of violence. Edkins, and most adepts of the language of trauma, emphasise how the outcome of this dispute often undermines – or rather *represses* – the stories of those who experienced violence themselves: how the account of survivors and witnesses of wars, terrorist attacks and other traumatic events 'have to be hidden, ignored, or medicalised'[49] so that a coherent lesson about what the violent past meant (what it 'wanted to say') can be drawn and disseminated. It is easy to see how this idea of the traumatic unintelligibility (of the unspeakable nature of violence) can also be turned against the victims themselves. As Caruth elucidates the question, any attempts to give meaning to a violently unintelligible event 'is always a matter of distortion, a filtering of the original event through *the fictions of traumatic repression*'.[50] It is through this distortion, via the exclusions and silences that it puts in place, that anxiety-driven acts of *unconscious repression* become acts of *political repression*.

The logic of the argumentation can be more clearly explained. An event is traumatic because it reminds subjects that there is always a form of alterity – always a different side – to any act of truth-telling. Hence, the recounting of an event is indissociated from an act to control its ultimate potentiality. It necessarily entails the silence of opposing interpretation that threatens one's idea of the event's 'wanting to say'. Representation – just like the dream of the burning child – is not meant to 'reproduce a presence': it is meant to *repress* the absolute and unbearable absence that emanates from our encounter with an unavoidable reality.

According to the language of trauma, it is this intrinsic and unescapable exclusion, caused by our very ability to make sense of our surroundings, that turns every human being into two things: a *tacit perpetrator of metaphysical violence* – the violence of excluding other possible interpretations of an event – and a *potential agent of repression*. Repression is here conceptualised as more than an instrumental action employed against political opposition by authoritarian regimes; it is the very condition of understanding of an always, already authoritarian form of subjectivity. It is the mechanism of defence upon which the good health and security of the psyche depends; the censorship that creates a façade, protecting consciousness from the outer world. If in *The Interpretation of Dreams* this possibility is posed by the structure of the unconscious – a system originally built to preserve an organism from excessive external stimuli – in Derrida, it rather becomes a consequence of language itself. It is language and the text (or the all-encompassing dynamics of representation) that lie in the source of repression. It is by our very capacity of *dicere* (speaking), by our potentiality to *dictum* (state) that we become somehow *dictatores* (dictators).

If Freud used the concept of political repression to illustrate the processes through which the unconscious represses 'inconvenient' truths, the language of trauma does the opposite. It is suggestive, through the concept of the traumatic, that practices of representation, particularly those related to the signification of violent events, inevitably lead to an act of repression. Paraphrasing Freud on the matter, representation can also work as a form of wish-fulfilment: it fulfils one's wish to be right.

CONCLUSION

This chapter provided an initial, introductory explanation of what I termed 'trauma talk', or the attempt to theorise and explain the phenomena of violence and political repression based on psychoanalytically inclined approaches. Throughout the text, I explained the medicalised origins of the concept of trauma and its transposition to the sociological and political arena in the course of the late twentieth century. Focusing on Caruth's conceptualisation of trauma as the *breakdown of the faculty of understanding* and expanding on her Freudian and Derridean bases, I described how the language of trauma leads to a depiction of *repression* as one of the foundational stones of human experience. Based either on the structure of the unconscious or on the nature of language itself, for theorists of trauma in the social sciences and the humanities, the fact remains that every single mind carries the potentiality for rejecting realities that disturb their peaceful stability. This is to say that every single individual faced with an incomprehensible 'event' risks perpetrating a form of metaphysical violence, thereby opposing interpretations of the event are excluded, ignored, silenced or simply *repressed*. Whereas a deeper critique of 'trauma talk' is beyond the scope of this work, the last sections have provided enough elements to elaborate a few concluding remarks.

This first problematic arising from the language of trauma is the idea of *incomprehensibility*. The whole theorisation of trauma as that which evades comprehension relies on the assumption that events, strictly speaking, lack an original meaning. Trauma comes from this disturbing absence posed by an encounter with a reality the mind cannot control – such as death, a tragedy of unfathomable proportions or the existence of something which disrespects prior knowledge. Aside from the philosophical questions regarding the event itself (how to define something that avoids definition?) a serious appraisal of the language of trauma begs the question, how about occurrences that *are easily understood?* What can trauma theorists say about instances where violence is deployed in a purely intelligible and crudely translucent way? Where violence is neither useless[51] nor related to subjective processes[52] but operates a logic described by Etienne Balibar as *super objective*, that is, as related to the basis of the capitalist system of excessive exploitation?[53] In this first, tentative conclusion it seems that although the triad anxiety-violence-trauma provides interesting ideas to work through a violence that arises out of subjective instances of repression, it lacks the theoretico-practical elements to address more structurally inclined notions of violence.

The second point is an extension of this question, further problematising the concept of violence as seen through the lenses of the traumatic. Almost every work on violence begins by pointing out the overwhelming abundance of things that could be called 'violent'.[54] By emphasising a Derridean idea of *metaphysical violence* trauma talk narrows down the scope of analysis to a violence connected to the exclusionary dynamics of representation. And by focusing on these dynamics, it risks falling into a Freudian-like, individualisable idea of political repression as interchangeable with the unconscious faculty of self-censorship. We can see this clearly in Žižek's analysis of terrorism as resentment.[55] To speak of violence via the language of unconscious drives is to make a choice; to decide to shift focus on one interpretation of the phenomenon, associated with the dimension of the *unspeakable*, to the detriment of other possible forms of understandings. This leads us to yet another question: what can we say about situations where the *traumatic has become the normal way of life*? How can we explain human suffering and destruction that are unrelated to subjective anxieties or *exceptional ruptures*, but are rather a normalised part of the society we live in? Take for example the situation in certain favelas in Rio de Janeiro, where in the mid-1990s a working group from the *Medicine san Frontieres* found that 90 percent of the local population harassed by an uninterrupted 'war on drugs' constantly experienced post-traumatic stress disorder symptoms.[56] In this sense it would be interesting to contrast the Freudian description of the wish-fulfilling function of dreams with that of another psychoanalyst, Frantz Fanon. Analysing colonialism as a form of psychopathology that structured the minds of the coloniser towards self-hatred, Fanon described a series of black patients who constantly dreamt of being white.[57] The question is whether Freud and Fanon were talking about the same phenomenon, or if the violence they described differed profoundly.

The third and final remark refers to an ethical dimension of critique. Are we as social scientists and researchers in the humanities prepared to take the consequences of trauma talk to its full potential? Can we explain *political repression* as deriving from the individual drive of *unconscious repression*? Are we comfortable with the suggestion that behind everyone – even behind survivors of the most horrific violations – there is a potential dictator? On a different, yet related, note, can we truly talk about terrorism in a depoliticised and abstract form of resentment? And, in case of a positive answer, is that not in itself a way of changing the conversation of moving focus away from the *structural dynamics of objective violence* into the individualisable sources of political repression?

NOTES

1. Sigmund Freud, 'Part Three: General Theory of the Neuroses. XXV: Fear and Anxiety', in *A General Introduction to Psychoanalysis* (New York: Boni and Liveright, 1920 [1917]).

2. Ibid.

3. Sigmund Freud, 'The Hysterical Proton Pseudos', in *Complete Psychological Works of Sigmund Freud. Vol. 1*, eds. James Strachey and Anna Freud (London: Vintage Classics, 2001 [1895]).

4. The phrase 'if you see something, say something' refers to the anti-terrorist campaign inaugurated by the US Department of Homeland Security in 2010. For more information see Homeland Security. 'If You See Something, Say Something', https://www.dhs.gov/see-something-say-something/about-campaign.

5. This refers to one of Freud's most famous patients, Emma Eckstein. Emma's hysteria expressed itself as a very peculiar fear of walking into shops by herself, which she explained as the consequence of a specific event in her childhood, when two shop assistants laughed at her childish clothes. Feeling embarrassed by the situation, Emma ran away from the precinct and developed her pattern of anxious behaviour. Nevertheless, Freud rejected Emma's explanation of her affliction as a senseless theory. If what she said made any sense (the connection between laughter

and her clothes), then the hysteric affliction would invariably attack her whether she was 'by herself' or not. Supposing Emma would still be wearing clothes whenever she walking into a shop, her fear of being laughed at would manifest itself. Besides, as a grown-up person, she would hardly wear the same childish outfits that once triggered her 'trauma'. Based on an enigmatic and seemingly disconnected fact – that Emma recalled being sexually aroused by the sight of one of the shop assistants – Freud creates another explanation. In fact Emma had been abused by a shopkeeper, even before the episode she recalled actually happened. It was the suppressed memory of this abuse that generated the seemingly *incomprehensible* neurosis.

6. Sigmund Freud, 'Beyond the Pleasure Principle', in *Beyond the Pleasure Principle and Other Writings*, ed. Adam Phillips (London: Penguin Books, 2003 [1920]), p. 50.

7. Slavoj Žižek, *Violence: Six Sideways Reflections* (London: Profile Books, 2009), p. 78.

8. Jenny Edkins, *Trauma and the Memory of Politics* (Cambridge: Cambridge University Press, 2003); 'Remembering Relationality: Trauma Time and Politics', in *Memory, Trauma and World Politics: Reflections on the Relationship between Past and Present*, ed. Duncan Bell (Basingstoke: Palgrave Macmillan, 2006); Ruth Leys, *Trauma: A Genealogy* (Chicago: The University of Chicago Press, 2000); Roger Luckhurst, *The Trauma Question* (London: Routledge, 2008); Jeffrey Alexander, *Trauma: A Social Theory* (Cambridge: Polity, 2012).

9. Claire Moon, 'Healing Past Violence: Traumatic Assumptions and Therapeutic Interventions in War and Reconciliation,' *Journal of Human Rights* 8, no. 1 (2009); David Mendeloff, 'Trauma and Vengeance: Assessing the Psychological and Emotional Effects of Post-Conflict Justice,' *Human Rights Quarterly* 31, no. 3 (2009); Marita Eastmond and Johanna Selimovic, 'Silence as Possibility in Postwar Everyday Life', *International Journal of Transitional Justice* 6, no. 3 (2012).

10. Kate Schick, 'Acting Out and Working Through: Trauma and (In)Security', *Review of International Studies* 37, no. 4 (2011); Erica Resende and Dovile Budryte, *Memory and Trauma in International Relations* (Oxon, NY: Routledge, 2013); Emma Hutchison and Roland Bleiker, 'Emotional Reconciliation: Reconstituting Identity and Community after Trauma', *European Journal of Social Theory* 11, no. 3 (2008); Emma Hutchison, 'Trauma and the Politics of Emotions: Constituting Identity, Security and Community after the Bali Bombing', *International Relations* 24, no. 1 (2010).

11. Ruth Leys, *Trauma: A Genealogy* (Chicago; London: University of Chicago Press, 2000); Karen Brounéus, 'The Trauma of Truth Telling: Effects of Witnessing in the Rwandan Gacaca Courts on Psychological Health', *Journal of Conflict Resolution* 54, no. 3 (2010).

12. Ian Hacking, 'Memoro-Politics, Trauma and the Soul', *History of the Human Sciences* 7, no. 2 (1994).

13. Cathy Caruth, 'Recapturing the Past: Introduction', in *Trauma: Explorations in Memory*, ed. Cathy Caruth (Baltimore, MD; London: The Johns Hopkins University Press, 1995), p. 153.

14. Bessel van der Kolk and Onno Van der Hart, 'The Intrusive Past: The Flexibility of Memory and the Engraving of Trauma', p. 161.

15. Ibid.

16. Van der Kolk and Van der Hart, 'The Intrusive Past: The Flexibility of Memory and the Engraving of Trauma', 161; Ruth Leys, *Trauma: A Genealogy* (Chicago; London: University of Chicago Press, 2000).

17. Van der Kolk and Van der Hart, 'The Intrusive Past: The Flexibility of Memory and the Engraving of Trauma', p. 161.

18. Hannah Arendt, *The Origins of Totalitarianism* (New York: Harcourt Brace & Company, 1973), p. 459.

19. Theodor Adorno, 'What Does Coming to Terms with the Past Mean?' in *Bitburg in Moral and Political Perspective*, ed. Geoffrey Harman (Bloomington: Indiana University Press, 1986).

20. Giorgio Agamben, *Remnants of Auschwitz: The Witness and the Archive* (New York: Zone Books, 2002).

21. Claude Lanzmann and Cathy Caruth, 'The Obscenity of Understanding: An Evening with Claude Lanzmann', in *Trauma: Explorations in Memory*, ed. Cathy Caruth (Baltimore, MD; London: The Johns Hopkins University Press, 1995), p. 204.

22. Dominick LaCapra, 'Revisiting the Historians' Debate: Mourning and Genocide', *History and Memory* 9, no. 1 (1997); Dominick LaCapra, *Representing the Holocaust: History, Theory, Trauma* (Ithaca, NY: Cornell University Press, 1996); Maja Zehfuss, *Wounds of Memory: The Politics of War in Germany* (Cambridge: Cambridge University Press, 2007).

23. Luckhurst, *The Trauma Question*.

24. Priscila Hayner, *Unspeakable Truths: Transitional Justice and the Challenge of Truth Commissions* (New York: Routledge, 2011).

25. Juliane Barnes, 'Horror, Alarm and Chaos Grip Downtown Manhattan', http://www.nytimes.com/2001/09/11/national/11CND-SCENE.html.

26. Natalie Nougayrède, 'Paris Attacks Leave France in Trauma, Fearing for the Future', https://www.theguardian.com/commentisfree/2015/nov/14/paris-attacks-leave-france-in-trauma-fearing-for-the-future.

27. Karl Marx and Frederick Engels, *The Communist Manifesto* (London: Vintage, 2010 [1948]), p. 25.

28. Jenny Edkins, 'Ground Zero: Reflections on Trauma, in/Distinction and Response', *Journal for Cultural Research* 8, no. 3 (2004).

29. LaCapra, *Representing the Holocaust*; Michael Mann, *The Dark Side of Democracy: Explaining Ethnic Cleansing* (Cambridge: Cambridge University Press, 2005).

30. Jacques Derrida, *Speech and Phenomena: And Other Essays on Husserl's Theory of Signs* (Evanston, IL: Northwestern University Press, 1973); *Of Grammatology* (Baltimore, MD: The Johns Hopkins University Press, 1997); *Positions* (London; New York: Continuum, 2004).

31. Jacques Derrida, *Of Grammatology* (Baltimore, MD: The Johns Hopkins University Press, 1997).

32. Jacques Derrida, *Limited Inc* (Evanston, IL: Northwestern University Press, 1988).

33. Luckhurst, *The Trauma Question*, p. 5.

34. Sigmund Freud, *The Interpretation of Dreams* (London: Wordsworth Editions Limited, 1997 [1899]).

35. Freud, *The Interpretation of Dreams*, p. 16
36. Ibid., p. 353.
37. Ibid., p. 408.
38. Ibid., p. 372.
39. Ibid., p. 53.
40. Claire Moon, 'Narrating the Present: Confessional and Testimonial Truth-Telling', in *Narrating Political Reconciliation: South Africa's Truth and Reconciliation Commission* (Lanham, MD: Lexington Books, 2008); 'Healing Past Violence: Traumatic Assumptions and Therapeutic Interventions in War and Reconciliation', *Journal of Human Rights* 8, no. 1 (2009); Michael Humphrey, 'Reconciliation and the Therapeutic State', *Journal of Intercultural Studies* 26, no. 3 (2005); Vanessa Pupavac, 'Human Security and the Rise of Global Therapeutic Governance', *Conflict, Security and Development* 5, no. 2 (2005); Michel Foucault, *Society Must Be Defended: Lectures at the Collège de France, 1975–76* (New York: Picador, 2003); Michel Foucault, *Security, Territory, Population: Lectures at the Collège de France, 1977–78* (New York: Picador, 2009).
41. Zehfuss, *Wounds of Memory*, p. 32.
42. Idith Zertal, 'From the People's Hall to the Wailing Wall: A Study in Memory, Fear, and War', *Representations* 69, no. 69 (2000); Patrick Pinkerton, 'Resisting Memory: The Politics of Memorialisation in Post-Conflict Northern Ireland', *The British Journal of Politics & International Relations* 14, no. 1 (2012); Jeffrey K. Olick, 'Collective Memory: The Two Cultures', *Sociological Theory* 17, no. 3 (1999); Aletta J. Norval, 'Memory, Identity and the (Im)Possibility of Reconciliation: The Work of the Truth and Reconciliation Commission in South Africa', *Constellations* 5, no. 2 (1998).
43. Jacques Derrida, 'Autoimmunity: Real and Symbolic Suicides: A Dialogue with Jacques Derrida', in *Philosophy in a Time of Terror: Dialogues with Jurgen Habermas and Jacques Derrida*, ed. Giovanna Borradori (Chicago: University of Chicago Press, 2004), p. 90.
44. Jacques Derrida, *Writing and Difference* (London: Routledge, 2001).
45. Derrida, 'Autoimmunity', p. 90.
46. Primo Levi, *The Drowned and the Saved* (London: Abacus, 2012 [1986]).
47. Emilio Crenzel, 'El Prólogo del Nunca Más y la Teoría de los Dos Demonios: Reflexiones sobre una Representación de La Violencia Política en la Argentina', *Contenciosa* 1 (2013).
48. Stéphane Baele, 'Are Terrorists "Insane"? A Critical Analysis of Mental Health Categories in Lone Terrorists' Trials', *Critical Studies on Terrorism* 7, no. 2 (2014).
49. Jenny Edkins, *Trauma and the Memory of Politics* (Cambridge: Cambridge University Press, 2003), p. 52.
50. Cathy Caruth, *Unclaimed Experience: Trauma, Narrative and History* (Baltimore, MD: The Johns Hopkins University Press, 1996), p. 15.
51. Levi, 'Useless Violence'.
52. Slavoj Žižek, *Violence: Six Sideways Reflections* (London: Profile Books, 2009).
53. Etienne Balibar, *Politics and the Other Scene* (London; New York: Verso, 2002).

54. Giorgio Agamben, Lorenzo Fabbri and Elisabeth Fay, 'On the Limits of Violence', *Diacritics* 4 (2009); Helen Dexter, 'Terrorism and Violence: Another Violence Is Possible?' *Critical Studies on Terrorism* 5, no. 1 (2012); Arendt, *On Violence*; Michel Wieviorka, *Violence: A New Approach* (London: SAGE Publications, 2009); Randal Collins, *Violence: A Micro-Sociological Theory* (Princeton, NJ: Princeton University Press, 2008); Charles Tilly, *The Politics of Collective Violence* (Cambridge: Cambridge University Press, 2003).

55. Žižek, *Violence*.

56. Nancy Cardia, 'Exposição à Violência: seus Efeitos sobre Valores e Crenças em Relação a Violência, Polícia e Direitos Humanos', (Exposure to violence: effects on values and belief in relation to political violence and human rights) *Lusotopie* (2003).

57. Frantz Fanon, *Black Skin, White Masks* (London: Pluto Press, 2008).

BIBLIOGRAPHY

Adorno, Theodor. 1986. 'What Does Coming to Terms with the Past Mean?' In *Bitburg in Moral and Political Perspective*, edited by Geoffrey Harman, 114–29. [s.l.]: Indiana University Press.

Agamben, Giorgio. 2002. *Remnants of Auschwitz: The Witness and the Archive*. New York: Zone Books.

Agamben, Giorgio, Lorenzo Fabbri and Elisabeth Fay. 2009. 'On the Limits of Violence'. *Diacritics* 4 (Winter): 103–11.

Alexander, Jeffrey. 2012. *Trauma: A Social Theory*. Cambridge: Polity.

Arendt, Hannah. 1970. *On Violence*. New York; London: Harcourt Brace Jovanovich.

Arendt, Hannah. 1973. *The Origins of Totalitarianism*. New York: Harcourt Brace & Company.

Baele, Stéphane J. 2014. 'Are Terrorists "Insane"? A Critical Analysis of Mental Health Categories in Lone Terrorists' Trials'. *Critical Studies on Terrorism* May (April): 1–20.

Balibar, Étienne. 2002. *Politics and the Other Scene*. London; New York: Verso.

Barnes, Juliane. 2001. 'Horror, Alarm and Chaos Grip Downtown Manhattan', available at: http://www.nytimes.com/2001/09/11/national/11CND-SCENE.html.

Brounéus, Karen. 2010. 'The Trauma of Truth Telling: Effects of Witnessing in the Rwandan Gacaca Courts on Psychological Health Karen'. *Journal of Conflict Resolution* 54 (3): 408–37.

Cardia, Nancy. 2003. 'Exposição à Violência : Seus Efeitos Sobre Valores E Crenças Em Relação a Violência, Polícia E Direitos Humanos'. *Lusotopie*: 299–328.

Caruth, Cathy. 1995. 'Recapturing the Past: Introduction'. In *Trauma: Explorations in Memory*, edited by Cathy Caruth, 151–157. Baltimore; London: The Johns Hopkins University Press.

Caruth, Cathy. 1996. *Unclaimed Experience: Trauma, Narrative and History*. Baltimore: The Johns Hopkins University Press.

Collins, Randal. 2008. *Violence: A Micro-Sociological Theory*. Princeton, NJ: Princeton University Press.

Crenzel, Emilio. 2013. 'El Prólogo Del Nunca Más E La Teoría de Los Dos Demonios. Reflexiones Sobre Una Representación de La Violencia Política En La Argentina'. *Contenciosa* 1: 1–19.
Derrida, Jacques. 1973. *Speech and Phenomena: And Other Essays on Husserl's Theory of Signs*. Evanston, IL: Northwestern University Press.
Derrida, Jacques. 1988. *Limited Inc*. Evanston, IL: Northwestern University Press.
Derrida, Jacques. 1997. *Of Gramatology*. Baltimore: The Johns Hopkins University Press.
Derrida, Jacques. 2001. *Writing and Difference*. London: Routledge.
Derrida, Jacques. 2003. 'Autoimmunity: Real and Symbolic Suicides: A Dialogue with Jacques Derrida'. In *Philosophy in a Time of Terror: Dialogues with Jurgen Habermas and Jacques Derrida*, edited by Giovanna Borradori, 85–136. Chicago: University of Chicago Press.
Derrida, Jacques. 2004. *Positions*. London; New York: Continuum.
Dexter, Helen. 2012. 'Terrorism and Violence: Another Violence Is Possible?' *Critical Studies on Terrorism* 5 (1): 121–37.
Eastmond, M., and J. M. Selimovic. 2012. 'Silence as Possibility in Postwar Everyday Life'. *International Journal of Transitional Justice* 6 (3): 502–24.
Edkins, Jenny. 2003. *Trauma and the Memory of Politics*. Cambridge: Cambridge University Press.
Edkins, Jenny. 2004. 'Ground Zero: Reflections on Trauma, In/distinction and Response'. *Journal for Cultural Research* 8 (3): 247–70.
Edkins, Jenny. 2006. 'Remembering Relationality: Trauma Time and Politics'. In *Memory, Trauma and World Politics: Reflections on the Relationship between Past and Present*, edited by Duncan Bell, 99–115. Basingstoke: Palgrave Macmillan.
Fanon, Frantz. 2008. *Black Skin, White Masks*. London: Pluto Press.
Freud, Sigmund. 1920 [1917]. 'Part Three: General Theory of the Neuroses. XXV: Fear and Anxiety'. In *A General Introduction to Psychoanalysis*. New York: Boni and Liveright.
Freud, Sigmund. 1997 [1899]. *The Interpretation of Dreams*. London: Wordsworth Editions Limited.
Freud, Sigmund. 2001 [1895]. 'The Hysterical Proton Pseudos'. In *Complete Psychological Works of Sigmund Freud. Vol. 1*, edited by James Strachey and Anna Freud, 352–56. London: Vintage Classics.
Freud, Sigmund. 2003 [1920]. 'Beyond the Pleasure Principle'. In *Beyond the Pleasure Principle and Other Writings*, edited by Adam Phillips, 42–102. London: Penguin Books.
Hacking, I. 1994. 'Memoro-Politics, Trauma and the Soul'. *History of the Human Sciences* 7 (2): 29–52.
Hayner, Priscila. 2011. *Unspeakable Truths: Transitional Justice and the Challenge of Truth Commissions*. New York: Routledge.
Humphrey, Michael. 2005. 'Reconciliation and the Therapeutic State'. *Journal of Intercultural Studies* 26 (3): 203–20.
Hutchison, E. 2010. 'Trauma and the Politics of Emotions: Constituting Identity, Security and Community after the Bali Bombing'. *International Relations* 24 (1): 65–86.

Hutchison, E., and R. Bleiker. 2008. 'Emotional Reconciliation: Reconstituting Identity and Community after Trauma'. *European Journal of Social Theory* 11 (3): 385–403.
LaCapra, Dominick. 1996. *Representing the Holocaust: History, Theory, Trauma.* Ithaca, NY: Cornell University Press.
Lacapra, Dominick. 1997. 'Revisiting the Historians' Debate: Mourning and Genocide'. *History and Memory* 9 (1): 80–112.
Lanzmann, Claude, and Cathy Caruth. 1995. 'The Obscenity of Understanding: An Evening with Claude Lanzmann'. In *Trauma: Explorations in Memory*, edited by Cathy Caruth, 200–220. Baltimore; London: The Johns Hopkins University Press.
Levi, Primo. 2012 [1986]. *The Drowned and the Saved.* London: Abacus.
Leys, Ruth. 2000. *Trauma: A Genealogy.* Chicago: The University of Chicago Press.
Luckhurst, Roger. 2008. *The Trauma Question.* London: Routledge.
Mann, Michael. 2005. *The Dark Side of Democracy: Explaining Ethnic Cleansing.* Cambridge: Cambridge University Press.
Marx, Karl and Frederick Engels. 2010 [1948]. *The Communist Manifesto.* London: Vintage.
Mendeloff, David. 2009. 'Trauma and Vengeance: Assessing the Psychological and Emotional Effects of Post-Conflict Justice'. *Human Rights Quarterly* 31 (3): 592–623.
Moon, Claire. 2008. 'Narrating the Present : Confessional and Testimonial Truth-Telling'. In *Narrating Political Reconciliation: South Africa's Truth and Reconciliation Commission*, 91–114. Lanham, MD: Lexington Books.
Moon, Claire. 2009. 'Healing Past Violence: Traumatic Assumptions and Therapeutic Interventions in War and Reconciliation'. *Journal of Human Rights* 8 (1): 71–91.
Norval, Aletta J. 1998. 'Memory, Identity and the (Im)possibility of Reconciliation: The Work of the Truth and Reconciliation Commission in South Africa'. *Constellations* 5 (2): 250–65.
Nougayrède, Natalie. 2015. 'Paris Attacks Leave France in Trauma, Fearing for the Future', available at: https://www.theguardian.com/commentisfree/2015/nov/14/paris-attacks-leave-france-in-trauma-fearing-for-the-future.
Olick, Jeffrey K. 1999. 'Collective Memory : The Two Cultures'. *Sociological Theory* 17 (3): 333–48.
Pinkerton, Patrick. 2012. 'Resisting Memory: The Politics of Memorialisation in Post-Conflict Northern Ireland'. *The British Journal of Politics & International Relations* 14(1): 131–52.
Pupavac, Vanessa. 2005. 'Human Security and the Rise of Global Therapeutic Governance'. *Conflict, Security and Development* 5 (2): 161–81.
Resende, Erica, and Dovile Budryte. 2013. *Memory and Trauma in International Relations.* Oxon, NY: Routledge.
Schick, Kate. 2011. 'Acting Out and Working Through: Trauma and (In)security'. *Review of International Studies* 37 (4): 1837–55.
Tilly, Charles. 2003. *The Politics of Collective Violence.* Cambridge: Cambridge University Press.

Van Der Kolk, Bessel and Onno Van Der Hart. 1995. 'The Intrusive Past: The Flexibility of Memory and the Engraving of Trauma'. In *Trauma: Explorations in Memory*, edited by Cathy Caruth, 158–82. Baltimore; London: The Johns Hopkins University Press.

Wieviorka, Michel. 2003. *Violence: A New Approach*. London: Sage Publication.

Zehfuss, Maja. 2007. *Wounds of Memory: The Politics of War in Germany*. Cambridge: Cambridge University Press.

Zertal, Idith. 2000. 'From the People' S Hall to the Wailing Wall: A Study in Memory, Fear, and War'. *Representations* 69 (Winter): 96–126.

Žižek, Slavoj. 2008. *Violence: Six Sideways Reflections*. London: Profile Books.

Part II

SECURITY: CONTROL

Chapter 4

Anxiety: Trauma: Resilience

Mark Neocleous

We live, apparently, in anxious times.* Nowhere is this clearer than in the idea that we live in an 'age of anxiety'. Wander into any bookshop and one finds the theme in just about every section: cultural studies (*The Age of Anxiety*, 1996); criminology (*Fear of Crime: Critical Voices in an Age of Anxiety*, 2008); the human sciences (*The Age of Anxiety: Conspiracy Theory and the Human Sciences*, 2001); corporate management (*Global Firms and Emerging Markets in an Age of Anxiety*, 2004); parenting (*Perfect Madness: Motherhood in the Age of Anxiety*, 2005; *Worried All the Time: Overparenting in an Age of Anxiety and How to Stop It*, 2003); religion (*Hope against Darkness: The Transforming Vision of St. Francis in an Age of Anxiety*, 2002; *For Our Age of Anxiety: Sermons from the Sermon on the Mount*, 2009; *Ancient Wisdom for an Age of Anxiety*, 2007); language (*At War with Diversity: US Language Policy in an Age of Anxiety*, 2000); drugs policy (*The Age of Anxiety: A History of America's Turbulent Affair with Tranquilizers*, 2009; *A Social History of the Minor Tranquilizers: The Quest for Small Comfort in the Age of Anxiety*, 1991); new age claptrap (*The Road Less Travelled: Spiritual Growth in an Age of Anxiety*, 1997); sexology (*Mindblowing Sex in the Real World: Hot Tips for Doing It in the Age of Anxiety*, 1995); food and drink (*Consuming Passions: Cooking and Eating in an Age of Anxiety*, 1998); terrorism studies (*The Age of Anxiety: McCarthyism to Terrorism*, 2005) and just plain old hope (*Hope in the Age of Anxiety*, 2009). This list could go on.

This huge intellectual labour and cultural production parallels developments in the psychiatric field, as indicated by the growth of the *Diagnostic and Statistical Manual of Mental Disorders* (DSM), the American Psychiatric Association's list of mental disorders and how to diagnose them. The first edition of the DSM in 1952 ran to 129 pages and contained just 106 diagnostic 'disorders'. The second edition was published in 1968, with 134 pages and 182 categories. DSM-III, published in 1980, was 494 pages long and contained 265 categories. DSM-IV, from 1994, had 886 pages and 297 diagnostic categories. DSM-V, released in 2013, runs to just under 1,000 pages. Part of the increase in size and proliferation of categories has been because disorders have been defined according to forms of behaviour and used to define clinical categories. For example, being a bit nervous or shy is a symptom of an underlying condition, which then becomes a clinical category such as social phobia, which is the term used as an explanation of what the manual calls 'social anxiety disorder'. Some of what it says about social anxiety concerns specific conditions, such as Parkinson's disease or disfigurement, but the term is also intended to capture fear or anxiety about one or more social situations in which the person is exposed to scrutiny by others, such as being observed or performing, fear that one will be negatively evaluated, and fear of situations which might provoke anxiety. 'Generalised anxiety disorder (GAD)' includes excessive anxiety and worry about two or more domains of activities or events such as family, health, finances and school/work difficulties; excessive anxiety on more days than not for three months or more; anxiety-showing symptoms such as restlessness, edginess and muscle tension; anxiety associated with behaviours such as avoidance of situations in which a negative outcome could occur, or marked time and effort preparing for situations in which a negative outcome could occur, or procrastination due to worries, or seeking reassurance due to worries. Most of us would therefore easily find ourselves in the pages of DSM through the category of anxiety. If one takes 'excessive anxiety about two or more domains of activities or events' such as family, health, finances and work, and one throws in some 'muscle tension' for good measure, it would be hard to find people who didn't fit the category. On the basis of the DSM it might actually be impossible to be human and avoid being diagnosed with a treatable mental disorder connected with anxiety.

This would be consistent with the fact that, according to the World Health Organization,[1] anxiety has emerged as the most prevalent mental health problem across the globe. With this expansion of the concept of anxiety, a process encouraged by the pharmaceutical industry and the banality of contemporary journalism, one finds it articulated as a problem just about everywhere one looks. For example, the Agoraphobia Society started life in the UK over thirty years ago with a fairly specific remit. It later became the National Phobics Society, with its remit duly extended. It has since been restyled Anxiety UK. Perhaps symptomatically, what used to be called hypochondria is now officially 'health anxiety'. Clearly the writers of all of those books about the 'age of anxiety' are on to something.

What is the relationship between this idea of an 'age of anxiety' and our contemporary political condition?

Some years ago Franz Neumann commented on the role of anxiety as one of the cornerstones of the political mobilisation of fear under fascism.[2] But Neumann was also sensitive to the ways in which anxiety could play a similar role in the formation of liberal political subjectivity, one which opened the door to authoritarian mobilisations and manoeuvres. Might not that be especially the case in an 'age of anxiety' which is also an age of neoliberal authoritarianism? And how might that be connected to the fact that the age is also, if anything, an 'age of security'? A glance at any security text, from the most mundane government pronouncement to the most sophisticated literature within academic 'security studies', reveals that through the politics of security runs a political imagination of fear and anxiety.[3] I want to first explore this relation between the politics of anxiety and the politics of security before connecting it to the question of trauma.

Along with anxiety, the idea of trauma is now deeply engrained in our political, cultural and intellectual universe. What in the seventeenth century was a surgeon's term to describe a physical wound, transformed in the nineteenth century to include psychic ailments comparable to shock, morphed into 'shell shock' and 'nervous trauma' by the end of the First World War, and from there eventually became a psychiatric category now used to describe experience of war, genocide and catastrophe. The history of the category 'trauma' could be described as moving from the idea of physical health to the idea of mental health and then on to the social management of major disasters.[4] This is most obviously apparent from the discourse surrounding war and conflict: at some point in the future, note the editors of one collection of essays on the trauma of war, historians looking back at the wars of the 1980s, 1990s and early twenty-first century will notice 'trauma projects' appearing alongside food, health and shelter interventions.[5] Yet the historians will also see a highly traumatised society in general, as trauma has become the discourse through which not only catastrophic events are articulated, but through which virtually all suffering is expressed: 'That was really traumatic!' is now thought to be an appropriate response to any event that would once have been described as 'rather unpleasant' or 'quite difficult'. Might we connect this trauma talk to the politics of anxiety and, from there, to the problem of security?

I suggest that the management of anxiety and trauma has become a way of mediating the demands of an endless security war: a war *of* security, a war *for* security, a war *through* security; a war which we are told has a permanence and universality to match the permanence and universality of our supposed desire for security. This chapter therefore seeks to understand the proliferation of discourses of anxiety and the emergence of a hypertrophied concept of trauma as ideological mechanisms deployed for the security crisis of endless war. Deployed, I will argue, as a training in resilience. As such, I want to suggest that the language of anxiety and trauma and the training in resilience that is associated with these terms weds us to a deeply conservative mode of thinking, with the superficial 'humanitarianism' supposedly captured in the discourse of anxiety and trauma in fact functioning as a means of cutting off political alternatives.

ANXIETY: DANGER

A notable feature of recent political discourse has been the proliferation of ideas and categories cantered on the claim that there is a disaster about to happen. Preparedness, prevention, planning and pre-emption have therefore become core ideas: everywhere one looks one finds emergency preparedness, contingency planning and pre-emptive action being addressed. Each of these is a concept with some scope, extending to war preparedness, disaster planning and terror attacks, and each of them resonates with and reinforces a whole gamut of associated security measures. They play heavily on the fear of potential 'natural' disasters, but their real power lies in the presentation of endless war in terms of the coming *political* disaster. They are intensely future-oriented, in that they seek to shape behaviour towards a future event beyond our control, but which we must be prepared to take under our control. The worst-case scenario must be prepared for, even though we don't know what it is yet and never can know what it is. The preparation becomes a technique of governance accommodating us to the security measures constantly established to deal with the catastrophe and disaster.[6] Or, put differently: the security measures help us deal with the anxiety over the catastrophe to come. Seen in this light, anxiety is a means of preparing us for the next attack in the permanent war on terror, the attack we are told time and again is bound to come – how many times does a politician, police chief or security intellectual tell us that an attack is highly likely, even just after (or *especially* just after) a supposed victory in the war? – and which could be and probably will be worse than the last attack and might even be worse than anything we can imagine, all of which enables an acceptance of the ubiquity of the war, its purported endlessness and the permanence of the security preparations carried out in its name.

Central to this is the concept of 'resilience'. In the last decade the idea of resilience has been elevated to one of the most significant buzzwords in the worlds of security and defence. But it has also become a key term within the wider cultural and intellectual zeitgeist. As a consequence, the resilience of everything from cities to infrastructures, local communities to national economies, individual people to collective peoples, systems to structures, has become a key idea on the political agenda.[7]

Resilience stems from the idea of a system (the term originates in ecological thought), which gives a certain scientific weight to ideas such as 'preparedness' and 'prevention' and, as Claudia Aradau and Rens van Munster point out, 'smoothly combines meanings derived from physiology (the capacity of material to return to a previous state), psychology (the capacity of an individual to return to normal after a traumatic event), ecology (the capacity of systems to continue functioning and renew themselves after a disruptive event) and informatics (the capacity of a system to keep on functioning despite anomalies and design flaws)'.[8] The official documentation on the term, of which there is now an enormous amount, plays on this: a 2008 OECD document on state-building, styled 'from fragility to resilience', defines the latter as 'the ability to cope with changes in capacity, effectiveness or legitimacy. These changes can be driven by shocks. . . or through long-term erosions (or increases) in capacity, effectiveness or legitimacy'.[9] A key United Nations document on disaster management suggests that resilience requires 'a consideration of almost every physical phenomenon on the planet'.[10] Note: *almost every physical phenomenon on the planet*. Although the overall argument is couched in terms of general risks, the UN links it explicitly to the wider security agenda in a way which politicises (and securitises) physical and systemic resilience. The document thus parallels national domestic legislation such as the UK's Civil Contingencies Act 2004, which involves contingency plans for anything which might be said to affect the 'welfare' of the UK.

As these examples suggest, in terms of state power huge resources are now expended mapping out potential disasters and in the apprehension of a disaster to come. Playing on the origins of resilience in systems thinking, the idea of planning out organisational and institutional resilience has become a central plank of action across central state agencies, local governments, emergency services and health authorities. In the UK, for example, this would stretch from the creation of 'UK Resilience' based in the Cabinet Office, through the resilience training offered to armed forces, right down to the fact that sniffer dogs, like their handlers, are now trained to be resilient. There has also developed a commercial rhetoric of 'organisational resilience' for corporations, not least through the 'International Consortium for Organizational Resilience': institutional activity enacted to manage organisational anxiety.

This increased prominence of the idea of resilience during the rise of neoliberalism is significant. Although this connection might seem odd given that more than anything resilience assumes a massive state role in planning for the future, the point of this future is that it is unknown and uncertain. Thus as a political category 'resilience' relies fundamentally on an anxious political psyche engaged in an endless war and preparing for the coming attack. Such a strategy foregrounds a politics of anticipation, in which the anticipation itself becomes both an exercise in and an expression of anxiety. This is why the term has been so easily expanded to straddle the private as well as the public, the personal as well as the political, the subjective as well as the objective, so that systemic, organisational and political resilience is connected to *personal* resilience in such a way that contemporary political subjectivity now has to be thought through 'the power of resilience'. Thus one finds texts about resilience as a personal attribute in which citizen-subjects are trained to 'achieve balance, confidence and personal strength', or, in the subtitle of another, 'find inner strength and overcome life's hurdles', or, better still, just 'bounce back from whatever life throws at us'.[11] And one finds workshops in resilience training to equip people for the endless war. In the contemporary cultural zeitgeist, then, the *anxious subject is acknowledged* as the *resilient subject is championed*.

In this acknowledgement and championing of the anxious subject one finds the relationship between the economic development of neoliberal subjectivity and the political development of resilient citizenship. Marx long ago spelt out the ways in which capital, as a system rooted objectively in permanent change and the constant revolutionising of production, promotes feelings of everlasting uncertainty in the subjectivity it generates; capital both generates and thrives on the anxiety that lies at the core of bourgeois subjectivity. The neoliberal intensification of this process, repackaged by politicians and employers as an inevitable fact of contemporary labour and exacerbated by the anxiety associated with the rise of consumerism, a decline of trust in public institutions and private corporations, and a collapse in pension schemes, has been compounded by this articulation of resilience as personal as well as systemic. Resilience is thus presented as a key way of *subjectively* working through the uncertainties, instabilities and anxieties of contemporary capital. The neoliberal subject can 'achieve balance' across the several insecure and part-time jobs they have, can 'overcome life's hurdles' such as facing retirement without a pension to speak of and just 'bounce back from whatever life throws at us' whether it be the collapse of welfare systems or global economic meltdown. The policing of the resilient subject coincides with the socio-economic fabrication of resilient yet flexible labour. 'Don't be scared, be prepared', a motto increasingly used by numerous organisations, becomes a guide by which subjects should manage their place in the market as well as in the security state. Neoliberal citizenship is nothing if not *a training in resilience*.

All of which is to say that anxiety and resilience are now core to the jargon of neoliberal authenticity.[12] Superficially, such jargon is full of 'recognition' for the complexities of human experience ('of course you are anxious'; 'we all share the same fears and anxieties'; it's only natural to be anxious'), but this merely encourages the naturalisation of a neoliberal subjectivity mobilised for security and capital. Hence, the jargon of neoliberal authenticity is the jargon of neoliberal authoritarianism. This is police power at its most profound, shaping subjectivity and fabricating order through psy-experts here, there and everywhere: counsellors within police departments, therapists within the community, psychologists in the media and analysts in the cultural field, all offering advice on our anxieties, coaching us in our resilience and thus, in a roundabout way, functioning as technologies of security. For if there is one abiding political purpose to be identified in the culture of anxiety, it is for that culture to function as a police power par excellence by closing down alternate possibilities: we are to learn that it is ok to be anxious about what might happen, but we are also expected to understand that our response must be resilience training rather than political struggle. We are expected and permitted (and maybe even *required*) to be collectively anxious and structurally resilient, but not mobilised politically. Or, to put it another way, prepared for trauma. Why trauma?

Towards the end of an essay titled 'Inhibitions, Symptoms and Anxiety' (1926), Freud explores the relationship between anxiety and danger, suggesting that we can distinguish realistic anxiety centred on known danger from neurotic anxiety centred on unknown danger. In this context, he introduces the concept of trauma: danger conjures up feelings of helplessness, and Freud suggests that a situation of helplessness that has been actually experienced is a traumatic situation. He therefore ends his comments with a dialectical triad that runs: 'anxiety-danger-helplessness (trauma)'.[13] Might there be a political implication in Freud's comment?

DANGER: TRAUMA

A few years before his essay 'Inhibitions, Symptoms and Anxiety', Freud published *Beyond the Pleasure Principle* (1920). Early in that text he writes about the lack of any analysis of war neuroses, which had been a major issue during and in the aftermath of the First World War. 'Shell shock' is that war's emblematic psychiatric disorder, but by 1916 the term 'shell shock' was being used as a synonym for 'war neuroses'.

Now, DSM-I, published in 1952, contained a category known as 'gross stress reaction', picking up on the experience of soldiers in World War II and trying to move beyond 'shell shock' and 'war neuroses'. DSM-II, however, published in 1968, no longer had a listing for any kind of psychiatric disorder produced by war. Rather, it was suggested that the symptoms formerly understood under 'gross stress reaction' should be reclassified under 'adjustment reaction to adult life'. This meant that war veterans returning from Vietnam after 1968 were being assessed using a diagnostic nomenclature that did not appear to have any terminology specific to war-related trauma. Vietnam veteran groups gradually mobilised around and against this, since they believed that the experiences of returnees from Vietnam were not being properly understood or appreciated by the authorities and, where they were recognised, it was not through the right prism (of war). The issue was finally resolved in 1980 with the *invention*, as Allan Young puts it, of 'post-traumatic stress disorder' (PTSD). In other words, the fate of the category 'trauma' was tied to the history of warfare, and one cannot understand PTSD without grasping it in the context of America's attempt to understand Vietnam and its own role (and 'traumatic' defeat) in that war. That is, we need to recognise from the outset that PTSD was a *politically driven psychiatric diagnosis*.[14]

One of the outcomes of this rise of PTSD was that as a label it meant abandoning the term 'neurosis' in dealing with the experiences of the people in question. Fassin and Rechtman point out that this was a huge conceptual shift with profound political implications, because it meant jettisoning the tradition of suspicion that had always surrounded the idea of trauma and which had been captured with the label 'neuroses'. This suspicion had its roots in the class politics of the terminology in question, for despite its long history in the English language 'trauma' came into its own as a category in the nineteenth century as a means of interpellating workers on railways who were thought to be malingering after an accident. In the early twentieth century it was then used for interpellating working-class soldiers thought to be malingering after war experience. The original 'trauma' victims were 'the workforce in a rapidly expanding industrial society and cannon fodder for its great international conflicts'.[15] In other words, the term 'trauma' was originally applied to what were thought to be the malingerers and shirkers of the working class, although at that point the term was not being with any sympathy for the workers in question.

The withdrawal of the neurotic paradigm and the end of the crusade to discover fraud or malingering with the invention of PTSD had a major impact, since not only was trauma no longer a mark of malingering or cowardice, it was also now something that could be grasped and sympathised with. That this occurred through the struggle for recognition of the trauma suffered by Vietnam veterans was crucial, since it meant that if American soldiers could be understood as genuine victims of trauma, then the implication was that the perpetrators of atrocity could be counted among its victims. Note that as it agitated for changes to DSM-III the Vietnam Veterans Working Group argued that the symptoms of Vietnam compensation victims were very similar to those of the victims of what is widely said to be the most politically significant trauma of a century of traumas: the concentration camp survivors. And when not invoking the Holocaust, the comparison was made with victims of other mass historical atrocities, such as the slave trade or Hiroshima. In the American context, classing perpetrators as victims was a move that satisfied both pacifists and supporters of the war because it meant that the war could be denounced by both sides and without directly condemning those who fought in it. In terms of healing and unifying a nation seriously divided by the war, not least given the historical moment in which more and more atrocities committed by American troops were being uncovered, the importance of the step taken in shifting the language of trauma perhaps cannot be overstated, for it generated an all-encompassing category of the 'survivor' and 'trauma-victim'.[16] Understood outside of the American context and in terms of the wider political and cultural shifts, we might say that by re-presenting trauma through a narrative of victimhood, psychiatry has played a crucial role in helping the state conceal the trauma that the state itself produces; experiences and memories understood as trauma come to play a central role in the reassertion of political authority.[17] Depoliticising a highly charged situation, 'trauma' replaces politics with a concept of psychic wounding, to be managed by the individual and the state.

From hereon psychiatry would treat the battlefield as a 'microcosm of trauma',[18] and war zones are now always already understood through the language of the traumatic: 'Iraqis are being traumatised every day'; 'within five years of the falling of the regime, all Iraqis will be traumatised' and so on. One of the features of 'contemporary' war, however, is that the battlefield is now global: the whole social order is understood to be the war zone, and there is no 'frontline' or 'battlefield' in any meaningful sense of the term. And so, trauma has moved away from the battlefield and into every walk of life. Not only has this made PTSD virtually indistinguishable from combinations of already established disorders such as depression, panic disorder and, of course, generalised anxiety disorder, it has also enabled the consciousness of trauma to penetrate all areas of social life and be applied to human experience in general.[19] On the one hand, 'traumatic memory' has become a way of unravelling people's experiences even when they do not think of themselves as traumatised. Bruno Bettelheim, for example, writes of concentration camp survivors who 'often do quite well in life' and who appear 'symptom-free', but adds that this is only 'as far as appearances go'. In fact, 'their life is in some essential respects . . . full of inner insecurity' which 'they usually manage to hide' (note the trope of security). Bettelheim knows this because 'the trauma (is) so horrendous' that real 'integration' requires 'acceptance of how severely one has been traumatised'.[20] On the other hand, people can now be traumatised by an experience such as watching TV – the term 'distant traumatic effects' is now widely used to describe people traumatised through a medium, the most common being TV (and very often through watching 'security crises' such as 9/11). The extent to which it would be hard to overestimate the plasticity, power and apparently universal applicability of the concept 'trauma' is illustrated by an observation made previously: the fact that the sentence 'that was really traumatic!' has become a common way of describing a whole gamut of ultimately rather mundane experiences.[21]

It is on this basis that traumatology has taken off. Encouraged by specialist organisations such as the International Society for Traumatic Stress Studies (founded 1985) and specialist outlets such as the *Journal of Traumatic Stress* (first volume: 1988), trauma talk has become everyday: Frank Furedi has revealed the proliferation of trauma talk in British newspapers, from just under 500 citations in 1994 to several thousand by the early twenty-first century.[22] UNICEF's 1996 report *The State of the World's Children* estimated that ten million children were psychologically traumatised.[23] Trauma, we might say, has become part of the jargon of neoliberal authenticity. But then might it not also be part of the jargon of neoliberal authoritarianism? And might this be so in a way similar to the relationship between anxiety and resilience, one which we saw was organised through the possibility of future (political) danger?

In a discussion in 2003 Jacques Derrida asked a pertinent question: 'imagine that the Americans and, through them, the entire world, had been told: what has just happened, the spectacular destruction of two towers . . . is an awful thing, a terrible crime, a pain without measure, but it's all over, it won't happen again, there will never again be anything as awful as or more awful than that.' Mourning would be possible, selves could be remade, pages would be turned and a line could be drawn under the trauma. But as Derrida suggests, the traumatism which followed, like all traumatism, 'is produced by the *future*, by the *to come*, by the threat of the worst *to come*, rather than by an aggression that is "over and done with"'.[24] Derrida's suggestion runs counter to the common trope of 'trauma and memory', an approach which encourages us to think of trauma in terms of a 'remaking of the self' in the light of the past, as 'unclaimed experience', as the 'redemptive authority of history', as 'forgetfulness and forgiveness', as 'struggles over representations of the past', as 'healing'.[25] This is especially the case following 9/11, an event which is presented to us as *the* collective trauma of our time – these are now 'the days after', as one character puts it in Don DeLillo's 'post-9/11' novel *Falling Man*. But Derrida's suggestion helps us read trauma in terms of the danger of the terror *to come*, or which *might* be to come. The trauma is the trauma of a future which is unknowable but imaginable, and *imaginable as traumatic*. The 'wound' of trauma is less than the wound of the past and much more, to paraphrase Derrida, a wound which remains open in our terror of the danger that we imagine lies ahead. The terror lies not in what has happened in the past but in the danger and the anxiety of what we imagine threatens to happen, and which we are encouraged to imagine as being worse than anything that has ever taken place.

In this light, the issue is not the remaking of the self in the light of past trauma but the *making of the self in preparation for the trauma to come*. And that making of the self is how an anxious political subjectivity now comes to be shaped: endlessly, just like the war itself. What we need to think about, then, is how and why so many acts are produced as 'trauma' and what that production does to contemporary political subjectivity. For the imagination of danger and terror is the contemporary psychopolitical condition of trauma politics. If the catastrophe must be imagined and the worst-case scenario considered so that contingency plans, emergency measures and, more than anything, the security arrangements be put in place, then trauma has become a means of integrating us into the security measures of endless war. Trauma, that is, has become a means of organising the anxious subject of (in)security within a social field defined as war. This is not liberation from past violence but preparation for future violence. If 'society must be defended', as we are now all fond of saying with Foucauldian irony (albeit with rather different levels of irony, depending on our politics), then it must be defended more than anything from its future traumas.

This is where trauma connects to the growth of resilience as a political concept.[26] If resilience has come to the fore in the context of an anxious political psyche engaged in a 'war on terror' and within the wider neoliberal authoritarianism confronting us, we might add that it has done so for a social order and international system understanding itself as traumatised and preparing for more trauma to come. 'Resilience training' represents a general preparation for events defined in advance as traumatic. As Pat O'Malley puts it, 'resilience does not seek only to render individuals able to "bounce back" after trauma, an essentially reactive model.' Rather, 'it aims to create subjects capable of adapting to, and exploiting to their advantage, situations of radical uncertainty'.[27] The biological and psychological frailty implied in the concept of trauma has to be somehow compensated for in advance by the strength and endurance implied in the concept of resilience. To be a viable political subject, now, means planning one's resilience to withstand the trauma to come.

It is for this reason that the psy-disciplines have been central to the growth of 'resilience'. The American Psychological Association (APA) launched a major 'Road to Resilience' campaign in 2002 to link 'those types of traumatic events' (i.e., 11 September 2001) with 'the hardships that define all of our lives, anytime that people are struggling with an event in their communities'. 'It became clear that these events helped to open a window to self discovery for many', said Jan Peterson, assistant executive director of public relations in APA's Practice Directorate. 'People were interested in learning more about themselves – and in particular, how to become more resilient.' The APA launched a 'multi-media approach', with a free toolkit including '10 ways to build resilience', a documentary video *Aftermath: The Road to Resilience* with three 'overarching messages' ('resilience can be learned'; 'resilience is a journey, not an event or single turning point'; 'there is no prescribed timeline for the road to resilience'), special phases of the campaign including 'Resilience for Kids and Teens' and resilience workshops for journalists.[28] The main theme to emerge is how individuals, communities and organisations might 'bounce back' from any attacks, setbacks or challenges.[29] A leading article titled 'Providing Direction on the Road to Resilience' by Russ

Newman, executive director at the APA, published in *Behavioral Health Management* in July 2003 to publicise the campaign, has been made available on websites run by and for business management.[30] Elsewhere one finds that resilience workshops are conducted in centres specialising in trauma.[31]

By pairing trauma with resilience, the subject's personal anxieties become bound up with the political dangers facing the nation; the trauma is individual and collective, and so the resilience training is the training in and of liberal subjects such that capitalist order might be properly secured. The fabrication of liberal subjectivity and its martial defence are to be achieved in one and the same moment. In this way the trauma-resilience couplet is now central to the politics of security: the measures proposed in the unsuccessful National Resilience Development Act in the United States in 2003 found their way into the ubiquitous powers of the Department of Homeland Security, and the UK's more recent *National Security Strategy* (2008) is structured around the same problematic – the concept of resilience runs through the text, encompassing the armed forces, the police, the British people, the private sector, 'human and social resilience', 'community resilience' and on it goes.[32]

This planned defence and its prior imagining of the community and its subjects as anxious and traumatised closes down alternate possibilities. Trauma and, relatedly, PTSD are themselves symptomatic of the way contemporary order is constituted as a certain kind of war, the mobilisation of anxiety within this war and the kind of responses we are allowed to have to it. We can be traumatised, we can prepare to be traumatised, we can be trained to be resilient against the trauma to come and we can obtain some therapy to help us cope in advance. But we must not be challenged to respond politically. 'Resilience' thereby designates an aptitude for little other than keeping things exactly as they are. We can expect to be traumatised collectively, but not mobilised politically.

Trauma talk, anxiety consciousness and the concept of resilience are thus part of the jargon of authenticity: pure ideology, just like the trope of the 'age of anxiety'. Seemingly responsive to real human need, the anxiety-trauma-resilience triad functions as a form of political administration. Politics has been reduced to the administration of anxious and traumatised subjects in their acceptance of and preparation for the permanent security war.

NOTES

* This chapter is a revised version of Mark Neocleous, '"Don't Be Scared, Be Prepared": Trauma-Anxiety-Resilience', *Alternatives*, Vol. 37, No. 3, 2012, pp. 188–98.

1. *The WHO World Mental Health Survey: Global Perspectives on the Epidemiology of Mental Disorders* (Cambridge: Cambridge University Press, 2008).

2. Franz Neumann, 'Anxiety and Politics' (1954), in Franz Neumann (ed.), *The Democratic and the Authoritarian State* (New York: Free Press, 1957).

3. See Mark Neocleous, *Critique of Security* (Edinburgh: Edinburgh University Press, 2008).

4. Didier Fassin and Richard Rechtman, *The Empire of Trauma: An Inquiry into the Condition of Victimhood* (2007), trans. Rachel Gomme (Princeton, NJ: Princeton University Press, 2009), 10.

5. Patrick J. Bracken and Celia Petty, 'Introduction', in Patrick J. Bracken and Celia Petty (eds.), *Rethinking the Trauma of War* (London: Free Association Books, 1998), 1.

6. Claudia Aradau and Rens van Munster, *Politics of Catastrophe: Genealogies of the Unknown* (London: Routledge, 2011); Stuart Price, *Worst-Case Scenario? Governance, Mediation and the Security Regime* (London: Zed Books, 2011).

7. For a longer critique see Mark Neocleous, 'Resisting Resilience', *Radical Philosophy*, Vol. 178, 2013, pp. 2–7; *War Power, Police Power* (Edinburgh: Edinburgh University Press, 2014), 204–13.

8. Aradau and Munster, *Politics*, 46–7.

9. OECD, *Concepts and Dilemmas of State Building in Fragile Situations: From Fragility to Resilience* (OECD, 2008), 17.

10. United Nations, *Living with Risk: A Global Review of Disaster Reduction Initiatives, Vol. 1* (New York and Geneva: UN, 2004), 37.

11. Robert Brooks and Sam Goldstein, *The Power of Resilience: Achieving Balance, Confidence, and Personal Strength in Your Life* (New York: McGraw-Hill, 2004); Karen Reivich and Andrew Shatté, *The Resilience Factor: 7 Keys to Finding Your Inner Strength and Overcoming Life's Hurdles* (New York: Broadway Books, 2003); Jane Clarke and John Nicholson, *Resilience: Bounce Back from Whatever Life Throws at You* (Richmond, Surrey: Crimson Publishing, 2010).

12. I am playing here on Theodor Adorno, *The Jargon of Authenticity* (1964), trans. Knut Tarnowski and Frederic Will (London: Routledge and Kegan Paul, 1973).

13. Sigmund Freud, 'Inhibitions, Symptoms and Anxiety' (1926), in *The Standard Edition of the Complete Psychological Works of Sigmund Freud, Vol. XX* (London: Vintage, 2001), 165–7.

14. Allan Young, *The Harmony of Illusions: Inventing Post-Traumatic Stress Disorder* (Princeton, NJ: Princeton University Press, 1995); also Wilbur J. Scott, *The Politics of Readjustment: Vietnam Veterans since the War* (New York: Aldine de Gruyter, 1993), 34, 238; Wilbur J. Scott, 'PTSD in DSM-III: A Case in the Politics of Diagnosis and Disease', *Social Problems*, Vol. 37, No. 3, 1990, pp. 294–310; Edgar Jones and Simon Wessely, *Shell Shock to PTSD: Military Psychiatry from 1900 to the Gulf War* (Hove, East Sussex: Psychology Press, 2005), 131. Also Ben Shephard, *A War of Nerves: Soldiers and Psychiatrists 1914–1994* (London: Pimlico, 2002); and Paul Lerner, *Hysterical Men: War, Psychiatry, and the Politics of Trauma in Germany, 1890–1930* (Ithaca, NY: Cornell University Press, 2003). Note also Philip Cushman's argument concerning psychotherapy's socio-political function, not least due to its reliance on trauma theory – *Constructing the Self, Constructing America: A Cultural History of Psychotherapy* (Cambridge: Da Capo Press, 1995), 343.

15. Fassin and Rechtman, *Empire*, 39; also Michael R. Trimble, 'Post-Traumatic Stress Disorder: History of a Concept', in Charles R. Figley (ed.), *Trauma and Its Wake, Vol. 1: The Study and Treatment of Post-Traumatic Stress Disorder* (New York: Brunner/Mazel, 1985), 5–14.

16. For a more recent and comparable case see Paula Gody-Paiz, '"Canada's Troubled Troops": The Construction of Post-Traumatic Stress Disorder and Its Uses by the Canadian Armed Forces', *Alternate Routes*, Vol. 20, 2004, pp. 6–23.

17. See Jenny Edkins, *Trauma and the Memory of Politics* (Cambridge: Cambridge University Press, 2003), xv. For a similar claim concerning the reassertion of the authority of the British state following the First World War, see Susan Kingsley Kent, *Aftershocks: Politics and Trauma in Britain, 1918–1931* (Houndmills, Basingstoke: Palgrave, 2009), 7. On the advantage that the powerful have over the powerless in the conduct of griefwork, see Jonathan Shay, *Achilles in Vietnam: Combat Trauma and the Undoing of Character* (New York: Scribner, 2003), 56.

18. Chester B. Scrignar, *Post-Traumatic Stress Disorder: Diagnosis, Treatment, and Legal Issues* (New Orleans, LA: Bruno Press, 1988), 2.

19. Young, *Harmony*; Derek Summerfield, 'The Social Experience of War and Some Issues for the Humanitarian Field', in Bracken and Petty (eds.), *Rethinking*; Austin Sarat, Nadav Davidovitch and Michael Alberstein, 'Trauma and Memory: Between Individual and Collective Experiences', in Austin Sarat, Nadav Davidovitch and Michael Alberstein (eds.), *Trauma and Memory: Reading, Healing, and Making Law* (Stanford, CA: Stanford University Press, 2007).

20. Bruno Bettelheim, 'Trauma and Reintegration', in *Surviving and Other Essays* (London: Thames and Hudson, 1979), 33–35.

21. Tana Dineen, *Manufacturing Victims* (Montreal: Robert Davies, 1996), 56; Ian Hacking, *Rewriting the Soul: Multiple Personality and the Sciences of Memory* (Princeton, NJ: Princeton University Press, 1995), 183; Kirby Farrell, *Post-Traumatic Culture: Injury and Interpretation in the Nineties* (Baltimore, MD: Johns Hopkins University Press, 1998), x.

22. Frank Furedi, *Therapy Culture: Cultivating Vulnerability in an Uncertain Age* (London: Routledge, 2004), 4.

23. UNICEF, *The State of the World's Children* (Oxford: Oxford University Press, 1996), 13.

24. Jacques Derrida, 'Autoimmunity: Real and Symbolic Suicides – A Dialogue with Jacques Derrida', in Giovanna Borradori (ed.), *Philosophy in a Time of Terror: Dialogues with Jurgen Habermas and Jacques Derrida* (Chicago: University of Chicago Press, 2003), 97.

25. Susan J. Brison, *Aftermath: Violence and the Remaking of a Self* (Princeton, NJ: Princeton University Press, 2002); Cathy Caruth, *Unclaimed Experience: Trauma, Narrative, and History* (Baltimore: Johns Hopkins University Press, 1996); Ruth Leys, *Trauma: A Genealogy* (Chicago: University of Chicago Press, 2000); Shosana Felman, *The Juridical Unconscious: Trials and Traumas of the Twentieth Century* (Cambridge: Harvard University Press, 2002); Allen Meek, *Trauma and Media* (New York: Routledge, 2010); Peter A. Levine, *Walking the Tiger: Healing Trauma* (Berkeley, CA: North Atlantic Books, 1997).

26. Allan Young, 'Posttraumatic Stress Disorder of the Virtual Kind: Trauma and Resilience in Post-9/11 America', in Austin Sarat, Nadav Davidovitch, and Michal Alberstein (eds.), *Trauma and Memory*, 21–48; Roger Luckhurst, *The Trauma Question* (London: Routledge, 2008), 210.

27. Pat O'Malley, 'Resilient Subjects: Uncertainty, Warfare and Liberalism', *Economy and Society*, Vol. 39, No. 4, 2010, pp. 488–509, 492.

28. J. Daw, 'Documentary on Resilience Set to Air Sept. 11', *Monitor on Psychology*, Vol. 33, No. 7, 2002, p. 12; Sara Martin, 'Building Resilience from the Grassroots Up: APA Members Take the "Road to Resilience" Campaign to the Public', *Monitor on Psychology*, Vol. 33, No. 11, 2002, p. 52.

29. Russ Newman, 'The Road to Resilience', *Monitor on Psychology*, Vol. 33, No. 9, 2002, p. 62.

30. For example: http://www.allbusiness.com/health-care-social-assistance/880919-1.html.

31. See www.traumaweb.org. For discussion see Keren Friedman-Peleg and Yehuda C. Goodman, 'From Posttrauma Intervention to Immunization of the Social Body: Pragmatics and Politics of a Resilience Program in Israel's Periphery', *Culture, Medicine and Psychiatry*, Vol. 34, No. 3, 2010, pp. 421–42.

32. Cabinet Office, *The National Security Strategy of the United Kingdom: Security in an Interdependent World* (London: HMSO, 2008).

BIBLIOGRAPHY

Adorno, Theodor. *The Jargon of Authenticity*. Translated by Knut Tarnowski and Frederic Will. London: Routledge and Kegan Paul, 1973.

Aradau, Claudia and van Munster, Rens. *Politics of Catastrophe: Genealogies of the Unknown*. London: Routledge, 2011.

Bettelheim, Bruno. *Surviving and Other Essays*. London: Thames and Hudson, 1979.

Bracken, Patrick J. and Petty, Celia. 'Introduction'. In *Rethinking the Trauma of War*, edited by Patrick J. Bracken and Celia Petty. London: Free Association Books, 1998: 1–8.

Brison, Susan J. *Aftermath: Violence and the Remaking of a Self*. Princeton, NJ: Princeton University Press, 2002.

Brooks, Robert and Goldstein, Sam. *The Power of Resilience: Achieving Balance, Confidence, and Personal Strength in Your Life*. New York: McGraw-Hill, 2004.

Cabinet Office. *The National Security Strategy of the United Kingdom: Security in an Interdependent World*. London: HMSO, 2008.

Caruth, Cathy. *Unclaimed Experience: Trauma, Narrative, and History*. Baltimore, MD: Johns Hopkins University Press, 1996.

Clarke, Jane and Nicholson, John. *Resilience: Bounce Back from Whatever Life Throws at You*. Richmond, Surrey: Crimson Publishing, 2010.

Cushman, Philip. *Constructing the Self, Constructing America: A Cultural History of Psychotherapy*. Cambridge, MA: Da Capo Press, 1995.

Daw, J. 'Documentary on Resilience Set to Air Sept. 11'. *Monitor on Psychology* 33 (2002): 12.
Derrida, Jacques. 'Autoimmunity: Real and Symbolic Suicides – A Dialogue with Jacques Derrida'. In *Philosophy in a Time of Terror: Dialogues with Jürgen Habermas and Jacques Derrida*, edited by Giovanna Borradori. Chicago: University of Chicago Press, 2003: 85–136.
Dineen, Tana. *Manufacturing Victims*. Montreal: Robert Davies, 1996.
Edkins, Jenny. *Trauma and the Memory of Politics*. Cambridge: Cambridge University Press, 2003.
Farrell, Kirby. *Post-Traumatic Culture: Injury and Interpretation in the Nineties*. Baltimore, MD: Johns Hopkins University Press, 1998.
Fassin, Didier and Rechtman, Richard. *The Empire of Trauma: An Inquiry into the Condition of Victimhood*. Translated by Rachel Gomme. Princeton, NJ: Princeton University Press, 2009.
Felman, Shosana. *The Juridical Unconscious: Trials and Traumas of the Twentieth Century*. Cambridge, MA: Harvard University Press, 2002.
Freud, Sigmund, J. Strachey (eds.). 'Inhibitions, Symptoms and Anxiety' (1926). In *The Standard Edition of the Complete Psychological Works of Sigmund Freud, Vol. XX*. London: Vintage, 2001: 165–7.
Friedman-Peleg, Keren and Goodman, Yehuda C. 'From Posttrauma Intervention to Immunization of the Social Body: Pragmatics and Politics of a Resilience Program in Israel's Periphery', *Culture, Medicine and Psychiatry* 34 (2010): 421–42.
Furedi, Frank. *Therapy Culture: Cultivating Vulnerability in an Uncertain Age*. London: Routledge, 2004.
Gody-Paiz, Paula. ' "Canada's Troubled Troops": The Construction of Post-Traumatic Stress Disorder and Its Uses by the Canadian Armed Forces', *Alternate Routes* 20 (2004): 6–23.
Hacking, Ian. *Rewriting the Soul: Multiple Personality and the Sciences of Memory*. Princeton, NJ: Princeton University Press, 1995.
Jones, Edgar and Wessely, Simon. *Shell Shock to PTSD: Military Psychiatry from 1900 to the Gulf War*. Hove, East Sussex: Psychology Press, 2005.
Kingsley Kent, Susan. *Aftershocks: Politics and Trauma in Britain, 1918–1931*. Houndmills, Basingstoke: Palgrave, 2009.
Lerner, Paul. *Hysterical Men: War, Psychiatry, and the Politics of Trauma in Germany, 1890–1930*. Ithaca, NY: Cornell University Press, 2003.
Levine, Peter A. *Walking the Tiger: Healing Trauma*. Berkeley, CA: North Atlantic Books, 1997.
Leys, Ruth. *Trauma: A Genealogy*. Chicago: University of Chicago Press, 2000.
Luckhurst, Roger. *The Trauma Question*. London: Routledge, 2008.
Martin, Sara. 'Building Resilience from the Grassroots Up: APA Members Take the "Road to Resilience" Campaign to the Public', *Monitor on Psychology* 33 (2002): 52.
Meek, Allen. *Trauma and Media*. New York: Routledge, 2010.
Neocleous, Mark. *Critique of Security*. Edinburgh: Edinburgh University Press, 2008.
Neocleous, Mark. 'Resisting Resilience', *Radical Philosophy* 178 (2013): 2–7.

Neocleous, Mark. *War Power, Police Power*. Edinburgh: Edinburgh University Press, 2014.
Neumann, Franz. *The Democratic and the Authoritarian State*. New York: Free Press, 1957.
Newman, Russ. 'The Road to Resilience', *Monitor on Psychology* 33 (2002): 62.
OECD, *Concepts and Dilemmas of State Building in Fragile Situations: From Fragility to Resilience*. Paris: OECD, 2008.
O'Malley, Pat. 'Resilient Subjects: Uncertainty, Warfare and Liberalism', *Economy and Society* 39 (2010): 488–509.
Price, Stuart. *Worst-Case Scenario? Governance, Mediation and the Security Regime*. London: Zed Books, 2011.
Reivich, Karen and Shatté, Andrew. *The Resilience Factor: 7 Keys to Finding Your Inner Strength and Overcoming Life's Hurdles*. New York: Broadway Books, 2003.
Sarat, Austin, Davidovitch, Nadav and Alberstein, Michael. 'Trauma and Memory: Between Individual and Collective Experiences'. In *Trauma and Memory: Reading, Healing, and Making Law*, edited by Austin Sarat, Nadav Davidovitch and Michael Alberstein. Stanford, CA: Stanford University Press, 2007: 3–20.
Scott, Wilbur J. *The Politics of Readjustment: Vietnam Veterans since the War*. New York: Aldine de Gruyter, 1993.
Scott, Wilbur J. 'PTSD in DSM-III: A Case in the Politics of Diagnosis and Disease', *Social Problems* 37 (1990): 294–310.
Scrignar, Chester B. *Post-Traumatic Stress Disorder: Diagnosis, Treatment, and Legal Issues*. New Orleans, LA: Bruno Press, 1988.
Shay, Jonathan. *Achilles in Vietnam: Combat Trauma and the Undoing of Character*. New York: Scribner, 2003.
Shephard, Ben. *A War of Nerves: Soldiers and Psychiatrists 1914–1994*. London: Pimlico, 2002.
Summerfield, Derek. 'The Social Experience of War and Some Issues for the Humanitarian Field'. In *Rethinking the Trauma of War*, edited by Patrick J. Bracken and Celia Petty. London: Free Association Books, 1998: 9–37.
Trimble, Michael R. 'Post-Traumatic Stress Disorder: History of a Concept'. In *Trauma and Its Wake, Vol. 1: The Study and Treatment of Post-Traumatic Stress Disorder*, edited by Charles R. Figley. New York: Brunner/Mazel, 1985: 5–14.
UNICEF. *The State of the World's Children*. Oxford: Oxford University Press, 1996.
United Nations. *Living with Risk: A Global Review of Disaster Reduction Initiatives, Vol. 1*. New York and Geneva: UN, 2004.
World Health Organization. *WHO World Mental Health Survey: Global Perspectives on the Epidemiology of Mental Disorders*. Cambridge: Cambridge University Press, 2008.
Young, Allan. *The Harmony of Illusions: Inventing Post-Traumatic Stress Disorder*. Princeton, NJ: Princeton University Press, 1995.
Young, Allan. 'Posttraumatic Stress Disorder of the Virtual Kind: Trauma and Resilience in Post-9/11 America'. In *Trauma and Memory: Reading, Healing, and Making Law*, edited by Austin Sarat, Nadav Davidovitch and Michael Alberstein. Stanford, CA: Stanford University Press, 2007: 21–48.

Chapter 5

The New Age of Suspicion

Emmanuel-Pierre Guittet and Fabienne Brion[1]

Suspicion and distrust have many faces. Ahmed Mohamed, a fourteen-year-old Texan student who in 2015 built a homemade clock mistaken for a bomb by one of his teachers, became rapidly known as 'clock boy'. Was he a Muslim youth mistreated by overzealous police officers in a town known for its resentment of Muslims or an example of vigilance against potential terrorism? His ingenuity has been praised by President Obama, among others, but for many it would be otiose to say that the danger of missing a real bomb means the threshold for doubt should always be low. While the United Kingdom is welcoming their first child refugees from Calais, a Tory MP has suggested that British authorities should give them dental tests to verify their age. This inappropriate stance by a British MP points to a normalising distrust for refugees' true identities and motives in a growing atmosphere of reluctance and animosity towards migrants across European countries. Perhaps one of the highlights of the ongoing popular American TV reality show *Cheaters* is when the betrayed lover is encouraged to call the deceiver so that everyone can see his or her verbal betrayal in real time. In a recent 2016 advertising campaign aimed at increasing awareness of dangerous and suspicious conduct among their young pupils, a Belgian school pictured a pear cut in half with a kiwi in disguise inside, accompanied with the following message: 'If you see something suspicious report it immediately.' A campaign that is reminiscent of the New York Metropolitan Transportation Authority's 'If you see something, say something' slogan. The phrase 'unattended baggage will be removed and may be destroyed' will be familiar to everyone who has ever boarded an aeroplane as much as the idea that officers working in an airport are now trained to detect behavioural clues of supposedly malicious intent. Since 2006, the US Transportation Security Administration (TSA) deploys officers to watch for suspicious behaviour. Whether or not the programme called *Screening Passengers by Observation Techniques* is scientifically sound and worth the cost, thousands of officers are daily deployed and engaging in casual conversation in order to measure reactions and looking for signs of stress or deception. In their attempt to inform and prevent radicalisation, the United Kingdom West Midland Police force reminds its readers on its website that 'There is no single way of identifying someone who is likely to be vulnerable to radicalisation' before adding a couple lines further down that someone who is asking for his passport, saving money, buying new clothes and researching travel plans online are warning signs that 'may provide an indication travel to Syria is being planned'. These different examples of security-awareness campaigns, practices of detection of untrustworthy conducts in public spaces and declarations about unreliable child refugees or deceiving lovers seem to participate to an all-too familiar ongoing normalisation of disbelief, distrust and suspicion across our liberal societies.

Suspicion is certainly a hallmark of police and intelligence services' cultures. Suspicion is their territory and a constitutive feature of their professional identities: people and situations are constantly read as if they are not what they appear to be.[2] 'A cop's talent is in seeing what is hidden or disguised, not what is there', as Crank suggests.[3] Suspicion as a capacity to recognise any kind of unexpected variations in what could be seen by non-professional as ordinary routine is highly regarded among police officers. A suspicion that something exists is more than idle speculation whether something exists or not; it is a positive feeling of actual apprehension or mistrust but without sufficient evidence. As such, suspicion is closely aligned with any modern scientific endeavour, hoping to unlock 'nature's secrets'. It is an invitation to look further or beneath the surface, to explore with a sense of curiosity what seems to be peculiar or unusual. The problem is not suspicion per se but the extent and consequences of a normalisation of suspicion that innervates the social and political fabric of our societies.

The aim of this chapter is to pinpoint how suspicion is the active ingredient of the precautionary principle at stake in our risk societies and the unfortunate, deeply entrenched driving force that leads to a blurring of the boundaries between rationality and panic, between anticipation and anxiety. We argue here that suspicion is the operating principle and modus operandi of security practices. Distrust and anxiety are its foreseeable social and political consequences. When suspicion governs security agencies' scripts and practices and permeates political discourse and ordinary daily practices, it produces an anxious alertness that perpetuates, rather than mitigates, past, present and potential fear.

It is helpful to begin with a brief summary of how Beck's notion of risk society has informed security studies. When the essence of risk is not what is happening but what might happen, it implies that perception of risks is intimately tied to understandings of what constitutes dangers, threats and for whom. When security can be defined as risk management, the quest for maximum information in order to reduce uncertainty and ultimately to eliminate it becomes central. In the second part, we take heed of the underpinning rationale of early detection and prevention one can found in de-radicalisation policies and resilience programmes. Among the different programmes that have been implemented across Europe, we focus primarily on the British 'Prevent' strategy and its early intervention scheme, 'Channel'. We then examine the Belgian resilience toolkits 'Bounce'. At the core of these policies, programmes and tools of de-radicalisation and resilience there is a problematic attribution of vulnerability and suspicion to individuals, groups, communities and spaces already stigmatised and identified as dangerous. The fact that these de-radicalisation and resilience policies and programmes include the establishment of partnerships with community representatives, the enrolment of vast and various professional segments of our societies in the detection of suspicious conducts and the referral of individuals to a de-radicalisation programme is central to the third part. We suggest, then, that suspicion has become a dispositif, a technique of governance which imposes a particular conduct, a new way to formulate truth, trust and normality.

RISK-SOAKED SECURITY: LOGICS AND CONSEQUENCES OF ANTICIPATION

Beck's powerful notion of 'risk society'[4] has significantly impacted upon the ways in which security has been understood and has led to timely and rich analyses. Scholars are now well aware of how risk, perceived as ascertainable, is about 'trying to turn uncertainties into probabilities'[5] and of how the allocation of risks is central to the modern security mantra. The dominance of probabilistic risk discourse against the threat of ambivalence and contingency as one of the main 'foci imaginarii of social order' of our modernity[6] has been the subject of heated academic debate. Eventually it became a key term of reference for scholars as well as a populist term, widely used in the media.[7]

The notion that both national and international security agendas no longer revolve around traditional conceptions of borders and territorialised protection but around anticipating and multifaceted threats stemming from an increasingly globalised and interconnected world is no longer disputed. 'The management of risk and the taming of chance'[8] constitutes the core tenet of how security is apprehended and produced. Security is a 'war bereft of temporal or spatial parameters'[9] where threats are, by their very nature, irregular, incalculable and, crucially, unpredictable.[10] Any understanding of a threat as both dispersed and uncontrollable fosters a mode of security that aims to identify a peril at an early stage and to intervene accordingly. It implies a more imaginative orientation towards the future and anticipatory devices such as storytelling and the construction of worst-case scenario.[11] As De Goede reminds us, 'Pre-emption does not endeavour to predict the future, but it premeditates the future by mapping and imagining multiple future scenarios that are made actionable in the present.'[12] When risk is presented in a way that includes the uncertain, it creates a reformulated model of risk management which can justifiably include everything from the minutiae of everyday mundane life up to actions on faraway battlefields.[13] This is to say that saying and doing security shifts from the figure of the perpetrator, where the act has been committed and should be punished, to the figure of the suspect, where the action has yet to be committed.[14] Since the publication of Beck's seminal risk society thesis, an increasing number of commentators and scholars place an emphasis upon the extent to which the pursuit of risk reduction contributes to the emergence of societies obsessively preoccupied with the search for safety, expressed in terms of anticipation and early detection. As Wilkinson[15] highlights, our societies are more anxious because they are more risk conscious.

Over the past decade, everyone has become accustomed to reminders that a new type of risk without boundaries has emerged. Precautionary governmental process and the rising cultural prevalence of risk have indelibly transformed our understanding of past, present and future through inductive and probabilistic reasoning on the danger to come.[16] The unpredictability of violence confounds the extents of regulatory institutions, forcing governments to concede that they cannot guarantee public safety unless one opts for an extension of surveillance and control. When the need to manage risk requires greater access to information, technological fixes become the security apparatus, and the language of security technologies becomes the language of risk, which in turn makes the deployment of ever more up-to-date technologies the only desirable and acceptable solution. Our daily lives have become besotted by biometrics, CCTV and new smart ID systems. As Lyon[17] highlights, consumer data are merged with those obtained for policing and intelligence, both nationally and across borders, contributing to the creation of an ever-widening web of surveillance. These forms of mass surveillance result in the aggregation of people who, without doing anything special, come under 'categorical suspicion'[18] or 'social sorting'[19] by virtue of their involuntary contribution to statistical algorithms.

Since the revelations of Edward Snowden in June 2013, no one can ignore the alarming extent of mass surveillance.[20] We know that the American National Security Agency and the British security services are routinely collecting, processing and storing huge quantities of digital communications. The British Government Communications Headquarters mass-surveillance programme, 'Tempora', was recently been declared perfectly legal.[21] Yet, its legitimacy and modus operandi are still highly dubious – and ultimately dangerous especially when members of the Executive themselves do not understand the process and its technicalities.[22] Perhaps the more crucial point is that these practices of surveillance and the underlying logic of anticipation have turned suspicion into legitimate, 'actionable' intelligence.[23] These surveillance programmes are enabled by a culture of fear and suspicion,[24] which mutually reinforce each other. Surveillance fosters suspicion and, in turn, suspicion supports the logic of maximisation of surveillance.[25]

The fact that everyone is always a potential suspect is reinforced by our reliance on automated forms of identification and verification and by the monitoring surveillance technologies we use nowadays. If there is no limit to suspicion, everything and everyone can logically be part of it. On this view, the realm of surveillance ought to extend to a class of putative suspects so large that, in order to monitor and pre-empt their possible future violations, it could be said that it is necessary to survey and scrutinise everyone. This point is sharpened further if one looks at the now-numerous government anti-terrorist and 'be alert' campaigns that have been implemented over the past decade; one should not only remain alert and be aware of one's surroundings at all times but should also report concerns about anything or anyone that might be out of place.

In the wake of 9/11 attacks in 2001, the number of 'be alert', 'see something, say something', 'every piece of information helps' or 'report suspicious activity' campaigns has grown exponentially across Western societies. The 2003 'see something, say something' New York Metropolitan Transportation Authority campaign became a national campaign supported by the US Department of Homeland Security in 2010 and has even been developed into a Smartphone app 'see something, send something'.[26] Every US and British local and national police forces have implemented 'report suspicious activity' campaigns on their websites. The 2002 Australian 'be alert, not alarmed' campaign was supported by television commercials and the production of a booklet on terror prevention. The production of an anti-terrorist brochure covering the basics of first aid, how to respond in the workplace to a major incident and what to have at hand in case of an emergency was also part of the 2004 British campaign.[27] Every single Western government has sought to communicate the risk of terrorism to the public, contributing to a state of constant alert,[28] reinforcing militaristic views about the fight against terrorism and underpinning the idea that every citizen has a new security role to play.[29] As the US TSA website underlines:

> Citizens play a pivotal role in reporting suspicious activities to law enforcement authorities, which may help prevent or deter an attack in places frequented by all of us. (TSA website)[30]

As Mythen and Walklate[31] posit, there is a visible moral dimension at play in these dominant representations of the terrorist risk and in the way citizens have been deputised. Alongside new surveillance technologies, requesting help from citizens is certainly an interesting inflection in how social control is engineered nowadays.[32] The key point here is what Andrejevic aptly highlights when he focuses on citizen-to-citizen surveillance or 'lateral surveillance'.[33] Following Andrejevic's argument, Chan underlines how these anti-terror campaigns legitimate a right to suspicion.[34] A right to suspicion is based on the argument that everyone being part of a community possesses a local knowledge of what is normal and abnormal, acceptable and suspicious.[35]

What we would argue here is that the problem is not one of a transformation of our Western societies into police states where everyone might be an informant, but much more the fact that these campaigns beget a double-edged vexing attitude towards the meaning of daily life and citizenship: there is no such thing as a normal situation for it is always and only seemingly normal one and, by extension, we are all watchers and suspects at the same time. The more incidents of distrust one might witness through the lens of computerised suspicion and patterns of deviance, the more it begets a generalised perception of natural human dishonesty and a tragic understanding of danger as permanent and dormant.

Sarraute's *Age of Suspicion* (originally published in 1956) marked durably the 1950s literary world, initiating what will be soon recognised as the *new novel*.[36] When writing against the assumptions of the classical novel of the nineteenth century, where the author and reader move in a common world of well-known entities and where easily identifiable characters can be understood through the qualities and possessions bestowed upon them, she initiated a new type of novel premised upon a new understanding of the reader.[37] A new reader instructed by very different narrative principles: there is no such thing as authenticity, sincerity and state of grace. Sarraute's assault on classical literature was concomitant to the emergence of behaviourism which dominated scientific psychology in the post-war decades. While behaviourists were inclined to claim that human conduct can be deciphered, analysed and translated, Sarraute's mistrust in the appearance of a cohesive plot and characters was an invitation to write differently about the unfathomable depths of the human mind, the subterranean feelings and thoughts on the outermost fringes of our consciousness. Yet, between the apparently opposed scientific and literary approaches summarised previously, there is a common point of departure: what people say, do (or write) cannot be trusted as such. How this sceptical and pessimistic anthropological assumption about human nature invaded our daily routines is central to our argument. It dovetails neatly with the rather generalised anxiety about transnational forms of violence expressed in terms of '(new) terrorism' and 'radicalisation'.

DE-RADICALISATION AND EARLY PREVENTION'S TOOLS

The evolving trend of deadly attacks carried out across Europe in the last fifteen years has contributed to the imposition of the issue of violent extremism and radicalisation – be it carried out in the name of Islam or originating in far right, far left, anti-Semitic or xenophobic ideologies – as a very guiding principle to the European political agenda. Identifying, detecting and addressing the underlying factors leading some individuals or groups, in particular among the disenfranchised youth of European cities, to participate in violent acts have become critical. In addition to counter-terrorism legislation, European countries have developed numerous policies and programmes for early detection and prevention aiming at preventing 'non-radicals' from being radicalised and to stop them from possibly joining violent groups in Europe and abroad.

In this European trend towards the development of counter-radicalisation policies, the United Kingdom led the way with the *Prevent* strand of its 2005 counter-terrorist strategy *Contest*. The *Prevent* programme came under considerable criticism and the original overall plan *Contest* has since been substantially revised. However, the core dimension of the programme is still very much the same: to identify those at risk of becoming radicalised, to assess the level of risk they might pose and to work with sectors and institutions where there are risks of radicalisation. Within this architecture, the 2007 Channel scheme is dedicated to providing support at an early stage to people who are identified as vulnerable and therefore referred to it.

The Belgian 2002 'Plan M' (M for surveillance of Mosques) and its successor, the 2005 'Plan R' (R for radicalisation), have received less scholarly attention. The linguistic division between French and Flemish as well as the inextricable tangle of Belgian local, regional and federal levels of decisions does not help. Nonetheless, the Belgian *Plan R* is very similar to *Prevent* and the overall British *Contest* strategy. They both aim at:

(1) detecting radicalising (key) actors in an early stage so as to be able (2) to take the necessary measures.[38]

The [Prevent] *strategy also means intervening to stop people moving from extremist (albeit legal) groups into terrorist-related activity.*[39]

Like *Prevent*, the Belgian *Plan R* stresses the importance of developing an integrated collaboration between various public services in the fight against radicalisation and the detection of early signs of radicalisation. The detection of early signs of radicalisation and the management of radicalised people take place within a solid territorial network of *Local Integrated Security Cells*

(*Lokale Integrale Veiligheidscel*, LIVC, in Flemish, and *cellule de sécurité intégrale locale*, CSIL, in French) set up by the mayors in order to exchange information between the various local social and prevention services on one hand, and with the federal level through a territorial network of *Local Task Forces* on the other. Key to the *Plan R* is the two-pronged approach: to deal with 'radicalised' individuals inasmuch as protecting potentially 'vulnerable' individuals from falling into radicalisation.

Under the 2011 European Commission Prevention of and Fight against Crime programme, the project Strengthening Resilience against Violent Radicalisation (STRESAVIORA I), conducted by the Belgian Federal Home Affairs authorities, led to the recent creation in 2015 of three resilience tools: 'Bounce^{young}' (i.e., resilience training programme for young people), 'Bounce^{along}' (awareness-raising tool for parents and front-line workers) and 'Bounce^{up}' (a tool to train the trainers). Within the next years, STRESAVIORA II will aim at implementing and diffusing these tools across European countries.

Prevent has generated a debate on whether the Muslim community has become a 'suspect community'. Pantazis and Pemberton[40] opened the debate when they argued that Muslims have been construed as the enemy within and counter-terror measures essentially directed against them. Being a member of the Muslim community can eventually lead to a suspicion by association. In recalling Hillyard's[41] seminal contribution on how once the Irish community was at the centre of all social and political preoccupations, Pantazis and Pemberton place an emphasis upon the extent to which Muslim communities have been constructed as threat to civil society, resulting in them becoming the subject of negative stereotyping, intelligence profiling and the violent expression of anti-Muslim sentiments. In contrast to the thrust of the argument being made here, Greer[42] emphasises the existence of an Islamist extremism threat and therefore questions the extent to which counter-terrorism measures have impacted negatively on Muslim community. For Greer, feeling under suspicion is significantly different from being under suspicion, whereas for Pantazis and Pemberton[43] the feeling and the experience of suspicion are consubstantial. Breen-Smyth[44] reinforces this point in her contribution to the debates. She argues that a suspect community is generated through national or state security policies and reproduced and reinforced by societal responses and social practices. Even the supposedly clear distinction between 'moderate' and 'extremist' Muslims reinforces the point. As Ragazzi[45] explains, the 'moderate Muslim' implicitly constructs the 'Muslim' as a threat. First, it posits that some Muslims are bound to be extremists and therefore dangerous. Secondly, it tends to stigmatise the Muslim community as harbouring terrorists and radicals. Finally, it tends to convey the idea that the Muslim community is simultaneously inside and outside British society and therefore its relationship to 'western values' is inherently tendentious. Thus, the expression 'British Muslim' can be understood as an exclusionary label despite its seemingly attempt to be inclusive.

The Belgian de-radicalisation strategy is clearly guided by the need to address the issue of foreign fighters and returnees. Belgium has been bashed for having the largest number of foreign fighters as a proportion of its population in the Western world. Recent estimates from both official and non-government sources range between 388 confirmed cases according to Bakker and De Bont,[46] 470 according to Coolsaet[47] and somewhere between 420 and 516, according to Van Ginkel and Entenman.[48] Quite a number of these foreign fighters have come back to Belgium. According to Coolsaet,

> Almost a third (some 130) have now returned, of which a third has been arrested and sent to jail.[49]

Across Europe, the fear of the returnees tipped the scale on the criminalisation side rather than logics of reintegration. In reaction to the November 2015 Paris attacks, the Belgian prime minister, Charles Michel, has declared his 'relentless firmness against the rise of radicalisation' and made it clear that returnees belong to jail.[50] For the purpose of our argument, it is worthwhile to mention here how the Belgian penitentiary administration is categorising these 'extremist inmates' since 2015. There are currently 85 convicted extremists in Belgian prisons, divided in two main groups: the *F section* for the 'foreign fighters' and the *T section* for 'terrorists'. The *F section* is subdivided into four subcategories: 'FA' for the recruiters and/or predicators, 'FB' for the militant returnees, 'FC' for the passive returnees and 'FD' for the facilitators, the ones who have helped in either the departure or the return of the foreign fighters. The *T* section is also subdivided into four subcategories: 'TA' for the 'terrorists' recognised as leaders, 'TB' for the militants who have contributed to an attack, 'TC' for the ones who have offered some logistics in the preparation of an attack and 'TD' for the ones who have offered some support more broadly. Key to these classifications is to separate these inmates into two broader categories: those whose extremist certainties are so ingrained that the system regards them as beyond hope and those who are dangerous but potentially and hopefully salvageable.

At the core of these de-radicalisation programmes and penitentiary classifications there are two implicit suggestions. The first suggestion is that our political institutions and values are fragile. The second one is that there are powerful and volatile social forces in our societies and beyond which, upon hearing a radical message of agitators, are likely to sweep all before them with unstoppable force. Asserting danger, therefore, is primarily focused on detecting early signs and categorising expression of grievances. The multiple indicators punctuating the alleged pathway to radicalisation are very similar between the different programmes. Whether one takes the three-edged *Prevent* programme,[51] the different *Bounce* resilience tools or even the more recent Canadian 'behaviour barometer' created by the Montreal-based Centre for the Prevention of Radicalisation Leading to Violence (CPRLV),[52] they work within the same rationale: to establish a line between behaviours that should be understood as a cause for immediate concern from the ones that, sooner or later, will be a cause for potential future worries. The CPRLV's four-colour-coded behaviour barometer offers a four-pronged framework: 'insignificant' (code green), 'troubling' (code yellow), 'worrisome' (code orange) *and* 'alarming' (code red). This attempt to clarify the different categories of conduct under suspicion raises yet more questions.

Between *Prevent*, *Channel* and *Bounce* there is a common understanding of de-radicalisation and resilience based upon a precarious definition of radicalisation. The 2014 Belgian *Ministerial Circular on Terrorism and Violent Radicalisation* (known as the 'Circulaire GPI 78') defines radicalisation in those terms:

> [radicalisation is] *a process whereby an individual or a group is so influenced that the individual or group in question is mentally prepared to commit extremist acts, including violent or even terrorist action.*

There has been considerable political and academic interest in studying radicalisation and, very often, radical, radicalism and radicalisation are used as interchangeable concepts and linear processes leading to violence. Yet, the threshold between holding radical views and becoming violent is still subject to discussion. Many scholars suggest that the notions of radicalism and radicalisation have contributed to obscure the scope of the debate rather than to clarify it.[53] The word 'radicalisation' is unsatisfactory for it fails to convey the complexity of a phenomenon that still affects only a small number of people. Part of the problem is that radicalisation is based upon a problematic fusion of certain dominant explanatory models of the 'causes of terrorism' (specifically, 'psychological vulnerability' to 'radicalisation') that have focused mostly on psychology (frustration/aggression, grievances), ideological factors (violence-prone ideologies) and perceived or real social inequality (the 'root causes' models). Radicalisation then works like an optical machine, producing 'visibilities' and 'invisibilities'. While radicalisation highlights the importance of one's opinions, views and ideas, portraying dangerous groups and/or individuals, outlining an escapable pathway to violence, it also ignores the political and social dimensions at stake.

The preventive logic of 'far better to prevent terrorism before it happens than to investigate and prosecute after a tragedy' is, unfortunately, largely shared across most segments of our societies. When looking at how de-radicalisation and resilience schemes rely heavily upon the vigilance and cooperation of social workers, youth workers, health workers and teachers, among others, we would like to argue that suspicion has become a dispositif, a technique of governance which imposes a particular conduct, a new way of formulating normality across society.

Universities, hospitals, educators, local government officials and social workers have been slowly but surely largely co-opted into a larger security apparatus. They have been redefined as the key actors at the 'front line' of the pursuit of de-radicalisation and resilience. The United Kingdom 2015 Counter-Terrorism Act (section 26) imposes new duties on National Health Service Trusts, schools and, more widely, public sector employers and employees. They are statutorily obliged to intervene if they suspect an individual is 'at risk of radicalisation'.[54] Enrolling practitioners into de-radicalisation and resilience schemes has been a consistent trend across European countries. Initiated with the British *Contest* counter-terrorist strategy, the idea that it is of paramount importance to include social workers, religious leaders, researchers and police officers together is also a core principle of the 2011 European Commission's Radicalisation Awareness Network. Training and raising awareness among first-line practitioners was initially received with resistance. Across Western countries, senior academics and academic-related staff have regularly raised strong concerns about the possible negative effects of such policies on academic freedom and freedom of speech. Regardless of these concerns about educators expected to identify and refer students 'at risk of radicalisation', the British education system is now subordinated to a security agenda.

According to recent British press reports putting the emphasis on how the government is stepping up its efforts in the fight against radicalisation, it is no less than 400,000 nurses, doctors, teachers and local government officials that have been trained to deal with individuals who are vulnerable to extremism.[55] In regard to Belgium, it is difficult to assess with precision the number of people who have been trained and/or who are currently contributing to the early-detection programmes and referring. However, like the United Kingdom where all local councils are operating *Channel* schemes, Belgian de-radicalisation programme is based on the territorial network of the *Local Integrated Security Cells*. While there are some disparities between the different Belgian cities, the *Local Integrated Security Cells* usually gather members of the local police, youth support and health department services, street workers, local schools, local houses of Justice and centres for mental healthcare.

Referrals to de-radicalisation programmes rise every year. Thanks to the British 2000 Freedom of Information Act (FOIA), we can ascertain the following figures in regard to the United Kingdom: In 2006, when *Channel* was launched, six people were referred. Between 2007 and 2015, no less than 6,306 individuals were referred (FOI request number 000098/15). For the year 2015 only, the National Police Chiefs' Council has established that 3,955 individuals were referred (FOI request number 000026/16).

SUSPICION AS A TECHNIQUE OF GOVERNANCE

In his thorough assessment of Danish counter-radicalisation efforts, Lindekilde convincingly shows how the lack of consensus on indicators of radicalisation and resilience increases inconsistency in initial assessment and 'constitutes a risk of potential under-reaction (false negatives) and over-reaction (false positives)'.[56] In sum, indicators of (pre)radicalisation and the terminology of radicalisation itself are inconsistent and theoretically impoverished. Nonetheless, these indicators are shaping decisions made by what have been designated as front-line workers.

Bernard de Vos, a well-established and regarded Ombudsman for Children's Rights in Belgium, recently declared in a radio interview that

> I don't think that we are facing a problem of radicalisation but rather a series of explosive individual situations because young people from migrant backgrounds are stigmatised and victimised.[57]

This declaration about 'radicalisation' on one of the major Belgian radio stations just a couple of weeks after the attack in Nice on the 14th of July and a few days after the killing of a priest in Normandy on the 26th of July 2016 sparked a series of immediate and violent rebukes. De Vos' declarations have been largely interpreted as a scandalous infringement of the compulsory expression of solidarity towards the victims of terrorism and immediately marked as off-limits. Collins shows how these rituals of solidarity in the wake of an attack are key elements in the production and reproduction of social order.[58] To defy such an order is to expose oneself to public odium. Clearly, and as can be seen in different interviews carried out since then with other practitioners enrolled in de-radicalisation, the reactions towards De Vos certainly inhibited them from expressing comparable concerns. Members of the Belgian penitentiary staff, probation officers and the social workers working in juvenile detention centres who were once keen on expressing their views have become much more reticent.[59] They were particularly concerned about discussing the inherently problematic dimensions of their daily work when they are required to do monitoring and reporting.[60]

This has important consequences beyond the possibility of being able to express oneself or not. It is how this chilling effect impacts upon professional decisions in regard to day-to-day early-detection and monitoring of radicalisation. It seems that, among the Belgian 'front liners', failing to recognise the possible danger to come – and therefore to report it – is largely perceived as an unsettling situation of potential liability. Belgian social workers are paralysed by the idea that they can forgo acting in a meaningful way, so they refer 'suspects'. They do not refer because they essentially believe in what radicalisation is and how it should be tackled, but rather as a professional defence mechanism. Mills shows how the public sphere is connected with the personal realm of experience.[61] When our daily environment is saturated with the risk of terrorism, the way these professionals encounter and cope with the pressure exercised upon them to be the first line in the defence of our societies is to apply – consciously or not – a strategy of risk displacement. Sharing information, referring an individual allows them to avoid both the present and future responsibility for failing to do it. It allows them to divert and shield themselves from the potential harm of being the subjects of suspicion themselves in the 'always probable case that missing a sign could end up in a bloody disaster'.[62]

This strategy of risk displacement is not an easy strategy to mobilise for most of these professionals. Whether this strategy is put in place and acknowledged or not by its actors, it is an ethical and professional dilemma that haunts them in their daily routines.[63] To refer someone or a situation is to contribute seemingly to the defence of society and the ultimate justification deployed here is very often expressed in terms of contributing solely to avoid a potential and future disaster. But at the same time, this imperative of referral is also understood as a cultivation of liability that undermines their professional identity. Social workers and teachers who share a particular professional *habitus*, a series of codes, traditions and sensibilities for which taking the risk of trusting someone and fostering trust plays an essential role are putting themselves at risk of not being able to carry out their assignments.[64] The dilemma and the anxiety about whether one is doing the right thing is neither cognitive nor affectual but ultimately driven by the necessity to mitigate an imperious command to refer an unusual situation and/or an individual with a necessity to secure a professional identity.

The different variations of 'if you see something, say something' have certainly resulted in plenty of seeing and saying, perhaps even more than the authorities might have expected to hear. The different early-detection schemes have also resulted in a rather spectacular growth in the number of referrals. Yet, the question one should ask is how much of this information has been turned into usable intelligence. Sheptycki[65] underlines that one of the main problems intelligence officers are facing is when they are simply inundated by data. In their well-documented analysis of daily practices within French domestic intelligence services, Bonelli and Ragazzi show

how in a high-tech intelligence-led environment some senior policing officers are turning low-tech; against information collected through referrals, they tend to go back to the old-fashioned technologies such as observation, informant and written memos.[66] When it comes to gathering information and converting that information into knowledge, it is has to be conceded that the different early-detection schemes are, for some analysts, essentially viewed as noise pollution. Bonelli and Ragazzi are not suggesting that this is a well-shared professional move with regard to the reliability of knowledge; it is one particular mode of reasoning combined with a particular set of strategies of enquiry. Furthermore, they underline how the use of low-tech technologies is still driven by a logic of anticipation. Their argument does not undermine the idea that potentiality of suspicion has acquired particular potency in our anxious societies craving for more security.

CONCLUSION

Tempting though it would be to speak of a 'normalisation of suspicion', what needs to be pinpointed here is the corroding influence of a spreading wariness on how we are collectively induced to understand ordinary action (and therefore inaction), the possibility of trusting someone and, last but not least, the presumption of innocence are slowly mutating into a presumption of guilt. As it has been suggested earlier, the different 'be alert campaigns' deployed over the years have given birth to the development of sensitivity towards unintended consequences of our actions. One can see how this sensibility that prides itself on its uncompromising wariness and vigilance is based on the conviction that appearances can deceive. One should question the motives that lie behind action (and inaction), disagreement (and agreement) and conduct. What is left of the rule of proof and the shield against premature punishment when the notion of innocence becomes more and more an inconvenient technicality as opposed to a valued principle? People registered on 'suspected terrorist lists' will inevitably struggle to prove their innocence because, apart from the extremely complex jurisdictional matters at stake, at the very core of these listings of suspicion lies the classic double problem of inductive principle and probabilistic reasoning. In calling attention to the possibility that the future could be different from the past and present in unforeseeable ways, it raises doubts about the very possibility of definitive refutations of grounds for suspicion.

Distrust is not only a central mechanism of how the risk society is policed but also a core component of our ways of seeing and being as ordinary citizens. The complex ways in which we have collectively become embedded in risk assessment technologies and generalised forms of suspicion towards unfamiliar persons, undesirable people and menacing outsiders have reinforced social fragmentation and the dangers of polarisation and exclusion. The overarching question of the efficiency and intended or unintended consequences of these counter-terrorism and de-radicalisation policies is very often left aside; the question of whether these measures could contribute to increase the risk of escalation of violence and the risk of further exclusion of a population already disenfranchised seems almost forgotten. How far can these duties of referral push those who are single out down a path that they may otherwise have rejected? Suspicion is the active ingredient of the precautionary principle at stake in our risk societies and the unfortunate, deeply entrenched driving force that leads to a blurring of the boundaries between rationality and panic, between anticipation and anxiety. When a more or less articulated set of grievances leads to a referral and when, on the other side, a referral is perceived as a rightly acceptable and desirable compliance, one might expect this suspicious posture to remain at the centre of national and international politics for the foreseeable future unless we question collectively the assumptions, presumptions and rationales that underpinned the evolution of contemporary risk society. Unfortunately, the complex mechanism of governance and social regulations are not historically known to be open to such a radical reflexivity.

NOTES

1. We would like to thank Amandine Scherrer and Peter Lawler for their comments on an early version.

2. Dunham, Roger G., Geoffrey P. Alpert, Meghan S. Stroshine and Katherine Bennett. 2005. Transforming Citizens into Suspects: Factors That Influence the Formation of Police Suspicion. *Police Quarterly* 8(3): 366–393.

3. Crank, John P. 2014. *Understanding Police Culture*. Abingdon: Routledge, 145.

4. Beck, Ulrich. 1992. *Risk Society: Towards a New Modernity*. London: Sage; Beck, Ulrich. 1999. *World Risk Society*. Malden, MA: Polity Press; Beck, Ulrich. 2002. The Terrorist Threat. World Risk Society Revisited. *Theory Culture Society* 19(39): 39–55; Beck, Ulrich. 2006. Living in the World Risk Society. *Economy and Society* 35(3): 329–345.

5. Douglas, Mary. 1986. *Risk Acceptability According to Social Sciences*. London: Routledge & Kegan, 19.

6. Bauman, Zygmunt. 1991. *Modernity and Its Ambivalence*. Cambridge: Polity Press, 16.

7. Furedi, F. 2002. *Culture of Fear: Risk-Taking and the Morality of Low Expectations*. New York: Continuum International.

8. Garland, David. 2001. *The Culture of Control*. Oxford: Oxford University Press, 194.

9. Reid, Julian. 2006. *The Biopolitics of the War on Terror: Life Struggles, Liberal Modernity and the Defence of Logistical Societies*. Manchester: Manchester University Press, x.

10. Amoore, Louise, and De Goede, Marieke. eds. 2008. *Risk and the War on Terror*. Abingdon: Routledge; Aradau, Claudia, and van Munster, Rens. 2007. Governing Terrorism through Risk: Taking Precautions, (Un)knowing the Future. *European Journal of International Relations* 13(1): 89–115.

11. Aradau, Claudia, and van Munster, Rens. 2011. *Politics of Catastrophe: Genealogies of the Unknown*. Abingdon: Routledge.

12. De Goede, Marieke. 2012. *Speculative Security. The Politics of Pursuing Terrorist Monies*. Minneapolis: University of Minnesota Press, 53.

13. Dal Lago, Alexandro, and Palidda, Salvatore. eds. 2010. *Conflict, Security and the Reshaping of Society. The Civilization of War*. Abingdon: Routledge.

14. Guittet, Emmanuel-Pierre, and Perier, Miriam. 2005. Suspicion et exception [suspicion and exception]. *Cultures & Conflits* 58: 5–12; Bigo, Didier, and Guittet, Emmanuel-Pierre. 2011. Northern Ireland as Metaphor: Exception, Suspicion and Radicalization in the 'War on Terror'. *Security Dialogue* 42(6): 483–498.

15. Wilkinson, Iain. 2001. *Anxiety in a Risk society*. London: Routledge.

16. Bigo, Didier, and Guittet, Emmanuel-Pierre. eds. 2006. *Antiterrorisme et Société* [Antiterrorism and Society]. Paris: l'Harmattan, 192.

17. Lyon, David. 2003. *Surveillance after September 11*. Cambridge: Polity.

18. Marx, Gary T. 1988. *Undercover: Police Surveillance in America*. Berkeley: University of California Press.

19. Lyon, *Surveillance*.

20. Bauman, Z., Bigo, D., Esteves, P., Guild, E., Jabri, V., Lyon, D., and Walker, R.B. 2014. After Snowden: Rethinking the Impact of Surveillance. *International Political Sociology* 8(2): 121–144.

21. Bowcott, Owen. 2014. UK Mass Surveillance Laws Do Not Breach Human Rights, Tribunal Rules. *The Guardian*, 5 December 2014.

22. Taylor, Matthew, and Ball, James. 2014. Philip Hammond 'Confused' about Extent of UK Surveillance Powers. *The Guardian*, 11 December 2014.

23. Gandy, Oscar H., K. Ball; K. Haggerty and D. Lyon (eds.) Jr. 2012. Statistical Surveillance. In *Routledge Handbook of Surveillance Studies*. Abingdon: Routledge.

24. Furedi, *Culture of Fear*.

25. Norris, Clive, and Armstrong, G. 1999. *The Maximum Surveillance Society*. Oxford: Berg.

26. Lovett, Kenneth. 2015. Andrew Cuomo Announces 'See Something, Send Something' Smartphone App for Reporting Suspicious Behaviour. *Daily News*, 23 November 2015.

27. Mythen, G., and Walklate, S. 2006. Communicating the Terrorist Risk: Harnessing a Culture of Fear? *Crime Media Culture* 2: 123–144.

28. Altheide, David. L. 2006. Terrorism and the Politics of Fear. *Cultural Studies-Critical Methodologies*, 6(4): 415–439.

29. Chan, Janet. 2008. The New Lateral Surveillance and a Culture of Suspicion. In M. Deflem (ed.) *Surveillance and Governance: Crime Control and Beyond*. JAI Press, 223–239.

30. https://www.tsa.gov/news/top-stories/2015/12/14/if-you-see-something-say-somethingTM.

31. Mythen and Walklate, *Communicating the Terrorist Risk*.

32. Norris, Clive. 2003. From Personal to Digital: CCTV, the Panopticon, and the Technological Mediation of Suspicion and Social Control. In *Surveillance as Social Sorting: Privacy, Risk and Digital Discrimination*, 249–281; Chan, Janet. 2008. The new lateral surveillance and a culture of suspicion. In M. Deflem (eds.) *Surveillance and Governance*: Crime control and Beyond, Bingley, UK: JAI Press.

33. Andrejevic, Mark. 2005. The Work of Watching One Another: Lateral Surveillance, Risk, and Governance. *Surveillance & Society* 2(4): 479–497.

34. Chan, *The New Lateral Surveillance*.

35. Norris and Armstrong, *The Maximum Surveillance Society*.

36. Jefferson, Ann. 2000. *Nathalie Sarraute, Fiction and Theory: Questions of Difference*. Cambridge: Cambridge University Press.

37. Sarraute, Nathalie. [1956] 1963. *The Age of Suspicion: Essays on the Novel*. New York: G. Braziller.

38. OCAM (Organe pour la Coopération pour l'Analyse de la Menace), Plan Radicalisation (plan R) (December 2004, revised May 2015) [confidential].

39. HM Government. Revised *Prevent* Duty Guidance: for England and Wales. Guidance for specified authorities in England and Wales on the duty in the Counter-Terrorism and Security Act 2015 to have due regard to the need to prevent people from being drawn into terrorism (March 2015, revised July 2015).

40. Pantazis, Christina, and Pemberton, Simon. 2009. From the 'Old' to the 'New' Suspect Community Examining the Impacts of Recent UK Counter-Terrorist Legislation. *British Journal of Criminology* 49(5): 646–666.

41. Hillyard, Paddy. 1993. *Suspect Community: People's Experience of the Prevention of Terrorism Acts in Britain*. Pluto Press.

42. Greer, Steven. 2010. Anti-Terrorist Laws and the United Kingdom's 'Suspect Muslim Community': A reply to Pantazis and Pemberton. *British Journal of Criminology* 50(6): 1171–1190.

43. Pantazis and Pemberton, From the 'Old' to the 'New' Suspect Community; Pantazis, Christina, and Pemberton, Simon. 2011. Restating the Case for the 'Suspect Community'. A Reply to Greer. *British Journal of Criminology* 51(6): 1054–1062.

44. Breen-Smyth, Marie. 2014. Theorising the 'Suspect Community': Counterterrorism, Security Practices and the Public Imagination. *Critical Studies on Terrorism* 7(2): 223–240.

45. Ragazzi, Francesco. 2014. Policed Multiculturalism? The Impact of Counter-Terrorism and Counter-Radicalization and the 'End' of Multiculturalism. In Baker-Beall, Christopher, Heath-Kelly, Charlotte, and Jarvis, Lee (eds.), *Counter-Radicalisation: Critical Perspectives*. London: Routledge, 156–174.

46. Bakker, Edwin, and de Bont, Roel. 2016. Belgian and Dutch Jihadist Foreign Fighters (2012–2015): Characteristics, Motivations, and Roles in the War in Syria and Iraq. *Small Wars & Insurgencies* 27(5): 837–857.

47. Coolsaet, Rik. 2016. Facing the Fourth Foreign Fighters Wave. What Drives Europeans to Syria, and to Islamic State? Insights from the Belgian Case. *Egmont Paper 81*. Brussels: Royal Institute for International Relations.

48. van Ginkel, Bibi, and Entenmann, Eva. eds. 2016. *The Foreign Fighters Phenomenon in the European Union*. The Hague: ICCT Research Paper, 25.

49. Coolsaet, Facing the Fourth Foreign Fighters Wave, 9.

50. http://www.premier.be/fr/lutte-contre-le-terrorisme-mesures-d%C3%A9cid%C3%A9es-par-le-gouvernement-f%C3%A9d%C3%A9ral-discours [in Flemish and in French]

51. http://www.npcc.police.uk/documents/TAM/2012/201210TAMChannelGuidance.pdf.

52. https://info-radical.org/wp-content/uploads/2016/08/BAROMETRE_EN_CPRLV_2016–1.pdf.

53. Baker-Beall, Christopher, Heath-Kelly, Charlotte, and Jarvis, Lee. eds. 2014. *Counter-Radicalisation: Critical Perspectives*. Abingdon: Routledge.

54. http://www.legislation.gov.uk/ukpga/2015/6/contents/enacted.

55. Ross, Tim. 2016. Extremists Will Be Forced onto 'Deradicalisation Programme' in New Terror crackdown. *The Telegraph*, 31 July 2016.

56. Lindekilde, Lasse. 2014. Refocusing Danish Counter-Radicalisation Efforts: An Analysis of the (Problematic) Logic and Practice of Individual De-Radicalisation Interventions. In Baker-Beall, Christopher, Heath-Kelly, Charlotte, and Jarvis, Lee (eds.), *Counter-Radicalisation: Critical Perspectives*. Abingdon: Routledge, 231.

57. Bel RTL, 10 August 2016; our translation http://www.rtl.be/belrtl/video/591832.aspx.

58. Collins, Randall. 2004. Rituals of Solidarity and Security in the Wake of Terrorist Attack. *Sociological Theory* 22(1): 53–87.

59. Series of meetings with Belgian social workers, penitentiary staff and youth workers during the preparation of a Belgian research grant application aiming at assessing Belgian de-radicalisation policies upon social cohesion and liberties. The different meetings were held in Brussels, between August and September 2016, and under the Chatham House rule. Thus, to avoid inadvertently ascribing views to people that they may not hold, but which they may have been simply reporting for discussion, comments are not attributed to any individuals.

60. Roundtable 1 and 2, Brussels, August 29, 2016

61. Mills, Wright. *The Sociological Imagination*. Oxford: Oxford University Press, 1959 [2000].

62. Roundtable 3, Brussels, 2 September 2016.

63. Roundtable 1 and 3, Brussels, 29 August 2016 and 2 September 2016.

64. Ouimet, Louis-Philippe. 2016. Radicalisation: Le lien de confiance ébranlé? *Radio Canada*, 27 October 2016.

65. Sheptycki, J. 2004. Organizational Pathologies in Police Intelligence Systems: Some Contributions to the Lexicon of Intelligence-Led Policing. *European Journal of Criminology* 1(3): 307–332.

66. Bonelli, Laurent, and Ragazzi, Francesco. 2014. Low-Tech Security: Files, Notes, and Memos as Technologies of Anticipation. *Security Dialogu* 45(5): 476–493.

BIBLIOGRAPHY

Altheide, David. L. 2006. Terrorism and the Politics of Fear. *Cultural Studies-Critical Methodologies*, 6(4): 415–439.

Amoore, Louise, and De Goede, Marieke. eds. 2008. *Risk and the War on Terror*. Abingdon: Routledge.
Andrejevic, Mark. 2005. The Work of Watching One Another: Lateral Surveillance, Risk, and Governance. *Surveillance & Society* 2(4): 479–497.
Aradau, Claudia, and van Munster, Rens. 2007. Governing Terrorism through Risk: Taking Precautions, (Un)knowing the Future. *European Journal of International Relations* 13(1): 89–115.
Aradau, Claudia, and van Munster, Rens. 2011. *Politics of Catastrophe: Genealogies of the Unknown*. Abingdon: Routledge.
Baker-Beall, Christopher, Heath-Kelly, Charlotte, and Jarvis, Lee. eds. 2014. *Counter-Radicalisation: Critical Perspectives*. Abingdon: Routledge.
Bakker, Edwin, and de Bont, Roel. 2016. Belgian and Dutch Jihadist Foreign Fighters (2012–2015): Characteristics, Motivations, and Roles in the War in Syria and Iraq. *Small Wars & Insurgencies* 27(5): 837–857.
Bauman, Z., Bigo, D., Esteves, P., Guild, E., Jabri, V., Lyon, D., and Walker, R.B. 2014. After Snowden: Rethinking the Impact of Surveillance. *International Political Sociology* 8(2): 121–144.
Bauman, Zygmunt. 1991. *Modernity and Its Ambivalence*. Cambridge: Polity Press.
Beck, Ulrich. 1992. *Risk Society: Towards a New Modernity*. London: Sage.
Beck, Ulrich. 1999. *World Risk Society*. Malden, MA: Polity Press.
Beck, Ulrich. 2002. The Terrorist Threat. World Risk Society Revisited. *Theory Culture Society* 19(39): 39–55.
Beck, Ulrich. 2006. Living in the World Risk Society. *Economy and Society* 35(3): 329–345.
Bigo, Didier, and Guittet, Emmanuel-Pierre. eds. 2006. *Antiterrorisme et Société* [Antiterrorism and Society]. Paris: l'Harmattan, 192p.
Bigo, Didier, and Guittet, Emmanuel-Pierre. 2011. Northern Ireland as Metaphor: Exception, Suspicion and Radicalization in the 'War on Terror'. *Security Dialogue* 42(6): 483–498.
Bonelli, Laurent, and Ragazzi, Francesco. 2014. Low-Tech Security: Files, Notes, and Memos as Technologies of Anticipation. *Security Dialogue* 45(5): 476–493.
Bowcott, Owen. 2014. UK Mass Surveillance Laws Do Not Breach Human Rights, Tribunal Rules. *The Guardian*, 5 December 2014.
Breen-Smyth, Marie. 2014. Theorising the 'Suspect Community': Counterterrorism, Security Practices and the Public Imagination. *Critical Studies on Terrorism* 7(2): 223–240.
Chan, Janet. 2008. The New Lateral Surveillance and a Culture of Suspicion. In M. Deflem (ed.), *Surveillance and Governance: Crime Control and Beyond*. Bingley, UK JAI Press, 223–239.
Collins, Randall. 2004. Rituals of Solidarity and Security in the Wake of Terrorist Attack. *Sociological Theory* 22(1): 53–87.
Coolsaet, Rik. 2016. Facing the Fourth Foreign Fighters Wave. What Drives Europeans to Syria, and to Islamic State? Insights from the Belgian Case. *Egmont Paper 81*. Brussels: Royal Institute for International Relations.
Crank, John P. 2014. *Understanding Police Culture*. Abingdon: Routledge.

Dal Lago, Alexandro, and Palidda, Salvatore. eds. 2010. *Conflict, Security and the Reshaping of Society. The Civilization of War*. Abingdon: Routledge.
De Goede, Marieke. 2012. *Speculative Security. The Politics of Pursuing Terrorist Monies*. Minneapolis: University of Minnesota Press.
Douglas, Mary. 1986. *Risk Acceptability according to Social Sciences*. London: Routledge & Kegan.
Dunham, Roger G., Alpert, Geoffrey P., Stroshine, Meghan S., and Bennett, Katherine. 2005. Transforming Citizens into Suspects: Factors That Influence the Formation of Police Suspicion. *Police Quarterly* 8(3): 366–393.
Furedi F. 2002. *Culture of Fear: Risk-Taking and the Morality of Low Expectations*. New York: Continuum International.
Gandy, Oscar H., Jr. K. Ball, K. Haggerty and D. Lyon (eds.) 2012. Statistical Surveillance. In *Routledge Handbook of Surveillance Studies*. Abingdon: Routledge.
Garland, David. 2001. *The Culture of Control*. Oxford: Oxford University Press.
Greer, Steven. 2010. Anti-Terrorist Laws and the United Kingdom's 'Suspect Muslim Community': A Reply to Pantazis and Pemberton. *British Journal of Criminology* 50(6): 1171–1190.
Guittet, Emmanuel-Pierre, and Perier, Miriam. 2005. Suspicion et exception [Suspicion and Exception]. *Cultures & Conflits 58*: 5–12.
Heath-Kelly, Charlotte. 2012. Reinventing Prevention or Exposing the Gap? False Positives in UK Terrorism Governance and the Quest for Pre-Emption. *Critical Studies on Terrorism* 5(1): 69–87.
Heath-Kelly, Charlotte. 2013. Counter-Terrorism and the Counterfactual: Producing the 'Radicalisation' Discourse and the UK PREVENT Strategy. *The British Journal of Politics & International Relations 15*: 394–415.
Hillyard, Paddy. *Suspect Community: People's Experience of the Prevention of Terrorism Acts in Britain*. London: Pluto Press, 1993.
HM Government. 2015. Revised *Prevent* Duty Guidance: For England and Wales. Guidance for specified authorities in England and Wales on the duty in the Counter-Terrorism and Security Act 2015 to have due regard to the need to prevent people from being drawn into terrorism (March 2015, revised July 2015).
Jefferson, Ann. 2000. *Nathalie Sarraute, Fiction and Theory: Questions of Difference*. Cambridge: Cambridge University Press.
Lindekilde, Lasse. 2012. Refocusing Danish Counter-Radicalisation Efforts: An Analysis of the (Problematic) Logic and Practice of Individual De-Radicalisation Interventions. In Baker-Beall, Christopher, Charlotte Heath-Kelly, and Lee Jarvis (eds.), *Counter-Radicalisation: Critical Perspectives*. Abingdon: Routledge, 223–241.
Lovett, Kenneth. 2015. Andrew Cuomo Announces 'See Something, Send Something' Smartphone App for Reporting Suspicious Behaviour. *Daily News*, 23 November 2015.
Lyon, David. 2003. *Surveillance after September 11*. Cambridge: Polity.
Lyon, David. 2016. Big Data Surveillance: Snowden, Every day Practices and Digital Futures. In Basaran, T., Bigo, D., Guittet, E. P., and Walker, R. B. J. (eds.), *International Political Sociology: Transversal Lines*. London and New York: Routledge, 254–271.

Marx, Gary T. 1988. *Undercover: Police Surveillance in America*. Berkeley: University of California Press.
Mills, Wright. 1959 [2000]. *The Sociological Imagination*. Oxford: Oxford University Press.
Mythen, G., and Walklate, S. 2006. Communicating the Terrorist Risk: Harnessing a Culture of Fear? *Crime Media Culture 2*: 123–144.
Norris, Clive., D. Lyon (eds.) 2003. From Personal to Digital: CCTV, the Panopticon, and the Technological Mediation of Suspicion and Social Control. In *Surveillance as Social Sorting: Privacy, Risk and Digital Discrimination*, London and New York: Routledge, 249–281.
Norris, Clive, and Armstrong, G. 1999. *The Maximum Surveillance Society*. Oxford: Berg.
OCAM (Organe pour la Coopération pour l'Analyse de la Menace). 2004. Plan Radicalisation (plan R) (December 2004, revised May 2015) [confidential].
Ouimet, Louis-Philippe. 2016. Radicalisation: Le lien de confiance ébranlé? Radicalization: the bond of trust shaken? *Radio Canada*, 27 October 2016.
Pantazis, Christina, and Pemberton, Simon. 2009. From the 'Old' to the 'New' Suspect Community Examining the Impacts of Recent UK Counter-Terrorist Legislation. *British Journal of Criminology 49*(5): 646–666.
Pantazis, Christina, and Pemberton, Simon. 2011. Restating the Case for the 'Suspect Community'. A Reply to Greer. *British Journal of Criminology 51*(6): 1054–1062.
Ragazzi, Francesco. 2014. Policed Multiculturalism? The Impact of Counter-Terrorism and Counter-Radicalization and the 'End' of Multiculturalism. In Baker-Beall, Christopher, Charlotte Heath-Kelly, and Lee Jarvis (eds.), *Counter-Radicalisation: Critical Perspectives*. London: Routledge, 156–174.
Reid, Julian. 2006. *The Biopolitics of the War on Terror: Life Struggles, Liberal Modernity and the Defence of Logistical Societies*. Manchester: Manchester University Press.
Ross, Tim. 2016. Extremists Will Be Forced onto 'Deradicalisation Programme' in New Terror Crackdown. *The Telegraph*, 31 July 2016.
Sarraute, Nathalie. [1956] 1963. *The Age of Suspicion: Essays on the Novel*. New York: G. Braziller.
Sheptycki, J. 2004. Organizational Pathologies in Police Intelligence Systems: Some Contributions to the Lexicon of Intelligence-Led Policing. *European Journal of Criminology 1*(3): 307–332.
Taylor, Matthew, and Ball, James. 2014. Philip Hammond 'Confused' about Extent of UK Surveillance Powers. *The Guardian*, 11 December 2014.
van Ginkel, Bibi, and Entenmann, Eva. eds. *The Foreign Fighters Phenomenon in the European Union*. The Hague: ICCT Research Paper, 2016.
Wilkinson, Iain. *Anxiety in a Risk Society*. London: Routledge, 2001.

Chapter 6

The Effects of Uncertainty: Anxiety and Crisis Preparedness

Carsten Baran

To ensure the continuity of core processes even in the event of external shocks is a key element of resilience. In the private sector, companies have started to build resilient organisations, which are able to continue their business operations and ensure the performance of the value chain, even in case of severe disasters. This refers directly to the consequences of anxiety regarding non-availability of critical resources due to both known and unknown threats. This intends to protect the company by elaborating crisis preparedness on a global level. The pandemic scenario has proved to be a major challenge for companies on the way to form a resilient organisation, as decisions have to be made with very limited information. The reaction of companies to pandemics has shown how sensitive their existing crisis response measures are to external influence and how anxiety paralyses appropriate handling. However, the lessons learned from the pandemic crisis reveals the necessity of improved risk mitigation strategies to fully establish a resilient organisation.

In the context of increasing political, societal and economic interdependences, a new reflection of organisations' risk perception and exposure has occurred. The awareness of international crisis events such as 9/11, pandemics or the Fukushima disaster has not only caused response actions of actors on multiple levels, but also created a narrative of uncertainty and anxiety. Altering values and increasing regulatory requests for security and service continuity have affected multinational companies in a way that has changed their self-reflection as well as their perspective on crisis preparedness. One example of crisis situations in which this relationship became visible are the recent pandemic waves, which increased the risk awareness regarding the effects of diseases on the continuity of business processes. A global spread of the bird flu and later the swine flu resulted in major challenges for companies' understanding of a resilient organisation. This included the experience of limited possibilities to react under the circumstances of uncertainty and the underlying presence of anxiety.

This contribution arranges the concepts of anxiety and uncertainty into the framework of corporate resilience during the crisis management of the recent pandemics in Germany. This addresses the fields of organisational sociology as well as risk management,[1] as a high degree of uncertainty forced decision makers to respond to this particular crisis situation under constant pressure. As the well-being and health of employees are not only an intrinsic interest of any organisation, it is also a product of the delegation of responsibility from the national authorities to the private sector, when regulators issued legal requirements for the implementation of corporate programs for effective resilience. During the crisis situation, anxiety clouded the process of decision making, as the available response strategy options were limited by insufficient knowledge about the effects of the measures taken and the fear of negative consequences as a result of decisions that had to be made. The transfer of responsibility from the public to the private is also central to this discussion.

This has resulted in two problems for the crisis management in affected companies: Firstly, how can a company develop response strategies with respect to evolving risks that might threaten the further existence of the company? And how can a company deal with limited information about the situation and vague knowledge about possible outcomes of decisions? Secondly, the need to comply with the fiduciary duties towards the employees that was required by the national regulators in Germany.[2] These two problems represent the agenda for this contribution. The empirical basis focuses on reactions of companies to the challenges of the pandemic waves between 2006 and 2011 in Germany, the recent high peak of this crisis scenario. This empirical material is primarily drawn from interviews with companies conducted by the author. The empirical basis will help to understand the theoretical concept of current methods of risk mitigation in companies and reveal the remaining challenges and problems for establishing a truly resilient organisation. In addition, this contribution seeks to highlight the new private-public partnership of shared responsibility when it comes to the safeguarding of employees. This chapter will thus further explain the connections between resilience and anxiety, and the effect on private organisations and public responsibility.

This chapter is organised as follows: First, it is important to understand the relationship between the wish to mitigate risks by implementing a resilient organisation on the one hand and the challenges to react to an incident under the circumstances of uncertainty, which will be the focus of the first section. Second, the theoretical groundwork will be enhanced by a closer look on the role of decisions for the understanding of risks and the possible risk mitigation strategies, which will be explained in the second section. In addition, it will be necessary to address the responsibility of resilience, by analysing the shared duties between the public and the private sector. As states incorporate companies more and more in their responsibility for protection and crisis preparation, the public and private sector became partners for the setup of resilience, which will be explored in the third section. This leads on to a case study of the reactions from companies to pandemics, namely the bird and swine flu waves in Germany between 2006 and 2011, which will give an example how the effects of uncertainty demanded advanced resilience planning and affected the area of fiduciary duty shared between national agencies and private enterprises in Germany.[3] This chapter will conclude that anxiety dominated the decision making of companies during this crisis, as they lacked experience for this particular scenario and depended on a few expert opinions, operated within an unclear area of shared responsibility and, most of all, feared to make an adverse decision. The transfer of responsibility is also particularly affected by anxiety, since decision making for the private sector is also concerned about minimising loss of profit.

RISK AND THE RESILIENT ORGANISATION

The global connection of production, communication and interaction is one of the core preconditions for the changing risk exposure of organisations. Under the impression of increasing complexity, the judgement of experts becomes crucial for society in order to define what is risky and what not, or to estimate what kinds of risks are of negligible magnitude.[4] Risk, in this case widely understood as a danger or a potential threat to the status quo of values, enables a prosperous business model. The private insurance industry sells products which are labelled with the provision of security, which serves an anthropological need.[5] Sophisticated methodologies of risk assessment and elaborated tools allow insurance companies to specify the individual premium according to the client's risk exposure. But how do organisations assess and respond to their own risk exposure? The 'resilient organisation' provides a term to describe such response strategies that promise stability and continuity, but have also proved to alter the organisation's self-conception.

The resilient organisation is the target model of an organisation to be resistant to external shocks. Here this means any external event that might result in a severe negative outcome for the organisation and threatens its own existence or capability to act. Resilience refers to the strategy to contain or prevent this external event from deploying an effect on the organisation and therefore to safeguard the organisation's continuity. The term is used by various disciplines to describe the capability to withstand external pressure, for instance in psychology, ecology or economics.[6] Thus, it includes two elements that define resilience: one is that the system, body or organisation is vulnerable to its environment; second, that the organisation possesses the capacity to adapt to the circumstances and can recover to its original status.[7]

From the perspective of a company this means especially to recover from any adversity that might jeopardise its ability to continue its core business processes and services. To achieve this one can build up high walls to provide protection against adverse shocks from the environment. This represents one element of resilience, which can be called a preventive strategy. For example, smoke detectors are a preventive strategy to increase resilience of an office building and reduce the risk that it might go up in flames. Another strategy is a mitigation of risks, which means the planning and testing of compensating strategies to respond to a shock, after it has occurred. For instance, if the office building has burned to the ground, the business processes might be recovered at a contingency site. As a summary, one can say that the first strategy intends to prevent a negative event from happening, and the second one mitigates the adverse effects of an incident. Additionally, a third element of resilience can be found, which states the reduction of time to recover from such an incident,[8] which implies extensive planning before the external shock commences. 'Crisis management' is the term for the active part of resilience and comes into play when the response plans need to be activated.

Speaking of preparation, it is important to keep in mind that all efforts of resilience are considered to be implemented before the incident occurs. Resilience covers a vast set of strategy options and planning, which allows a company to prepare for an incident before it becomes reality. Such strategy options can include different responses to a certain scenario, for example the loss of office spaces due to an incident that could disrupt normal operations. In this case, and according to the severity of the damage, different mitigations can be chosen. Key personnel can recover a minimum required level of service by moving to an alternate site and continuing their tasks over there. Or some employees could work from home, while others shift their workload to external service providers until the normal operations can be established again. All of this requires a detailed analysis of business processes, supply chain dependencies, customers' and regulator's requirements and of course sufficient allocated resources, which were reserved for this eventuality before it occurs. If this prerequisite is applicable, the company is prepared for external shocks and can be seen as resilient. But if the respective scenario is not covered by the company's resilience planning – for example, because it has not occurred before in this region or to this extent – confidence in the appropriate mitigation decreases. A disruption of normal operations due to the possible loss of personnel suddenly seemed possible during the bird and swine flu breakouts, which rapidly affected people on several continents. In fact, this scenario resulted in the urgent need for crisis management, in order to find an appropriate approach to deal with the severe incidents.[9]

RISK AND DECISION

When talking about risks, it is necessary to address the role of decisions in order to differentiate risks from dangers. According to Niklas Luhmann, risks must be seen as the consequence of a decision. For instance, the decision to use potential hazardous technologies embraces a concrete responsibility because it is an explicit choice.[10] In contrast to this, dangers refer to a damage that is caused by external sources without any human interference, for example, by a hurricane.[11] This differentiation is very helpful in order to analyse the role of decisions in the context of uncertainty.

The differentiation implies that any kind of assumption about potential future damages cannot be definite.[12] In fact, uncertainty enables a whole industry of risk monitoring and assessment to exist. But, even if the organisation runs its own risk management, it can only achieve a situation in which it deals with the consequences of uncertainty as best as possible. Absolute security about future damages cannot be realised.[13] As a result the term 'risk' 'reshapes the relation to what is knowable by introducing uncertainty and the unknowable at the heart of governing processes'.[14]

Nevertheless, the anthropological need for security does not correspond to this fact. One of the potential risk mitigation options is to insure the potential negative outcome of a risk.[15] However, risk insurance does not primarily aim to eliminate the risk itself, but to manage and control the symptoms. The actual risk remains and ensures future business for the insurance company. The private sector is thus focused on selling a 'subjective' feeling of security and not erasing the source of insecurity. Insurance against a potential negative outcome is of course limited by two aspects: Firstly, there is the inherent risk of insuring a valuable good without any purpose, for example, if the insured case never happens. Then the risk is to pay insurance premium without any use. Secondly, there are certain risks that cannot be insured.[16] One of them refers to events that can threaten the existence of the organisation itself. Such a risk as, for instance, the interruption of the value chain – especially in case of a multinational company – exceeds the insurance capabilities of even the biggest re-insurance companies.[17] In case of this very specific issue, the remaining risk mitigation is based on the development of the organisation's own crisis preparedness and results in the targeted resilient organisation. This relatively new mitigation option is related to a shift of responsibility, which also affects the realm of the state.

DELEGATION OF RESPONSIBILITY

Resilience understood as risk mitigation can be seen not only as process continuity, but also as protection of an organisation's assets. It aims to protect the crucial resources of the organisation, which mainly refers to the employees, added value, information assets and infrastructure. Of course, the core task is to ensure the continuity of business and allow the organisation to endure its capability to act and work. All measures of resilience like response plans, recovery strategies, financial reserves and risk capital are seen in the very context of business continuity.

Meanwhile, government agencies are supposed to care for the security of the population and its assets. This responsibility is the justification of the special position of the state and its exclusive right to the use of force. The state and its institutions are thus authorised to intervene in peoples' lives and to regulate cohabitation. This responsibility corresponds to the protection of the citizens and the warranty of their physical integrity. Preventive and reactive measures have been added over time and fill today's penal codes.[18] The same applies for the protection of individuals against the force of government. In accordance to the development of society, regulation has been extended in order to match the public need for centrally organised security. Thus, the state's regulation contains, besides the area of physical security, also economic, social or cultural protection.[19]

As such, we have seen how the modern social interventionist state in Europe has increased its involvement and regulation of individuals' lives. Not only the life and limb of the citizens, but also the protection against nearly any kind of harm, are included. Governments organise, for example, the construction of flood protection facilities against the threat of flooding, control the norms for dust particles in city areas or set the speed limits on highways. The increasing activities of states over the past centuries have reached an extensive level of care. This development has been possible only by sharing responsibility with semi-national institutions and private function owners, which have joined the organisational division of labour, for example, technical supervisory associations.

In terms of civil protection, the main direction of planning under the circumstances of the Cold War was based on a scenario of military confrontation between the two blocs of power. The provision of required goods for civilians was planned upon a military scenario. The circumstances changed after 1990 and the state's crisis plans became orientated towards a civil dimension and corresponding scenarios. The protection of so-called critical infrastructure emerged from a military understanding to a consideration of relevant institutions and facilities crucial to safeguard the status quo of modern societies.[20]

According to the trend of the time, privatisation of former public enterprises raised the question of continuous protection of this critical infrastructure. Such infrastructure involves privately owned companies that provide essentials goods and services needed to maintain society, for example the production of electricity, telecommunication or health care.[21] However, the state was seen as responsible for civil protection. Thus, it needed to implement standards and controls to ensure the inclusion of the recently privatised companies into the national plans for crisis preparedness. In this way, the private organisation became partners of the state's security concept, which also marked a significant transfer of responsibility. This delegation affected mainly companies which operated within the area of critical infrastructure. This includes organisations that provide special goods or possess relevant facilities that are needed for national well-being.

But the transformation from public to private ownership alone does not easily ensure compliance of the new partners to the protection standards of critical infrastructure. For instance, the compromise contains specific regulations for companies that are listed as providers of critical infrastructure. They must fulfil certain requirements for resilience, for example response plans to provide necessary service level and prevent a severe disruption of, for instance, electricity or telecommunication services. For example, financial institutions in Germany are also covered by legal regulation and required to implement resilience strategies, as defined in the supervision laws and international norms.[22]

The responsibility of the state to fulfil the public request for security is expressed in the form of regulatory bodies which control private enterprises. They compensate the transfer of accountability from the former national ownership into private hands. The major part of critical infrastructure and services is today provided by private enterprises in Germany, including the banking and finance area, telecommunications, parts of the health-care system, as well as electricity providers and transportation.[23] A difference remains between direct responsibilities in terms of accountability by immediate control of the state itself, or just the control of compliance by national regulatory bodies. If a company fails to prepare for a crisis properly, this could cause damage which probably affects the public, but the accountability remains with the management of the respective enterprise. The regulatory body in charge would be criticised for failing to effectively control the company, but it would not be the same in terms of responsibility according to the state's claim to protect its citizens and their assets.[24]

The depth of detail varies between different types of business and responsible regulatory body. Whereas some parts of the industry are regulated intensively by the supervisory authorities, other parts are more or less motivated by the civil contracts with customers and partners in order to recover their business rapidly. This delegation of responsibility is continued inside the organisation even further. The formally responsible board of management delegates this task to a senior manager, who asks one of the teams to prepare for a crisis and provide the regulatory bodies with the requested documentation. As a result, the state's responsibility is divided several times. It is this kind of delegation of responsibility that questions the national mission to protect its people by saving the status quo of civilisation (e.g., by the provision and maintenance of critical infrastructure) as well as to safeguard the economic assets of the taxpayer (e.g., compare the regulation in case of the system-relevant financial institutes). Private companies are hence challenged to comply with the relatively new area of responsibility, while a clear modus operandi between both public and private sector with regard to the safeguarding of people is not yet fully implemented. On the one hand, companies that provide critical infrastructure are obliged to prepare properly to potential risks but are on the other hand not fully integrated into a working concept of response activities. As a consequence, uncertainty about consequences of concrete risk mitigation measures is stated in the form of anxiety, which can cloud decision-making processes during crises.

This ambiguous nature is acutely expressed in the case of the pandemic scenarios, as demonstrated during the bird flu and the later swine flu crisis. National authorities, like in Germany, shifted parts of their responsibilities to private companies, which in this case included the responsibility to take precautionary actions for the welfare of the employees. The lessons learned of the first bird flu wave (pandemic influenza H5N1) in Germany were analysed and resulted in the 2009 German Influenza Pandemic Preparedness Plan, a document that addressed the tremendous consequences, which could be caused by a widely spread disease like this.[25] The private sector was involved in national action plans, as large organisations could contribute to the preventive and reactive strategies to contain the disease. This relatively new nature of the scenario, as well as a lack of standard approaches to deal with pandemics, put companies in a difficult position to comply with the requirement to prepare for this scenario as the precise guidelines were not defined at this time.[26] Under the circumstances of uncertainty, anxiety about possible consequences of decisions changed the perception of resilience with sustainable effects. The following case study will address this problem in detail. The role of anxiety will be analysed according to three categories of decisions that had to be made during the crisis: definition of pandemics, response actions and crisis communication. All three include the necessity of pending decisions in an environment of a high uncertainty, with a possibly negative outcome of a decision itself as the actual risk.

PANDEMICS

In contrast to past experiences of business disruptions, the emergence of a pandemic scenario revealed the anxious reaction patterns according to the risk of a loss of employees. Other risks as the loss of building were well known and handled almost with routine. Irrespective of the source of the risk – for example, a fire, terrorist attack or flooding – it was clear that the required measures in order to continue business relied on the quick recovery of business processes at a previously defined contingency location. The risk perception regarding viral infections in Western societies was already triggered by the SARS pandemic in Asia. The mutation of influenza types, which could be transferred from animals to humans, raised the public awareness for the upcoming threat and correlated with intensive media coverage. The same anxious reception of the phenomenon recurred when the first infection of humans with the swine flu was reported and the World Health Organization (WHO) proclaimed the highest level of escalation according to its pandemic model.[27]

The pandemic waves of the past decade are interesting with respect to the given question. How should companies respond to an unknown situation like the worldwide observed outbreak of an influenza? And how does the transfer of responsibility from the state to the private company affect the response? Enterprises were suddenly confronted with a risk, which they had seen to be within the sole responsibility of state authorities, for example, the national health departments. Hence, pandemics reveal a crucial problem for companies' resilience, because the risk lies with the decision that has to be made. It is not a danger that strikes down from the sky or suddenly occurs without any human interference or causal relation. The risk for the company is not related with the decisions that might have caused or accelerated the diseases' outbreak. The specific risk of pandemics is based on decisions that have to be made in order to handle the crisis and react to its development. The necessary decisions are categorised in the following three areas: First, the definition of pandemics including the role of experts, which mainly triggered a loss of confidence in existing plans and increased anxiety in the decision-making process. Second, the area of response actions, such as taking hygienic measures, which represent the ambiguous nature of unknown consequences of response strategy options. Thirdly, the area of crisis communication, which involved the role of reputation and external perception.[28]

Definition of Pandemics – The Pandemic Escalation Model

The first area concerns the mismatch between the pandemic escalation model of the WHO and the difficulty to implement the corresponding actions in reality. Many strategies to handle a pandemic scenario and the assumed threats were based on the escalation model of the WHO. Strategies that included the provision of medicines relied on objective criteria to plan the appropriate initiation of such measures. This incorporated medicines which would be used after the exposure to the flu, as soon as the highest escalation level was reached. Stockpiles of medicines, for example 'Tamiflu', were gathered around the globe. Until 2007, the number of treatment units in the USA was estimated at around 81 million pieces; in Germany there were 16 million units stored by the public and private sectors.[29]

However, crisis plans were difficult to use as the swine flu pandemic showed. The initiation of active measures was bound to the fulfilment of the criteria of the WHO escalation model. The plans premised the proclamation of the highest escalation level as necessary and appropriate for the prearranged measures. The development of the situation caused the decision makers in many companies and public authorities to stray off course and to refrain from planned actions. The plans were based on the six levels of the WHO escalation model, which can be differentiated into three stages. The first one contains the pre-pandemic phase, consisting of two levels, and describes the development of a flu, like seasonal infections. The second stage is the warning phase and includes the levels 3 to 5, which is seen as an escalation phase before the actual outbreak on a global scale. In this stage, the preparation for active measures would be initiated in order to have options at hand as soon as the last level would be proclaimed by the WHO. The third stage, containing the sixth level, describes the actual pandemic.[30]

For the proclamation of this final stage of the pandemic, the required threshold is considered to allow the provision of medicines in order to prevent the spreading of a disease. This stage is defined by an increasing and continuous transmission of the virus across the population in at least two regions, as defined by the WHO, and it would therefore be necessary to start immediate action in order to anticipate further escalation of the situation.[31] The escalation model is based on constant development and gradually increasing intensity. The actual spread of the disease across more than one continent in less than one month formally matched the requirements of the criteria catalogue, but did not materially qualify as an outbreak of a pandemic as imagined by the WHO. The pending decision in this moment was to find an answer to the urgent question: Should one stick to the original plan and initiate the provision of medicaments within the organisation, or leave the pre-defined path and make a decision ad hoc?

In other words, the risk was based on the decision to either follow the steps of the crisis plan, even though the indicators for this step were not confirmed, or to improvise. Both options implied significant advantages as well as disadvantages. If the window of opportunity for the provision of medicines would be missed, the chance to prevent the loss of employees through an infection could be missed. The only way to benefit from the stored medicines would be ensured if they are used in time, which means immediately after an infection (as in the case of the post-exposure prophylaxis), or before the exposure to the virus in case of vaccination.[32]

However, if the respective medicines would be issued at an early stage, the post-exposure prophylaxis could be useless. To provide and recommend these medicines to employees and their families could cause unknown side effects, which could provoke an unavailability of employees or result in massive lawsuits against the company.[33] At the time of the decision that had to be made, management of companies were forced to decide between two options with uncertain consequences. For both options, it was necessary to seek advice from experts. This implied internal and external consultations in order to achieve a more or less clear picture of the situation and possible outcomes. However, internal medical experts of the organisations are mostly specialised in occupational medicine and thus offer little expertise in the area of virology or immunology.

Therefore, external expertise was required. Especially pharmaceutical corporations offered their knowledge and help in this situation; however, it can be supposed that this was not offered solely by altruistic motivation, but also to make profitable sales market accessible. The quantity of sales regarding flu medicines was in fact increasing during the pandemic phases. With the outbreak of the bird flu in Asia in 2003 and the swine flu in 2009, the profit of the vaccination and post-exposure medicaments raised tremendously.[34] This fact altered the view of pharmaceutical experts, also because public opinion accused the authorities that the relationships and contacts to the pharmaceutical industry were not publicised properly.[35] As a result, the difficulty during the pandemic crises was based on a lack of experience with such a scenario and the mismatch of the pre-crisis plans, based on the WHO model. Thus, the risk to decide resulted in a limitation of the crisis management teams' capacity to act due to anxiety.

Response Actions – Appropriateness of Hygienic Measures

The second problem was to determine the right moment to achieve a preventive limitation of an outbreak by initiating hygienic measures within the organisation. A lesson learned from the bird flu pandemic was that a significant part of the population showed insufficient understanding and awareness of hygiene.[36] Thus, preparation included preventive measures as a crucial step to anticipate the spreading of disease and intended to raise staff awareness of this issue. As mentioned, the trigger for hygienic measures was linked to a certain level of the WHO escalation model and proved to be a hard decision to make.

The original intention was to initiate hygienic measures at an early stage of the pandemic escalation, whereas the provision of medicines would be scheduled to a later stage of the crisis according to the WHO model. This category would contain an increased frequency of professional cleaning and disinfection of office spaces and provide germicides at the sanitary installations and populated areas, such as the canteen or main entrances.[37] Thus, special information and awareness campaigns should also be rolled out, including posters, articles and addresses by the superiors in order to motivate staff to adapt their behaviour.

A further step would be the provision of face masks.[38] This would in fact be a critical issue, because masks are interpreted differently across cultures. Whereas it is more or less common to use a mask in public life in cities like Hong Kong or Tokyo, it is rarely seen in Düsseldorf or Milan. Where the masks are rare, they are likely to be seen as a threat of infection and their usage in corporate environment would have an effect on people's perception of the crisis. In other words, to recommend certain hygienic measures would therefore not only transport the message of prevention but could also induce certain fears in the population or eventually even increase them.[39] This means that the point of time for any intensification of the hygienic measures would be crucial and could also prove to be a difficult decision on the basis of uncertainty.

The risk was again expressed in form of the decision to either follow the original plan or to improvise. If the hygienic measures would be initiated too early, the awareness could be lost over time or, even worse, could not have been suitably anchored. Also, attention to appropriate hygienic behaviour was considered to decline over time. On the other hand, if the measures would be implemented too late, the whole concept of prevention would be lost. Under these uncertain circumstances, the risk of the decision disabled a proper crisis handling, because the lack of information about the actual development of the crisis as well as the lack of expertise slowed down every kind of activity. In both cases, either too early or too late, the prevention of the staff from developing an infection would affect the desired outcome.

Crisis Communication

Besides the threat of an infection of staff causing an interruption to business, the reputational risk also had to be considered. Any decision or activity would have an effect on the organisation's reputation and therefore an impact on the future of the company. The planning of internal and external crisis communication must be aware of the critical condition of the published information and keep the perspective of the audience and target groups in mind. The customers, partners, providers, regulatory bodies or the own employees are relevant stakeholders and possible recipients of any form of communication. In general, communication of a risk or a crisis intends to keep the trust of all possibly affected groups and to ensure the support for further actions.[40]

Both kinds of communication differ by the nature of their subjects. Risk communication includes the articulation of a prior assessment of a risk and is considered to convince a group of the correctness of the conclusion. Risk communication is the linkage between both groups, the one which has evaluated the risk and the other that needs to be informed about it. This act of translation can be used to address new categories of risks that might be relevant for society and public discourse. This can be an emerging risk, as international terrorism[41] or already known, continuously existing risks, which need to be remembered (e.g., the risk of driving under the influence of alcohol).

The nature of risk communication is described as a reciprocal one, which 'is typically defined as an interactive process that involves the exchange of information between parties about a sensitive issue'.[42] This exchange is an important element of bargaining about a risk subject. By discussing the nature of the risk as well as the available control and mitigation options, society can agree on a practical handling of the issue. This can support an overall acceptance of the risk and the agreed measures, which also allows the affected groups to anticipate the risk according to their own perception. Risk communication regarding HIV/AIDS is seen as the decisive reason for the declining numbers of new infections in Western Europe. In fact it is the lowest infection rate worldwide.[43] In other words, risk communication fulfils a preventive task by explaining the issue and anticipating the possible damage.[44]

Crisis communication in contrast focuses on concrete events and triggers. It considers reactive measures to contain the consequences of an occurring or already existing crisis. According to its nature, it is designed to limit the damage and intends to include all affected or interested groups in order to maintain the confidence and trust in the actions taken.[45] Today's society emphasises the capability to react to a crisis with a fast response in order to keep the stakeholders' confidence, which presumes media competence and communication skills.

What does this mean in the context of pandemics? Risk communication can be seen as an objective, which was mainly seen as the responsibility of the authorities. Crisis communication, in contrast, was an inevitable task of any company affected by the crisis and linked to important decisions. Every public statement would be treated as critical and its content, timing and wording needed to be selected carefully. The pressure for public crisis communication increased as the media reported intensively about the current status of the new infections across the globe and the mortality rate. The lack of relativisation and reflection was tangible. In such a tense situation, the crisis communication to the internal and external stakeholders grew in importance.[46]

However, the timing for any communication is key in order to reduce the risk of reputational damage by missing the right point of time as well as the appropriate way of communication. This inherent risk to crisis communication was caused by the lack of expertise. The expertise in the technical handling of communication in the corporate organisation can be assumed, given the high level of professionalism in corporate communication departments. Even though national authorities transferred a part of their responsibility for crisis preparedness to the private sector, it was somehow unclear what would be the appropriate share of corporate communication. Would it be the responsibility of the state and its institutions to initiate and run the communication on this issue of national health, or should companies act proactively in order to tranquilise customers, investors and staff?

The pending decision about the right way of communication as well as the uncertainty of the situation built up a risk in itself. As a conclusion, there are two important experiences for companies' crisis preparedness. One is the detachment of crisis planning on external expertise by investing in in-house risk assessments and defining thresholds for the activation of response plans and procedures as, for example, when to start preventive or reactive measures. The second refers to the differently perceived logics and paces of the crisis in the media, public awareness and national as well as private responses. In addition, the lack of reliable sources of information is significant for the understanding of anxiety. For example, estimations previous to the pandemic waves expected tremendous fatalities. The WHO calculated the global number of deaths between 2 and 7.4 million caused by the H1N1, the swine flu epidemic. Luckily only 18,366 cases could be confirmed in total and were related directly to the bird flu.[47] This explains the high degree of uncertainty due to missing expertise that could support the decision-making process and an active crisis management. In the end, the global scale of the pandemic stayed away, but the risk awareness regarding this topic was established and organisations learned about the possible damage to their own business.

Both events, the bird flu and the swine flu, were finally an essential step towards further development of the resilient organisation. It was concluded that dependency on response planning of specific scenarios proved to be hindering. Preparation should be more orientated towards a resource-based approach, focusing on the loss of resources as, for example, staff rather than over detailed scenarios. Based on this, the operational risk methodology advanced and changed the way to evaluate risks. The classification of risks into the loss of essential resources as staff, facilities, infrastructure, and service providers established the roadmap towards a resilient organisation.

CONCLUSION

By the logic of anxiety, the late modern society reflects the emergence of risks on a global scale and the de-bounding of the local space. At the same time, the state started to share its responsibility for the protection of the population with the private sector, which operates privatised critical infrastructure. The dependency of society on the continuous availability of this infrastructure demands an effective crisis planning, but also reveals an area of conflict between both involved partners. As a consequence, a relatively new form of risk mitigation has been established within companies, which focuses on risks regarding the value chain. This form seeks to build a resilient organisation, which is able to continue its business operations and therefore ensuring the performance of the value chain, even in case of severe disasters. It refers to a possible non-availability of critical resources due to both known and unknown threats and intents to protect the organisation by elaborating crisis preparedness on a global level.

Past events as the pandemics showed the necessity of resilience, but also the challenges to effectively respond to such a scenario under the circumstances of uncertainty. The differentiation between risk and danger has to be considered, when thinking about the role of decisions. Risks are to be seen as the result of someone's decision, either to act in a certain way or to neglect any activity. Especially under the circumstances of uncertainty, the anxiety of a 'bad' choice influences the decision-making process tremendously. The dependence on external expertise on a specific risk topic can influence the perception of the situation. In this case, the reaction of companies to the pandemics showed how sensitive their existing crisis response measures were to external influence and how anxiety paralysed appropriate handling. Uncertainty was also increased due to the shared responsibility for public health between public and private actors. As a result, the effects of uncertainty required new forms of risk mitigation and the realisation of a resilient organisation.

NOTES

1. This contribution addresses, on the one hand, the role of risk management in companies with the focus on mitigation of risks by the means of contingency plans and recovery measures. In the field of pandemic crisis preparedness, only little empirical work has been done with regard to the response plans of companies for this particular scenario as well as their specific perspective on risk mitigation. On the other hand, the organisational structure and understanding were altered by the risk perception and mitigation measures. One example is the shared responsibility for the well-being of the employees between public and private area. Both together trigger

interesting questions regarding the existing partnership and the role of decision making in companies under the circumstances of uncertainty.

2. There are several regulators on federal level responsible in Germany for certain industry branches. The regulation for the financial industry are of most interest, because they define concrete measures of crisis preparedness. These legal requirements will be detailed in the following.

3. The case study bases on empirical data that was collected in the form of interviews with experts and practitioners in corporate crisis management in Germany between 2012 and 2015 by the author of this contribution.

4. Lupton, Deborah, 'Sociology and Risk'. In: *Beyond the Risk Society: Critical Reflections on Risk and Human Security*, ed. Gabe Mythen and S. Walklate (Maidenhead: Open University Press, 2006), 12.

5. Ewald, Francois, 'Die Versicherungs-Gesellschaft'. In: *Politik in der Risikogesellschaft. Essays und Analysen*, ed. Ulrich Beck (Frankfurt am Main, 1991), 289

6. Pike, Andy, Stuart Dawley and John Tomaney, 'Resilience, Adaption and Adaptability'. *Cambridge Journal of Regions, Economy and Society*, 3 (2010), 60.

7. Brunsdon, Dave and Erica Dalziell, 'Making Organisations Resilient: Understanding the Reality of the Challenge.' Resilient Infrastructure Conference, Rotorua, 8–9 August 2005, 28.

8. Rose, Adam, 'Defining and Measuring Economic Resilience to Disasters.' *Disaster Prevention and Management*, 14(4) (2004), 308.

9. Günther, Lars, Georg Ruhrmann and Jutta Milde, Pandemie. Wahrnehmung der gesundheitlichen Risiken durch die Bevölkerung und Konsequenzen für die Risiko- und Krisenkommunikation. *Berlin: Forschungsforum Öffentliche Sicherheit Schriftenreihe Sicherheit* Nr. 7 (2011), 31.

10. Luhmann, Niklas, *Soziologie des Risikos* (Berlin: de Gruyter, 1991), 30.

11. One could argue that the damage caused by a natural catastrophe might be related to human activities, as for example, air pollution or fracking. The differentiation here should be seen in the difference of the ones that make a decision and those who suffer from the potential consequences.

12. Luhmann, *Soziologie des Risikos*, 31.

13. Luhmann, *Soziologie des Risikos*, 197.

14. Aradau, Claudia and van Munster, Rens, 'Governing Terrorism through Risk: Taking Precautions, (Un)knowing the Future'. *European Journal of International Relations*, 13(1) (2007), 150.

15. Jarvis, Darryl, 'Theorising Risk and Uncertainty in International Relations: The Contributions of Frank Knight'. *International Relations*, 25(3) (2011), 300.

16. Luhmann, Niklas, *Organisation und Entscheidung* (Wiesbaden: VS Verlag, 2000), 274.

17. There are insurance policies that cover the disruption of business or the incidents that can trigger interruptions as for example cyber insurance or supply chain insurance. Nonetheless, reinsurance companies such as Swiss Re or Munich Re as well as the direct insurance branch require the implementation of resilience programs in order to reduce the probability of a claim request. The insurance of a whole company with the size of a Fortune 500 or DAX30 listed enterprise can't be done, given the average revenue profit of around 50 billion EUR per year. (See Umsaetze

der DAX-Konzerne, Statista, accessed 30 September 2016, https://de.statista.com/statistik/daten/studie/75495/umfrage/umsaetze-der-dax-konzerne/.)

18. Public agencies regulate issues based on laws and ensure their compliance by enforcing penalties. This aims to establish a regulated area within which the individuals can trust on the security of public services or traded goods such as medicaments, banking transactions or data privacy.

19. The state and its institutions take care of a diverse spectrum of fields in the form of regulation. Laws and rules for the setup of the economy or laws for the preservation of cultural heritage represent the state's intention to comply with its responsibility for protection. However if the state can't fulfil the people's expectations, maybe due to limited resources or because there is no political will to intervene, confidence in and support towards the state decrease dramatically; see Krahmann, Elke, 'Risk Markets: The Commodification of Security and the Risk Society'. Paper presented at 6th Pan-European International Relations Conference, Turin, 12–15 September 2007, 9.

20. Church, Richard L., Maria P. Scaparra and Richard S. Middleton, 'Identifying Critical Infrastructure: The Median and Covering Facility Interdiction Problems'. *Annals of the Association of American Geographers*, 94 (2004), 491.

21. LaPorte, Todd, 'Critical Infrastructure in the Face of a Predatory Future: Preparing for Untoward Surprise'. *Journal of Contingencies and Crisis Management*, 15(1) (2007), 60.

22. Supervision laws for the banking or insurance industry are defined, for example, by Solvency II (Directive 2009/138/EC of the European Parliament and the Council) or by the German Insurance Supervision Act (VAG). International standards for the continuity of critical processes and services are defined by industry norms, such as ISO 22301 for business continuity management or ISO 22316 for security and resilience.

23. Fischer, Wolfgang, *Analyse und Simulation strategischer Angriffe auf die kritische Infrastruktur Internet*. Analysis and Simulation of strategic attacks on critical Internet infrastructure. (Jülich: Forschungszentrum Jülich, 2007), 34.

24. Momani, Naill, 'Business Continuity Planning: Are We Prepared for Future Disasters'. *American Journal of Economics and Business Administration*, 2(3) (2010), 274.

25. Defined in the 2009 updated version by the German institute for infectious disease control in Berlin (Robert Koch Institut, 'German Influenza Pandemic Preparedness Plan', 2009).

26. Ferguson, Neil et al., 'Strategies for Mitigating an Influenza Pandemic'. *Nature*, 422 (2006), 448.

27. Günther et al., Wahrnehmung, 31.

28. The following description of actions and measures is based on interviews with experts and practitioners in corporate crisis management in Germany between 2012 and 2015 by the author of this contribution.

29. Singer, Andrew C., 'Potential Risks Associated with the Proposed Widespread Use of Tamiflu'. *Environmental Health Perspectives*, 115(1) (2007), 102.

30. Robert Koch Institut, 'Wissenschaftliche Zusammenhänge der Pandemieplanung in Deutschland'. In: *Nationaler Pandemieplan Teil III*, ed. Robert Koch Institut (Berlin, 2007), 32f.

31. Günther et al., Wahrnehmung, 16.
32. Ferguson et al., 'Strategies for Mitigating', 448.
33. The acceptance for vaccination in European societies can be seen as elevated. However, the pandemics showed a decreasing acceptance of the flu vaccination, which was based on the low numbers of newly infected and a bad tolerance of patients as well as the public debate about the sense of the flu vaccination in general (Günther et al., Wahrnehmung, 28).
34. Handelsblatt, Tamiflu-Kritik und starker Franken setzen Roche unter Druck. Handelsblatt, 15 April 2014 accessed 15 December 2015. http://www.handelsblatt.com/unternehmen/industrie/pharmakonzern-tamiflu-kritik-und-starker-franken-setzen-roche-unter-druck/9764560.html.
35. Günther et al., Wahrnehmung, 31.
36. Ibid., 28.
37. Robert Koch Institut Wissenschaftliche Zusammenhänge, 89.
38. Facial masks were considered, for example, in the German national pandemic plan of 2007 just as additional measures to prevent an infection. However, the plan stated the eventuality of an opposed effect, if people might feel well protected by wearing a facial mask and could neglect other standard hygienic measures (Robert Koch Institut, Wissenschaftliche Zusammenhänge, 91).
39. Günther et al., Wahrnehmung, 19.
40. Frewer, Lynn, 'The Public and Effective Risk Communication'. *Toxicology Letters*, 149 (2004), 393.
41. Aradau, Claudia et al., 'Security, Technologies of Risk, and the Political: Guest Editors' Introduction'. *Security Dialogue*, 39(147) (2008), 33.
42. Meredith, Lisa et al., 'Analysis of Risk Communication Strategies and Approaches with At- Risk Populations to Enhance Emergency Preparedness, Response, and Recovery'. RAND Health working paper series (2008), 4.
43. Elbe, Stefan, 'HIV/AIDS: The International Security Dimensions'. In: *New Threats and New Actors in International Security*, ed. Elke Krahmann (New York, 2005), 113.
44. Günther et al., Wahrnehmung, 19.
45. Frewer, 'The Public and Effective Risk', 395.
46. Günther et al., Wahrnehmung, 42f.
47. Günther et al., Wahrnehmung, 31.

BIBLIOGRAPHY

Aradau, Claudia and Rens van Munster. 'Governing Terrorism through Risk: Taking Precautions, (Un)knowing the Future.' *European Journal of International Relations*, 13(1) (2007): 89–115.
Aradau, Claudia et al. 'Security, Technologies of Risk, and the Political: Guest Editors' Introduction.' *Security Dialogue*, 39(147) (2008): 147–154.
Brunsdon, Dave and Erica Dalziell. 'Making Organisations Resilient: Understanding the Reality of the Challenge.' Resilient Infrastructure Conference, Rotorua, – August 2005, 27–34.

Church, Richard L., Maria P. Scaparra, and Richard S. Middleton. 'Identifying Critical Infrastructure: The Median and Covering Facility Interdiction Problems.' *Annals of the Association of American Geographers*, 94 (2004): 491–502.

Elbe, Stefan. 'HIV/AIDS: The International Security Dimensions.' In: *New Threats and New Actors in International Security*, ed. Elke Krahmann (New York: Palgrave 2005): 111–130.

Ewald, Francois. 'Die Versicherungs-Gesellschaft.' In: *Politik in der Risikogesellschaft. Essays und Analysen*, ed. Ulrich Beck (Frankfurt am Main Suhrkamp Verlag: 1991): 288–302.

Ferguson, Neil et al. 'Strategies for Mitigating an Influenza Pandemic.' *Nature*, 422 (2006): 448–452.

Fischer, Wolfgang. *Analyse und Simulation strategischer Angriffe auf die kritische Infrastruktur Internet*. Analysis and Simulation of strategic attacks on critical Internet infrastructure. (Jülich: Forschungszentrum Jülich, 2007).

Frewer, Lynn. 'The Public and Effective Risk Communication.' *Toxicology Letters*, 149 (2004): 391–397.

Günther, Lars, Georg Ruhrmann, and Jutta Milde. *Pandemie. Wahrnehmung der gesundheitlichen Risiken durch die Bevölkerung und Konsequenzen für die Risiko- und Krisenkommunikation* Pandemics. Awareness of health risks for the population and the consequences for risk and crisis communication. (Berlin: Forschungsforum Öffentliche Sicherheit Schriftenreihe Sicherheit Nr. 7, 2011).

Handelsblatt. Tamiflu-Kritik und starker Franken setzen Roche unter Druck. Handelsblatt, 15 April 2014, accessed 15 December 2015. http://www.handelsblatt.com/unter nehmen/industrie/pharmakonzern-tamiflu-kritik-und-starker-franken-setzen-roche-unter-druck/9764560.html.

Jarvis, Darryl. 'Theorising Risk and Uncertainty in International Relations: The Contributions of Frank Knight.' *International Relations*, 25(3) (2011): 296–312.

Krahmann, Elke. 'Risk Markets: The Commodification of Security and the Risk Society.' Paper presented at 6th Pan-European International Relations Conference, Turin, 12–15 September 2007.

LaPorte, Todd. 'Critical Infrastructure in the Face of a Predatory Future: Preparing for Untoward Surprise.' *Journal of Contingencies and Crisis Management*, 15(1) (2007): 60–64.

Luhmann, Niklas. *Soziologie des Risikos* (Berlin: de Gruyter, 1991).

Luhmann, Niklas. *Organisation und Entscheidung* (Wiesbaden: VS Verlag, 2000).

Lupton, Deborah. 'Sociology and Risk.' In: *Beyond the Risk Society: Critical Reflections on Risk and Human Security*, eds. Gabe Mythen and S. Walklate (Maidenhead: Open University Press, 2006): 11–24.

Meredith, Lisa et al. 'Analysis of Risk Communication Strategies and Approaches with At- Risk Populations to Enhance Emergency Preparedness, Response, and Recovery.' RAND Health working paper series (2008).

Momani, Naill. 'Business Continuity Planning: Are We Prepared for Future Disasters.' *American Journal of Economics and Business Administration*, 2(3) (2010): 272–279.

Pike, Andy, Stuart Dawley and John Tomaney. 'Resilience, adaption and adaptability'. *Cambridge Journal of Regions, Economy and Society*, 3 (2010): 59–70.

Robert Koch Institut. 'Wissenschaftliche Zusammenhänge der Pandemieplanung in Deutschland.' In: *Nationaler Pandemieplan Teil III, ed.* Robert Koch Institut (Berlin 2007).

Robert Koch Institut. German Influenza Pandemic Preparedness Plan. Accessed 30 September 2016. https://www.rki.de/DE/Content/InfAZ/I/Influenza/Pandemieplanung/Downloads/pandemic_preparedness_plan_scientific_part_summary.pdf?__blob=publicationFile.

Rose, Adam. 'Defining and Measuring Economic Resilience to Disasters.' *Disaster Prevention and Management*, 14(4) (2004): 307–314.

Singer, Andrew C. 'Potential Risks Associated with the Proposed Widespread Use of Tamiflu.' *Environmental Health Perspectives*, 115(1) (2007): 102–106.

Statista. Umsaetze der DAX-Konzerne. Accessed 30 September 2016. https://de.statista.com/statistik/daten/studie/75495/umfrage/umsaetze-der-dax-konzerne/.

Part III

RESISTANCE: RECLAIMING

Chapter 7

The Politics of Anxiety and the Rise of Far-Right Parties in Europe

Norma Rossi[1]

Far-right parties seem to be knocking at the doors of every national parliament in Western Europe, urging reflection on the reasons for their rise and their success. The Front National in France, the Independence Party in the UK and the Alternative Fur Deutschland Party in Germany are just three examples of a more general advance of these parties across Europe. A growing literature has referred to this phenomenon as a form of 'radical revolt', an 'insurgency'[2] that challenges the established mainstream parties.

The dominant explanation of this phenomenon is that in times of anxiety, uncertainty leads to the growth of right-wing extremism. This understanding implies that extremism 'fills the voids' left empty by mainstream parties who are perceived as unable to offer effective responses to this anxiety. This chapter calls this diffused understanding into question by enquiring into the interplay between the 'far' right and (neo)liberal politics. I argue that the terms of the dominant debate in which this rise has been understood are misleading, because they work to conceal the link between mainstream (neo)liberal politics and those of the far right. Instead, by focusing on the political meaning of anxiety, I shall show that when anxiety becomes the driver of European politics, far-right parties enter into in a relation of mutual constitution with neoliberal politics rather than a zero-sum opposition to them.

By understanding anxiety as a political practice which enables a specific logic of security, it is possible to unravel the ways in which mainstream neoliberal politics are intimately linked to the rise of far-right movements and how they often profit from them. While they reject far-right solutions they often co-define the same sources of anxiety. In this way, neoliberalism can claim to act as a 'responsible' and 'rational' mediator between the need to tackle this anxiety and the authoritarian solutions which the far-right parties propose. Making anxiety the driver of security decisions has the effect of reproducing mainstream (neo)liberal parties as the proponents of an a-political solution. This different understanding of the rise of far-right movements is of great importance in enabling us to re-think the ways in which the politics of anxiety are currently at play in many European countries.

This chapter proceeds, first, by exploring further the assumptions at work and the implications of understanding the relationship between far-right and mainstream parties as an insurgency. It then elaborates on how this understanding can be revised by looking at the ways in which anxiety shapes a specific logic of security within which a productive dynamic between mainstream and far-right parties can develop. Finally, the chapter draws upon the case of Italy to illustrate this alternative understanding.

FILLING THE VOIDS?

European politics has been experiencing, at least in the last decade, a consistent rise of far-right extremisms which challenge mainstream (neo)liberal parties, in what has been defined as an 'insurgency' and 'an earthquake'.[3] These parties, it is generally claimed, spring up and flourish by exploiting the fear and anxiety of people disillusioned by the incapacity of the 'systemic' parties to respond to their insecurities, specifically in relation to economic and social phenomena such as the economic crisis, criminality and immigration. On the one hand, this understanding is sustained by the leaders of these movements, who 'present themselves as political outsiders, and claim that established parties do not listen to ordinary citizens [*which explains why*] these parties form an attractive alternative for dissatisfied citizens'[4] On the other hand, the mainstream parties also sustain this understanding. If we take the case of the UK, immigration, according to former prime minister David Cameron, is one of the issues which 'created the space for extremist parties to flourish, as they could tell people that mainstream politicians weren't listening to their concerns or doing anything about them'.[5] This was confirmed by what George Osborne told the BBC in the aftermath of the last European elections: 'the Conservatives *had to listen* to the "anger and anxiety" of those who voted for UKIP in Thursday's local and European elections'.[6] In this perspective, the rise of far-right parties is a symptom of times of anxiety against which mainstream parties must react. In this way, the understanding of the far right as an 'insurgency' functions to produce a specific role for the mainstream neoliberal parties: far-right parties are extreme and ideological in their solutions, whereas the established mainstream neoliberal political parties claim that certain measures are necessary not for ideological reasons, but in response to objective concerns dictated by the state of anxiety of the electorate.

However, does this perspective bear closer scrutiny? First, we need to think about the key assumption which sustains it. This argument rests on a specific assumption about a relationship of zero-sum opposition between liberalism and any form of authoritarian ideology, which is labelled as 'extremism from the right or from the left'. The recent statement in David Cameron's extremism speech in which he opposes 'basic liberal values' to Islamist ideology, seen as analogous to 'many ideologies that have existed before – whether fascist or communist',[7] is a case in point. Specifically, defining fascism as 'the other' has long been and remains central to the constitution of liberal identity; this is true in the academic discourse of international relations[8] as well as the diffused political language in which 'fascism' works as a signifier of the zero-sum enemy of liberalism, as, for example, when the UK minister of defence, Michael Fallon, defined ISIS as 'fascist enemy'.[9] Despite the fact that far-right parties have tried to detach their image from that of their predecessors, this ideal of the liberal battle against any form of fascism is reflected in the narrative of the 'insurgency', which re-proposes the same logic of the zero-sum game between mainstream (neo)liberalism and far-right extremism.

The idea of a far-right insurgency conceals the long-term tension and relation between mainstream (neo)liberalism and what has been defined as its opposite, on the right and on the left – extremism. However, this understanding works to erase the more complex interplay between (neo)liberalism and the far right by reproducing the narrative of their eternal opposition. It also reproduces the claim that liberalism occupies the centre of the political spectrum, a position which often makes appeals to democratic 'values' and 'ways of life' but rejects an ideological stance, which instead is made to appear the monopoly of the authoritarian extremist. A central effect of this understanding is that it identifies and emphasises similarities between 'extremes', such as the claim that the far left and the far right share a common Euroscepticism.[10] This means that understanding the rise of the far right as an insurgency promotes a comparative analysis of the rise of different extremist parties across Europe, thereby always eluding an analysis of the 'moderate middle' mainstream parties.[11] In this way, both epistemological and ontological priorities are given to liberalism instead of questioning how (neo)liberalism defines and is defined by the political locations that are presupposed by this assumption.

In order to challenge this assumption, this chapter argues that 'anxiety' is not a collective and individual psychological condition produced by the unfortunate contingencies of uncertain times; instead, anxiety is understood as a political practice which informs a distinctive logic of security, within which this dynamic between mainstream neoliberalism and the far right can unfold. The next section specifically illustrates this understanding of anxiety.

ANXIOUS SECURITY

As has been widely observed, public discourse on contemporary politics makes constant appeals to security issues, expanding the logic of risk and threat to cover ever broader realms.[12] This makes the analysis of the role of emotions like fear and anxiety in politics increasingly important. In this sense, the study of anxiety 'can stand as a genuine contribution to questions that are being posed in the culture at large'.[13] Specifically, anxiety pertains to questions of security, since it is through anxiety that 'we learn threatening information, we trust certain expert or relevant figures at the expense of others, and we hold political attitudes that are framed as protective.'[14] This means that if we do not take security as a 'given object or value' but consider the security-ness of an issue to be the result of a political and social construction,[15] we can ask how anxiety legitimises specific claims about security threats and specific solutions to those threats. In other words, it is possible to investigate how anxiety entails a distinctive logic of security, allowing and legitimising specific ways 'through which the security-ness of situations is created'.[16] Thus we can say that anxiety 'makes' security in a specific way, which means that anxiety is not only a psychological concept with which to study the emotions of individuals but also a political and social practice embodying and enabling a specific logic of security.

This section loosely borrows from Jacques Lacan's concept of anxiety in order to expand on how anxiety works as a political practice which informs a distinctive security logic. The relevance of Lacan's concept of anxiety for the study of security is given by the central importance in his work of the way time is tied to the meaning-making process of security. The distinctive way anxiety makes security is based on the idea that anxiety operates within 'discontinuity' in time[17] thereby breaking with the linearity of time and instead constructing the present as an interweaving of past and future. The etymology of the word *anxiety* can be traced back to the Latin *angere*[18] which means *tighten*, and indicates something that gives a sense of insecurity, unsettlement and anguish (*angoisse*), but that also *keep or hold fast*. Anxiety attacks therefore violently irrupt but are also destined to persist beneath the surface, once the crisis has passed, in the form of traumatic memories as well as a 'compulsion to repeat'.[19] Thus anxiety is related to the past 'and Freud himself points out . . . the subject who wakes up in the middle of the night, troubled by a nightmare that brings him back to a traumatic situation'.[20] However, anxiety is also related to the future, since it involves a constant 'search' for its next triggers, because 'anxiety constantly expects its next trigger, constantly searches for the next object upon which to fix its attention'.[21] In other words, anxiety is articulated through a triple temporality, in which the present is the result of an interweaving of past and future. With anxiety, it is the diachronic interweaving of memory and anticipation, past and future, that constitutes the present, rather than it existing independently as the central part of a linear temporal sequence stretching from past to future. As Bowie has explained, presence in anxiety 'comes into being at the point of intersection . . . between what-is-no-longer-the-case and what-is-not-yet-the-case'.[22] To be sure, anxiety works on three main temporal moments, as the etymology itself reveals: the presence of the threat, the repetition of the threat and the constant possibility of the return of the threat. This means that if we consider the constructed-ness of security, past and future become what grounds presence in anxiety, and this has important implications for how anxiety shapes security.

First, the security logic of anxiety can be distinguished from a logic driven by fear, for after the moment of its irruption, anxiety is destined to remain below the surface once the crisis has passed, both in the form of past traumatic memory and possible future return. As a consequence, this logic of security re-reads the security crisis as always in the process of re-emerging and in need of constant control.

Second, this has strong implications for the object of anxiety, since the construction of the threat which triggers anxiety in the present becomes characterised by 'discontinuity' in time; as noted earlier, in anxiety presence is constructed through an interweaving of past and future, which works to produce a constant sense of the potential possibility of imminent and threatening objects.[23] Indeed, following Harari, 'anxiety is distinguished from fear in having no object, and being rather in relation to the nothing.'[24] Anthropologist Kathleen Stewart notes something similar when she writes, 'Anxiety ranges without object. But so too does the sense of potential.'[25] This means that a logic of security which is informed by anxiety does not have a fixed object, and since the logic of anxiety generates an always-impending sense of potentiality; this implies that security can potentially be extended to any object.

To conclude, a security logic of anxiety is based upon a distinctive temporal articulation which relies on the past and the future to construct the present, and it has a distinctive relation to its object(lessness), whose absence potentially multiplies the possible triggers of anxiety; this makes security discourses potentially very resilient, and resisting them very difficult, as we shall examine in more depth in the empirical analysis.

This section explored how anxiety is produced and productive of a specific logic informing the construction of security. The next section shows how this security logic, legitimised and developed through the politics of anxiety, fuels a synergy between mainstream parties and the far right.

ITALY AND THE CRISIS OF ANXIETY

A growing literature on security practices post-9/11 has put the authoritarian tendencies inherent in (neo)liberalism under scrutiny. Specifically, the literature studying the use of exceptional and extra-legal means by liberal regimes has picked up on the ambiguous nature of liberalism as well as on the growing emergence of authoritarian tendencies within it. This is increasingly manifested through a blurring of the line between norm and exception in neoliberal security policies, which exposes these illiberal temptations as a constitutive part of liberalism. The empirical analysis which follows corroborates this literature by showing how the mutually constitutive dynamic between mainstream and far-right parties produces and is produced by the distinctive security logic of anxiety analysed in the previous section. This allows the normalisation of exceptional security measures and disrupts (or undermines) the mainstream narrative of a far-right 'insurgency', which, as argued earlier, is based on a zero-sum opposition between liberalism and authoritarian solutions.

This chapter examines the case of the Italian state in the context of its so-called war against the Sicilian Mafia in the 1990s. In Italy, a complex dynamic has developed over the last 25 years between the far-right and mainstream parties. Thus an analysis of the Italian case offers a perspective on the long-term effects of such a dynamic, and also provides potential insights into the changing character of the political system. Specifically, examining a timing antecedent to the events of 9/11 frames this analysis within more long-term processes of the transformation of security through the politics of anxiety. The empirical examination consists of a discourse analysis of the parliamentary debate on the ratification of government-led exceptional legislation.[26]

In 1992, the Italian government presented to Parliament a series of exceptional legislative provisions to authorise sending the Italian Army to Sicily to fight the Sicilian Mafia. It was to be the first time since the end of the Second World War that a major law enforcement operation was carried out by the Italian Army on national territory. The 'Sicilian Vespers' Operation involved more than 6,000 soldiers. In the course of the Parliamentary debate on converting the government's original emergency decree into law, the logic of security driven by anxiety informed the dynamic between the 'moderate' centre and the 'extreme' right.

From the outset, the political significance of the parliamentary debate was articulated through the deployment of a specific temporal image of immediacy and exceptionalism; an MP in favour of the security measures opened the debate by saying, 'The historical moment is decidedly one of emergency

... [in the face of] the advance of organised crime.'[27] The discourse of emergency relied on apocalyptic imaginaries: the Italian State was sitting on the 'edge of the abyss'.[28] The minister of the interior declared that 'what is at stake is the stability, the continuity and the persistence of the State in its unity and sovereignty.'[29] Here fear of the present is constructed through past traumatic images which provoke anxiety about the return of the past; indeed, the Italian State is described as at risk of 'barbarization'[30] while Sicily is defined as a 'terra infidelium',[31] a term which designates a territory where Christian bishops failed in their mission of evangelisation in the 15th and 16th centuries because the uncivilised natives expelled them. The MPs and members of cabinet relied on metaphors evoking the First and Second World Wars: Italy was defined as being in the 'trenches'[32] and the mafia was called 'a force of occupation controlling part of the [Italian national] territory'.[33] Giulio Di Donato, of the PSI (Italian Socialist Party), claimed that 'there is no need to repeat ourselves yet again ... *we are at war*.'[34] The logic of anxiety emerges from an analysis of the way in which the mafia is constructed as a threat. The mafia is at once extremely close, since it occupies part of the Italian territory, while representing as the object of anxiety an unquantifiable risk. This threat is constructed through a discontinuous temporality which simultaneously involves images of a future that recall the ultimate temporal image of the apocalyptic end of all times and the risk of a return to dark times of the past, as the use of metaphors of pre-civilisation and memories of the Second World War suggest. Yet, despite this exceptional situation, the main objective of the government remained, in the words of the prime minister, Giulio Andreotti:

> fight[ing] the mafia with the tools of democratic institutions ... being aware that any division between us constitutes a menace to the credibility of the institutions *in which dangerous authoritarian temptations can then arise*.[35]

Hence, the main logic driving this debate implies that in such moments of extreme emergency, there is always the risk of an authoritarian involution that can be referred to fascism. This move again makes the threat at once extremely present and potentially overwhelming, but also increasingly broad and comprehensive; that is, a possible resurgence of the fascist past and the collapse of the democratic state. This allowed the government to justify the exceptional legislation authorising the deployment of the army as necessary to protect democracy not only from attacks by the mafia, but also from possible internal authoritarian temptations. Indeed, although the far-right party, the Movimento Sociale Italiano (MSI), accused the government of collusion with the mafia, it nevertheless supported the decisions of the majority regarding the exceptional measures and indeed reinforced the governmental parties' definition of the mafia as a subversive force by arguing for the need 'to respond to acts of war with acts of war'.[36] It also claimed that the mainstream parties were too soft and invoked additional measures such as the declaration of martial law and the adoption of the death penalty for the Mafiosi.[37] This enabled the 'moderate' parties to claim not only that the decree-law was absolutely necessary to fight 'the war' against the mafia, but also that if the 'democratic' forces did not appear strong enough to react effectively to these threats, then authoritarian and extreme solutions such as those proposed by the far right would find their way through. This is where the dynamic between the 'far right' and the 'moderate centre' emerges. The far-right parties, by incarnating the authoritarian temptations, served the purpose of reproducing the discourse of the government in favour of the decree-laws and validating its role as the protector of the Italian Democratic State from the truly extreme measures they proposed.

Consequently, the exceptional measure was posed as both a response to an objective threat requiring a fight against the mafia *and* an urgent matter of contrasting rising extremism. Through this combined narrative, any opposition to the measures could be excluded as irresponsible. Indeed, during the parliamentary debate, a small minority of MPs were opposed to approving the emergency legislation, and specifically to the necessity of sending the army to Sicily. Their argument was that using the army to fight the mafia was of little use, because 'the mafia is in the institutions of the State, it lives in its institutions'.[38] This was branded as unreasonable and factionalist, and, in other words, disqualified from being 'proper' political discourse.

The parliamentary debate shows how the deployment of exceptional legislation in the face of an existential threat fuels the dynamic between the far-right and mainstream parties. However, this dynamic cannot work only through fear of the present; it needs a logic of anxiety, which simultaneously overlays fear of the present with the traumatic memory of a past threat – fascism – and anticipation of the possibility that this past might return in the future. What informs this dynamic is not simply fear of the exceptional threat, but anxiety that operates on this triple temporal level. In this way, anxiety defines the moment of exception which disqualified any opponent to the emergency legislation; 'anxiety animates these reckonings of who is "in" and who is "out," who belongs and who does not.'[39] These reckonings operate through a twofold exclusion, an absolute exclusion of any opposition to the exceptional legislation based on images of the existential threat, and the discounting of any 'extremist' reaction through the simultaneous presentation of the mainstream party as representing an objective and reasonable solution. The next section shows how this logic of anxiety operates to normalise the exception and how this further informs the relationship between liberalism and the far right.

STAYING ANXIOUS

As the previous analysis has demonstrated, neoliberal politics are intimately linked to the rise of far-right movements because they mutually constitute the political agenda and profit from it. Therefore, the initial question about the rise of extreme right-wing parties requires a very different answer to the one given by those who see the extreme right as simply 'filling the voids' left by the mainstream parties. Although mainstream parties reject far-right solutions, they identify the same threats. In this way, mainstream parties can claim to act as 'responsible' and 'rational' mediators between the need to tackle a threat and the authoritarian solutions proposed by the far-right parties. Paradoxically, this 'middle way' is manifested, as in the Italian example, by making the case for exceptional measures which simultaneously tackle the emergency but also impede anti-democratic solutions.

This last section expands on the implications of this co-constitution when anxiety becomes the driver of political decisions. First, anxiety changes the logic of security into an ever-emerging exceptional moment. Second, by making the exception a de-politicised objective decision, anxiety sustains the mutual constitution of the far right and the mainstream parties through this logic. Third, this synergy between mainstream and far-right parties has long-term effects of changing the political system.

First, when anxiety permeates the making of security, this allows the blurring of the lines between norm and exception by informing a logic of security based upon a triple temporality of past, present and future. Indeed, anxiety works to reproduce the constant possibility of a return to the dramatic conditions which led to the necessity of the exception. Anxiety asks us to exercise ceaseless vigilance, both against the risk of a future return of the threat and because a lack of response to the threat could fuel authoritarian solutions. In this way, anxiety makes the normalisation of emergency[40] become a de-politicised long-term necessity. Anxiety works by making the emergency always in the process of re-emerging, or, better, it erodes the thin line between normality and the exception through its triple temporality, which entails at once past, present, and future. Moreover, because of the potentially object-less nature of the threat, exceptional measures can be inflated to cover any possible domain. Indeed, we can see this logic at play in the reshaping of Italian security and defence policy in the aftermath of the Cold War period through the extension of the exceptional legislation authorising the use of the army in space, time and domain. Initially, the decree-law authorising the use of the army on national territory was due to expire on 31 December 1993. Instead, new decrees progressively extended its deployment, not only in Sicily, but also to Calabria, Naples and the north-eastern border of Italy with Slovenia in order to contrast illegal immigration. Through the mechanism of continually issuing new decree-laws, the Sicilian Vespers military mission ended only on 8 July 1998. At the same time, on 29 August 1994, another law-decree (No. 521) was issued and this time it was converted into Law No. 599 on 27 October 1994. This law included the effects of the previous decrees and allowed the use of the army 'for the control of the national territory and for humanitarian missions abroad',[41] constituting the basis for the participation of the Italian Army in the NATO mission in Kosovo.

Second, anxiety significantly changes the politics of exceptionalism, which would work through a specific temporality of the present if it followed only a logic of fear in the face of an imminent threat. Instead, when entangled with anxiety, *the politics of the exception* is understood as a long-term 'objective' necessity and thus calls for exceptional measures can be removed from an authoritarian agenda labelled as too extreme and too threatening by adopting an economic and managerial language that 'purifies' the exception of its own excess. In the Italian case, the excessively authoritarian rhetoric of the far-right party was purified and made compatible with notions of liberal democracy by arguments based instead on the 'objectivity' of the threat. In this way, even though their solutions were rejected, the far right could end up co-constituting the political agenda with the mainstream parties in the name of responding to an objective state of anxiety. In this sense, the narrative of the 'far-right insurgency' is functional to this dynamic, since it reinforces the call for objective and reasonable policies. It is easy to see how very present this type of logic is in the contemporary discussion on immigration in various European countries. Cameron justified a tougher approach to immigration as a way to 'starve extremist parties of the oxygen of public anxiety' so that they could no longer say that 'mainstream politicians weren't listening to their concerns'.[42] In this way, the allegedly zero-sum opposition between mainstream parties and the far right can be re-read more effectively as a process of mutual constitution.

Third, the logic of anxiety potentially has a very important effect on the structure of the political system. In the case of Italy, the emergency anti-mafia law(s) contributed to the re-admission of the far-right MSI party to the political scenario as a legitimate actor. Up until then, the MSI had been considered as being outside the so-called 'arco costituzionale' or constitutional spectrum; this expression included all the parties that had taken part in the Resistance and contributed to writing the Italian Constitution of 1948.[43] As noticed in studies on other contemporary far-right parties,[44] adopting a more technical and neutralising language allowed the MSI to present a 'detoxified' image, making it fit to govern.[45] We can see this pattern emerging in the parliamentary debate on the use of the army. For instance, in the discussion about whether the Sicilian Vespers mission should be confirmed, the MSI deputy Nino Sospiri addressed those who disagreed with the decree with these words: 'speaking objectively and truthfully[46]. . . it seems impossible to understand

... the position of certain [parliamentary] groups who are still opposed ... to the Sicilian Vespers operation, despite the evidence of the incontestably positive results obtained so far.'[47] It must be a matter of 'preconceived ideological aversion',[48] he concluded, since in Sicily there is 'an objectively exceptional situation'.[49] Although the informal re-inclusion of the MSI had already begun in the 1980s, in particular when the Christian Democrat Francesco Cossiga was prime minister, the MSI entered the national government for the first time only in 1994 under the name of Alleanza Nazionale, a party constituted by the more moderate wing of the MSI. In the meantime, its members had learnt to moderate and adapt their tone to the new language of objectivity in relation to security issues, to the extent that the same Nino Sospiri was able to become deputy minister of transport in Berlusconi's government.

ANXIETY AND THE TIME OF REASONABLE POLITICS

The final part of this chapter expands upon the most important consequence of reading the rise of the far right as part of the politics of anxiety. The mutually reinforcing dynamic between far-right and mainstream parties has strong implications for the changing meaning of engaging in political discourse and its limits.

If the rise of the far right is understood as an insurgency which is the result of the contemporary times of anxiety, the implication is that being objective, moderate and reasonable, rather than factionalist and ideological, are the qualities needed in such times. Anxiety thus becomes an enduring logic of security; invoked by contemporary politics as the effect of our unfortunate present circumstances, anxiety helps check and ban dissent. Dissent can then no longer be expressed, because dissenting becomes a sign of being unreasonable and factionalist rather than objective, moderate and 'technical'. In the Italian case, this was clearly demonstrated by the way opposition to the exceptional laws was defined as unreasonable and therefore improper political discourse. The politics of anxiety, which is predicated on the abiding memory of the threat as well as the eternal possibility of its return, makes this initially exceptional ban on dissent the rule, justified by the exceptional situation. This is clearly reflected in the extension of the emergency and its gradual normalisation. Moreover, the politics of anxiety shapes political discourse through a language of technicality and efficiency. In times of anxiety, all those who are sufficiently reasonable are supposed to unite against the rise of extremisms as well as contrast and respond to this anxiety. In this way, as Slavoj Žižek has argued, the mainstream parties claim to have become 'post-political' and 'technocratic' as opposed to their factionalist, ideological and 'politically passionate' extremist counterparts.[50]

Following this logic, dissent is automatically branded as opposed to necessary changes because it is unreasonable, factionalist and ideological. And being 'ideological' in times of anxiety, so the narrative goes, is counterproductive, because it does not deal with the danger of the always possible return of the threat(s) and it fuels dangerous extremism. In this context, the appeal to anxiety fuels the increasing dominance of emotional references, which contribute to shifting the debate to a further level of de-politicisation. This leads to more de-politicising appeals to other emotions opposed to anxiety, such as, in the Italian case, hope. Particularly interesting in this regard is the current centre-left and centre-right coalition government of Matteo Renzi for whom the emotional aspect is paramount; according to Renzi, the aim of his government is to give back 'hope' to the citizens as a cure for their anxiety,[51] and he has defined the positive results of his party at the last European elections as 'the vote of hope'.[52] In such a context, anyone expressing dissent is easily accused of being a 'killjoy', to borrow Sarah Ahmed's expression,[53] or defined as a 'gufo', a jinx who brings bad luck, as Renzi has often labelled his opponents.

Consequently, nowadays the politics of anxiety has a powerful impact on European politics and not just in terms of the party system. In actual fact, everything, at first sight, remains the same, since, as a recent study has shown, the extreme right parties have not so far managed to visibly alter the party system in most European countries.[54] If anything, they make the system even more cohesive: the moderate and reasonable parties have to 'join forces against the common enemy'[55] in order to tackle the anxiety and marginalise extremism, and consequently 'grand' coalitions between centre-right and centre-left parties flourish, as in the cases of contemporary Italy and Germany. However, on the other hand, this chapter has shown that the process of neutralising the authoritarian tendencies of the far right enables them to penetrate even further into the mainstream parties, shaping the political agenda and the meaning of what is considered 'reasonable' while excluding any possible alternative. This has direct consequences for the further homogenisation of the centre-left and centre-right mainstream parties around a neoliberal agenda, which neutralises any opposition from the left, increasingly unable to express a different political agenda to that of the more conservative part of the spectrum. This contributes to what Žižek has defined as the double death of the Left, 'as if the European Left had to die twice: first as the "totalitarian" Communist Left, then as the moderate democratic Left, which over recent years has been gradually losing ground in Italy, France, in Germany'.[56] In this sense, the neutralisation and homogenisation of the political debate revolve around a neoliberal 'centrist' agenda which claims to encompass all that is reasonable given the difficult condition of living in times of anxiety.

CONCLUSION: THE POLITICS OF ANXIETY AND THE ERADICATION OF POLITICS

This chapter started by asking how understanding anxiety as a form of politics rather than as an objective condition of our times allows us to understand the rise of far-right parties in Europe. It showed that this issue can be approached in a productive fashion if we challenge the narrative that far-right parties work as an insurgency, a revolt against mainstream neoliberal parties. My analysis has shown how, instead, mainstream neoliberal politics works well with the far right to shape the political agenda using anxiety as a way to inform a distinctive security logic based on a triple temporal dimension. In this way, anxiety becomes a distinctive logic of security which extends and normalises a state of exception. While fear of the threat refers to the present, sharply separating norm/exception, anxiety produces a crisis and then remains latent, opening to a security logic which blurs the line between norm and exception in the name of an ever-present object-less threat. In this logic of security dominated by an anxiety which unfolds simultaneously in the present, past and future, the politics of exception and normality unfolds in a distinctive way which shapes the mutually constitutive dynamic between neoliberalism and the far right. This mutually constitutive relation simultaneously opens and closes spaces for resistance. Indeed, while far right parties seem to resist (neo)liberal politics, the security logic fuelled by the politics of anxiety closes the space down for any other forms of resistance precisely because of the risk of rising extremism. As we saw in the previous section, this has long-term effects on shaping the political system and its winners and losers in favour of mainstream neoliberal parties and the exclusion of alternative discourse from the left. To conclude, there are two final implications that this analysis raises.

First, co-constituting the political agenda with a far-right party on the assumption that it can be kept under control seems a rather dangerous gamble. Since these parties increasingly dominate political discourse, far-right propositions regarding immigration, surveillance and counterterrorism measures are anything but defeated. The attempt to neutralise them through a politics of anxiety represents a very dangerous gamble indeed, and is bringing the far-right agenda to the very centre of the political spectrum. Again, the assumption at work on the part of the mainstream neoliberal parties is based on market economics which asserts that the market naturally tends towards equilibrium so the far right will not prevail, will stay where it is and will fuel the system. The question is, what if this principle fails? what if this automatism does not work? Indeed, neoliberalism does not seem to offer any guarantees against this possibility; as was noted quite a long time ago, the idea that the market economy offers any guarantees against authoritarianism 'may be good propaganda but it is poor political sociology'.[57]

Second and even more important, it is necessary to think about how anxiety is shaping the meaning of politics. We have seen how its logic of security changes the meaning of the exception; it does so because it promises the potential eternal return of what made the exception necessary in the first place and on this basis calls for a technicalisation and, in fact, a neutralisation of the political debate which needs to be efficient and reasonable rather than ideological and 'political'. In this sense, it transforms political questions into questions of economic equilibrium by applying the logic of the market, as Rob Walker and Didier Bigo have explained in the case of the neoliberal approach to the relationship between security and liberty.[58] In this case, this exigency of equilibrium translates into needing, on the one hand, to tackle the objective anxiety of the people and, on the other, to remain moderate and not fall into extremism and the unreasonable. In the course of the present analysis we saw how in the Italian case the accusation of being unable to find the right balance between these two needs resulted in charges of excessive factionalism and consequent expulsion from 'proper' political debate. This means, following R.B.J. Walker, that by inserting 'a logic of markets into a logic of state law', politics is eradicated.[59] Finally, what the politics of anxiety profoundly changes is the meaning of participating in the political arena, the conditions of access, or, in other words, the conditions under which one can be considered 'reasonable enough' to take part in the political process. It changes these terms in a direction which is shaped by a market logic that rejects politics in the name of technicality and objectivity. This translation of the political debate into market terms, however (barely), hides authoritarian tendencies rather than defeating them, as the Italian case clearly shows.

NOTES

1. The views expressed in this chapter are those of the author and do not reflect the views or policies of the Ministry of Defence.
2. Ford, Robert and Goodwin, Matthew. 2014. *Revolt on the Right. Explaining Support for the Radical Right in Britain*, London and New York: Routledge.
3. Parker, G., Stacey, K., Carnegy, H. and Fontanella-Khan, J. 2014. 'Ukip and Front National Lead Populist Earthquake'. *Financial Times*, 26 May 2014.
4. Rooduijn, Matthij. 2015. 'The Rise of the Populist Radical Right in Western Europe'. *European View*, 14, 3–11, 5; see also Barr, R.R. 2009. 'Populists, Outsiders and Anti-Establishment Politics'. *Party Politics*, 15:1, 29–48.
5. 'David Cameron on Immigration: Full Text of the Speech', 14 April 2011, http://www.theguardian.com/politics/2011/apr/14/david-cameron-immigration-speech-full-text.
6. 'I respect Nigel Farage, Says George Osborne', 24 May 2014, http://www.bbc.co.uk/news/uk-politics-27554556.

7. 'David Cameron Extremism Speech. Read the Transcript in Full', 20 July 2015, http://www.independent.co.uk/news/uk/politics/david-cameron-extremism-speech-read-the-transcript-in-full-10401948.html#gallery.
8. Steffek, Jens. 2015. 'Fascist Internationalism'. *Millennium: Journal of International Studies*, 1–20.
9. '"Battle of Britain": Defeating "Fascist" Enemy ISIS a Priority', 16 July 2015, https://www.rt.com/uk/310042-battle-of-britain-defeating-fascist/.
10. Halikiopoulou, Daphne, Kyriaki, Nanou and Sofia, Vasilopoulou. 2012. 'The Paradox of Nationalism: The Common Denominator of Radical Right and Radical Left Euroscepticism'. *European Journal of Political Research*, 51:4, 504–539.
11. A good example of this logic is the study by Golder Matt, 'Explaining Variations in the Success of Extreme Right Parties in Western Europe', 432–466.
12. Albertson, Bethani and Shana, Gadarian K. 2015. *Anxious Politics. Democratic Citizenship in a Threatening World*, New York: Cambridge University Press, xx.
13. Harari, Roberto. 2001. *Lacan's Seminar on Anxiety: An Introduction*, New York: Other Press, 3.
14. Albertson, Bethani and Shana, Gadarian K. 2015, *Anxious Politics*, xxi.
15. Aradau, C., Huysmans, J., Neal, A. and Voelkner, N. 2015, *Critical Security Methods. New Frameworks for Analysis*, New York: Routledge, 3.
16. Ibid., 3.
17. Lacan, J. 1960. 'The Subversion of the Subject and the Dialectic of Desire in the Freudian Unconscious'. Contribution to the 'Colloques philosophiques internationaux', 793–828.
18. 'Angoscia', http://www.treccani.it/enciclopedia/angoscia_(Universo-del-Corpo)/.
19. Harari, Roberto. 2001. *Lacan's Seminar on Anxiety*, 15.
20. Ibid., 15.
21. Middleton, T. 2013. 'Anxious Belongings: Anxiety and the Politics of Belonging in Subnational Darjeeling'. *American Anthropologist*, 115:4, 612.
22. Bowie, M. 1991. *Lacan*, Cambridge: Harvard University Press, 184 in Solomon, Ty. 2014. 'Time and Subjectivity in World Politics'. *International Studies Quarterly*, 58:4, 674.
23. Middleton, T. 2013. 'Anxious belongings', 612.
24. Harari, Roberto. 2001. *Lacan's Seminar on Anxiety*, 16.
25. Stewart, K. 2007. *Ordinary Effects*, Durham and London: Duke University Press, 94.
26. This is how the Italian constitution, art. 77, defines a 'decree law': 'When the Government, *in the case of necessity and urgency*, adopts under its own responsibility a temporary measure, it shall introduce that measure to Parliament for transposition into law. During a dissolution period, Parliament shall be convened within five days of such an introduction. The measure shall retrospectively cease to have effect if it is not transposed into law by Parliament within sixty days of its publication'. Once a decree-law is issued by the government, it immediately acquires the effect of law, and remains in force until parliamentary debate has been concluded. At the end of that period, either the decree-law is promulgated as a law by Parliament or else it lapses.

27. Atti Parlamentari (APP), seduta del 20 Luglio Camera dei Deputati, 1992, 2377.
28. APP, 2377.
29. APP, 1277.
30. APP, 105.
31. APP, 1992, 1280.
32. APP, 1277.
33. APP, 1280.
34. APP, 1281.
35. APP, 102–103, my emphasis.
36. See the intervention of the leader of the MSI, Gianfranco Fini, APP, 1286.
37. APP, 1286.
38. APP, 1292.
39. Middleton, T. 2013, 'Anxious Belongings', 608.
40. On the normalisation of the exception, see A.W. Neal. 2012. 'Normalization and Legislative Exceptionalism. Counterterrorist Lawmaking and the Changing Times of Security Emergencies'. *International Political Sociology*, 6:3, 260–276; A.W. Neal. 2012. *Exceptionalism and the Politics of Counter- Terrorism. Liberty. Security, and the War on Terror*, New York: Routledge.
41. For the text of the law, see: http://www.normattiva.it/uri-res/N2Ls?urn:nir:stato:legge:1994-10-27;599@originale, accessed on 8 August 2016.
42. 'In full: David Cameron Immigration Speech', 14 April 2011, http://www.bbc.co.uk/news/uk-politics-13083781.
43. Cerri, A. 2012. 'Spunti e riflessioni sulla Costituzione nella storia dell'Italia Repubblicana e nel presente momento'. In D'Atena A. (ed.), *Studi in onore di Pierfrancesco Grossi*, Torino: Giuffrè Editore, 412.
44. Mudde, C. 2007. 'Populist Radical Right Parties in Europe'. Cambridge: Cambridge University Press; Rydgren, J. 2005. 'Is Extreme Right-Wing Populism Contagious? Explaining the Emergence of a New Party Family'. *European Journal of Political Research*, 44, 413–437.
45. Mudde, 2007, and Rydgren 2005 in 'The Rise of the Populist Radical Right in Western Europe', 8.
46. APP, Nino Sospiri, 2968.
47. Ibid., 2968.
48. Ibid.
49. Ibid., 2976.
50. Žižek, S. 2001. *Living in the End Times*, London and New York: Verso, ix.
51. 'Idee', http://www.matteorenzi.it/idee/.
52. 'Renzi: Ora il nostro peso in Europa cambia, no siamo più a rimorchio', 26 May 2014, http://www.corriere.it/politica/speciali/2014/elezioni-europee/notizie/renzi-non-era-voto-di-me-ora-riforme-basta-alibi-fca59524-e4bb-11e3-8e3e-8f5de4ddd12f.shtml.
53. Ahmed, S. 2007/2008. 'Multiculturalism and the Promise of Happiness', *New Formations*, 121–137.
54. Mudde, C. 2014. 'Fighting the System? Populist Radical Right Parties and Party System Change'. *Party Politics*, 20:2, 217–226.

55. Žižek, S. 2001. *Living in the End Times*, ix.
56. Ibid., viii.
57. Miliband, R. 2009. *The State in Capitalist Society*, London: Merlin Press, 17.
58. Walker, R.B.J. 2014. 'Which Democracy for Which Demos?'; Fichera, M., Hanninen, S. and Tuori, K. *Polity and Crisis*, Farnham: Ashgate, 171–188; Bigo, D. 2010, 'Delivering Liberty and Security? The Reframing of Freedom When Associated with Security'. In Bigo, D., Carrera, S., Guild, E. and Walker, R. (eds.), *Europe's 21st Century Challenge: Delivering Liberty and Security*, London and New York: Routledge, 263–288.
59. Walker, R.B.J. 2014. 'Which Democracy for Which Demos?'

BIBLIOGRAPHY

Ahmed, S. 2007/2008. 'Multiculturalism and the Promise of Happiness', *New Formations*, 121–137.

Albertson, B. and Gadarian, K.S. 2015. *Anxious Politics. Democratic Citizenship in a Threatening World*, New York: Cambridge University Press.

Barr, R.R. 2009. 'Populists, Outsiders and Anti-Establishment Politics', *Party Politics*, 15(1), 29–48.

Bigo, D. 2010. 'Delivering Liberty and Security? The Reframing of Freedom When Associated with Security'. In Bigo, D., Carrera, S., Guild, E. and Walker, R. (eds.), *Europe's 21st Century Challenge: Delivering Liberty and Security*, London and New York: Routledge, 263–288.

Cerri, A. 2012. 'Spunti e riflessioni sulla Costituzione nella storia dell'Italia Repubblicana e nel presente momento'. In D'Atena, A. (ed.), *Studi in onore di Pierfrancesco Grossi*, Torino: Giuffrè Editore.

Ford, R. and Goodwin, M. 2014. *Revolt on the Right. Explaining Support for the Radical Right in Britain*, London and New York: Routledge.

Golder, M. 2003. 'Explaining Variations in the Success of Extreme Right Parties in Western Europe', *Comparative Political Studies*, 36(4), 432–466.

Halikiopoulou, D., Nanou, K. and Vasilopoulou, S. 2012. 'The Paradox of Nationalism: The Common Denominator of Radical Right and Radical Left Euroscepticism', *European Journal of Political Research*, 51(4), 504–539.

Harari, Roberto. 2001. *Lacan's Seminar on Anxiety: An Introduction*, New York: Other Press.

Lacan, J. 1960. 'The Subversion of the Subject and the Dialectic of Desire in the Freudian Unconscious'. Contribution to the 'Colloques philosophiques internationaux', 793–828.

Middleton, T. 2013. 'Anxious Belongings: Anxiety and the Politics of Belonging in Subnational Darjeeling', *American Anthropologist*, 115(4), 608–621.

Miliband, R. 2009. *The State in Capitalist Society*, London: Merlin Press.

Mudde, C. 2007. *Populist Radical Right Parties in Europe*, Cambridge: Cambridge University.

Mudde, C. 2014. 'Fighting the System? Populist Radical Right Parties and Party System Change', *Party Politics*, 20(2), 217–226.

Neal, A.W. 2012. *Exceptionalism and the Politics of Counter-Terrorism. Liberty, Security, and the War on Terror*, New York: Routledge.
Neal, A.W. 2012. 'Normalization and Legislative Exceptionalism. Counterterrorist Lawmaking and the Changing Times of Security Emergencies', *International Political Sociology*, 6(3), 260–276.
Parker, G., Stacey, K., Carnegy, H. and Fontanella-Khan, J. 'Ukip and Front National Lead Populist Earthquake', *Financial Times*, 26 May 2014.
Rooduijn, M. 2015. 'The Rise of the Populist Radical Right in Western Europe', *European View*, 14, 3–11.
Rydgren, J. 2005. 'Is Extreme Right-Wing Populism Contagious? Explaining the Emergence of a New Party Family', *European Journal of Political Research*, 44, 413–437.
Solomon, Ty. 2014. 'Time and Subjectivity in World Politics', *International Studies Quarterly*, 58(4), 674, 671–681.
Steffek, J. 2015. 'Fascist Internationalism', *Millennium: Journal of International Studies*, 44(1), 1–20.
Stewart, K. 2007. *Ordinary Effects*, Durham, NC and London: Duke University Press.
Walker, R.B.J. 2014. 'Which Democracy for Which Demos?' In Fichera, M., Hanninen, S. and Tuori, K. (eds.), *Polity and Crisis*, Farnham: Ashgate, 171–188.
Žižek, S. 2001. *Living in the End Times*, London and New York: Verso.

PARLIAMENTARY DOCUMENTS

Atti Parlamentari, Camera Dei Deputati, Discussioni 25 Maggio 1992.
Atti Parlamentari, Camera dei Deputati, Discussioni, 20 Luglio 1992.
Atti Parlamentari, Camera dei Deputati, Discussioni, 30 Luglio 1992.
Atti Parlamentari, Camera Dei Deputati, Discussioni, 31 Luglio 1992.
Atti Parlamentari, Camera dei Deputati, Discussioni, 3, Agosto 1992.
Atti Parlamentari, Camera dei Deputati, Discussioni, 8 Settembre 1992.
Atti Parlamentari, Camera de Deputati, Discussioni, 10 Settembre, 1992.

Chapter 8

Indignation as Resistance: Beyond the Anxiety of No Future Alternatives

Paolo Cossarini

On Sunday 24 May 2015, Ada Colau, the most visible and influential face in Spanish society's struggle to stop house evictions, was elected mayor of Barcelona. With a clear message in support of social justice, participatory democracy and citizens' empowerment, Colau and her political group – *Barcelona en Comú* (Catalan for Barcelona in Common) – obtained a simple majority that allowed them to govern the city. Over the last few years Colau has been the spokesperson of the platform of those affected by mortgages (in Spanish, *Plataforma de Afectados por la Hipoteca*, PAH). This networked association, which has expanded throughout the entire country, emerged in 2009, and since has become the most important organisation involved in the movement against evictions. Since 2011 the emergence of anti-austerity mobilisations, also known as the *Indignados* movement in the Spanish context, the protests and action taken by the PAH acquired new visibility. Despite the differences and peculiarities of the variegated protest mobilisations, the shared aim of these phenomena was to establish a vector of political and social change, demonstrating a lack of faith in traditional political processes and official actors. Five years after the beginning of these contentious practices, some of their members are leading the current changes on the Spanish political landscape.

It is worth remembering that housing in Spain has been at the centre of recent economic developments and a key part of every political movement over the last decade. Both financial institutions and political parties supported the neoliberal tendency of ever-growing prices for housing as the engine of the Spanish economy during the 1990s and the 2000s. 'Between 1998 and 2007, the number of formalised mortgages rose annually to 822,000, more than 8 million mortgages in total.'[1] Over the last decade, 'the equivalent of a new home for every newborn person in the country has been constructed.'[2]

Exacerbated by structural deficiencies of the economic system and widespread corruption, the consequences of the economic recession have immediately caused profound social grievances. In the specific case of housing, the result has been the inability of homeowners to pay their mortgage or their rent. Mortgages acquired in the context of the housing bubble had led to a considerable private debt that left huge numbers of people unable to meet their mortgage payments as unemployment skyrocketed. Although it is difficult to get figures on the social magnitude of the housing crisis in Spain, the housing issue certainly acquired tragic dimensions. According to the Spanish Land Registry, since the beginning of the financial and economic crisis, more than 350,000 foreclosure processes have been applied. Only in 2014 there were 212 mortgage foreclosures and 159 evictions produced each day throughout Spain or, putting it differently, every 15 minutes a family has been evicted from their home, left on the street and in debt for life.[3] In this context, Ada Colau and the movement she has been representing have tenaciously pointed at the relationship between the financial, economic and political elites as one of the main obstacles in achieving a change in the Spanish housing policy. They claimed to disrupt the current neoliberal practices and policies that have led housing into a speculative sector,[4] and to observe the constitutionally anchored 'right to decent and adequate housing' (Art. 47 of the Spanish Constitution). In this regard, the platform of those affected by mortgages – within the broader wave of mobilisation that emerged since 2011 – has actively engaged against neoliberalism, promoting the right to housing, and cracking the property myth of homeowners that defined the Spanish economic boom.[5]

Since their manifestation, Spanish protests against austerity measures originated in the aftermath of the 2008 crisis, as well as mobilisations against house evictions, have caught the scholarly attention. A copious amount of literature has particularly focused on topics such as the organisational resources and networks these movements employed to mobilise citizens, the type of mobilisations, and their inner structure.[6] Moreover, beyond the mobilisation per se, scholars have pointed out that social movements reveal meta-questions about the political realm, and have a critical role about the concrete ways in which politics 'is done'. Among other things, scholars have highlighted the anti-austerity discourses, the struggle against economic inequalities and the growing precariat,[7] the relationships between movements and democratic theory,[8] the rise of (left-wing) populism in Europe[9] and the central critique of representation.[10]

Given this context, the focal point of this chapter is developed from an angle that relates these questions to the increased attention that is paid to the role of emotions in politics. Indeed, it is argued that delving into the specific emotional dynamics as highlighted by the recent cycle of mobilisation is a fruitful way of considering this phenomenon. It has not gone unnoticed that much of the recent wave of protests against austerity politics in Europe was shaped by, and contributed to shape, emotional reactions. If 2011 has been defined as the year of global indignation, a vast array of emotions – such as indignation, resentment, humiliation, anger, anxiety, fear and so forth – were at play in the mobilisations and are key defining features of the current state of affairs.

Here it is contended that recent anti-austerity mobilisations can be analysed through the lens of emotions and their role in politics. Besides the micro-politics of social mobilisation, recent contentious phenomena are part of a broader conjunction in which the emotional dimension plays a central role. Additionally, emotions are pivotal in the process of subject formation that takes place within these movements, and beyond. Mostly formed by young unemployed and indebted homeowners, protesters and activists are the symbol of the neoliberal subjectivity, representing the junction of current political, social and economic trends: anxious, precarious and indebted lives, and political powerlessness. Specifically, key emotional elements appear as central vectors of this process, both in their inhibiting and empowering sides. Special focus will be paid to the affirmative forms of confrontation these contentious practices articulate through the same emotional dynamics. In this regard, negative emotions such as anxiety and insecurity are turned into practices of resistance against political and financial institutions: negative paralysing emotions can lead to mobilisation. Moreover, the democratic *milieu* of the recent cycle of protest, as witnessed by the discourse of the new political parties that have been born as result of these mobilisations, marked the return to 'inequality' and 'injustice' as master frames.[11] The slogans and mottos used during the protests unambiguously targeted capitalist greed, precariousness, political corruption, and those such as bankers and politicians who were judged guilty of making the 'common people' suffer. It is this suffering and the vulnerability of people, it will be argued, that characterises a common ground for identity formation, and the construction of an alternative political discourse. Lastly, it is contended that the different forms of mobilisation stress the dysfunctions of our current democracies, setting not only unconventional forms of mobilisation that challenge the role traditionally performed by political institutions; rather, they constitute an alternative form of political action that opens up a social horizon that goes beyond the logic of denial of future/alternative possibilities, led by financial institutions.

In order to deal with this series of problems, we first need to delve into the relationship between emotions and politics. We then need to undertake a short exploration of neoliberal subjectivity that characterises current times and political struggles. Finally, specifically focusing on the Spanish context since 2011 – the *Indignados* movement and the PAH – we will highlight the political vision and social possibility these movements entail. Throughout our argument, it will be clear that anxiety represents an essential vector for current political dynamics. Often being a paralysing emotion that goes along with social and economic uncertainty, it also opens the path to variegated emotional reactions and triggers an active, and alternative, form of political engagement.

MAPPING THE EMOTIONS–POLITICS NEXUS IN NEOLIBERAL TIMES

Political science has often seen emotions, and similar concepts such as passions, feelings and so forth, as the enemies of reason. Passions have been somehow derided as anti-political by the modern and contemporary rational project of government. In this sense, the marginalisation of emotions in the Western tradition is to be traced back to the reason/emotion dualism, which also triggered the association of reason with the realm of institutionalised exercise of power.[12] Yet, passions matter in politics: fear, anger, guilt, pity, envy, anxiety and shame, among other feelings, play a key role in many aspects of social life, from the formation of collective identities, and the economic and markets dynamics, to the birth of social movements, and the strategies of political parties. Although the modern reason/emotion dichotomy and the contemporary epistemology of social sciences contributed to the (often deliberate) marginalisation of passions, it is worth bearing in mind that classical liberals, such as Locke, Mill, Smith and Madison, demonstrate an 'acute awareness of human irrationality' – or the possibility that human beings will often be motivated by 'irrational desire'[13] – and that the basic assumptions of rationalism, with special relation to the place of passion, only begin with neoclassical economic theories. All in all, from an epistemological and political point of view, the rise of rationalism has often meant in modern history the removal of emotions from the core of the political realm.

However, in recent years a wide range of disciplines, such as in neurology[14] and cognitive psychology,[15] and philosophy,[16] have given new prominence to the role of emotions in social and political sciences.[17] Drawing on these different traditions of thought, and on the relatively new 'affective turn',[18] several critical approaches have developed a vast cross-disciplinary literature on emotions that opens up thought-provoking interrogatives about the relationship between emotional and political dimensions. This heterogeneous literature has been undermining the traditional dichotomies between reason and passion, trying to find a location for emotions and affective dimensions in social and political investigation.

The nature, definition and political role of emotions are the core subjects of a great deal of contemporary literature,[19] which has constituted variegated field of theoretical research. Commonly, questions have converged around whether there are positive and negative, political and non-political emotions; how the cultural and contextual levels influence individual and collective emotions; and how emotions shape politics. Dealing with these questions, many philosophical, psychological and political traditions have developed different perspectives.[20] Moreover, the idea that there are certain emotions that are *essentially political* is present in the scholarship.[21] Among others, loyalty, solidarity, anger, fear, anxiety, resentment and shame – without exhausting the list of 'political' emotions – are often seen as the key emotions that construct and support social structures, as well as relations of domination. It is well known, for instance, that Max Weber associated loyalty with the legitimate systems of domination. He thought of loyalty as a key element that links the powerless to the powerful: the loyalty to the powerful is at the base of every legitimate form of domination and, together with fear, constitutes a field that shapes obedience. In this context, emotions do not exclusively belong to the realm of the micro-politics of individual behaviour and social movements – and thus they should not be treated merely in an instrumental and functionalist manner. Rather, as Flam highlights, we should connect the micro-politics to the macro-politics. In this vein, emotions such as loyalty, anger, shame and fear are inner features of both social structures and relations of dominations. Within this framework, the role of passions becomes essentially political, being interpreted as *cementing*, and *activating*, or as *sanctioning*, and *subversive* emotions.[22]

From Cementing the Liberal Society to the Neoliberal Subjectivity

Dealing with this issue, one should bear in mind that liberalism was born out of the fires of civil and religious wars, and the social and economic uncertainty that characterised the beginning of modernity. Most of the key concepts of the intellectual fathers of modern political thought were a set of responses to the violent and fearful conditions in which they lived. As Judith Shklar[23] emphasised, the 'politics of fear' dramatically informed classical liberal theorising at the beginning of modernity, and still strongly influences contemporary debates about the nature of our political organisation. In this vein, one can consider liberalism as a radical security project, which has been concerned, from its outset, essentially with the provision of security measures.[24]

Accordingly, the idea that certain emotional states and dynamics are at the core of political organisations has been developed in the political thinking of the twentieth century. For instance, while for Weber fear is an essential emotion for every form of legitimate domination – he argued that individual and collective action in a given community is 'determined by highly robust motives of fear and hope'[25] – the concept of risk later became the common ground of a great deal of scholarship. In this sense, fear relates to the world 'risk society',[26] in which the 'unpredictable, uncontrollable and ultimately incommunicable' consequences of risks increasingly circulate at a global scale.[27] According to Beck, it is not that life has become more dangerous. It is that risk has now de-bounded, in spatial, temporal and social terms, so that 'the hidden central issue in world risk society is *how to feign control over the uncontrollable* – in politics, law, science, technology, economy and everyday life'.[28] Nonetheless, the risk society is still based on the idea that dangers and fears, once identified as such, can be controlled. All this has encouraged social scientists and political theorists to dig into the patterns of fear, highlighting different perspectives of analysis: the paradoxes of contemporary insecurity,[29] the risks of industrialised societies[30] or the fluid nature of current fears.[31] Frank Furedi,[32] for his part, argues that, as this fear is often irrational, exaggerated or misplaced, it is not simply a reasonable response to the conditions of a risk society, but the result of a debilitating obsession with safety or the outcome of a media-produced perception of heightened risk. The idea that governments are increasingly manufacturing, drawing upon and reproducing fear has become the predominant focus of attention in scholarly works. Some tend to assume the effects of fear result in creating fearful masses, stating that 'fear has become the emotion through which public life is administered'.[33] Engin Isin,[34] for his part, argues that Anglophone neoliberal state societies are now governed through neurosis: 'the culture of fear' underplays 'the fact that people not only conduct their lives with affects and emotions but also in the absence of capacities for evaluating full and transparent information'.[35] As Joanna Bourke argues in *Fear: A Cultural History*, our understanding of, response to and even subjective feeling of fear are historically determined. That is, fears, risks and dangers are fundamentally constituted through a dynamic process with the social and, at the same time, contribute to shape it.

What these reflections show is that individual and collective emotional states are constitutive of political organisations. The contemporary world is no exception, although one might question that neoliberalism's emotional bases are the same of modern liberalism. Regardless of the perspective one adopts – neoliberalism as an ideology,[36] as a state form[37] or as a form of transnational governmentality[38] – it seems clear that neoliberalism defines contemporary politics, permeating into everyday life of Western societies and beyond, and marking a moral agenda. The market is seen as the only effective horizon for freedom and emancipation, as well as risk is considered as a condition of possibility for societal enrichment. Here, the core idea is that there is no possibility of escaping from danger as such; rather, exposing oneself to risks is what enables freedom and, combined with state withdrawal, determines the efficient functioning of society. This goes beyond the economic reasoning, implying consequences for political issues such as political organisation and legitimacy, and social action. Moreover, this belief in the necessity and positivity of risks and danger is what informs the basic ontology of neoliberalism, that is precariousness and vulnerability. Investigating the neoliberal subjectivity means recognising their fundamental role. In this context, if risk and danger are permanently at work, there is no possible insurance system that could remove insecurity. Every aspect of life is uncertain, and living on the edge of chronic, unmanageable debt is the concrete *nomos* of precariousness and vulnerability.

Drawing on Guy Standing,[39] it can be affirmed that today a new global class structure is taking shape: precariat. Although it is clear that social formations are overlapped on previous configurations, the social democratic consensus of the middle decades of the twentieth century – in which capital, the trades unions and labour found a common ground for developing a welfare state – has now gone through a deep transformation that has led to a bourgeoning form of hierarchical social organisation. While at the top of the structure is the effective ruling class – formed by both a plutocracy linked in part to financial capital, and the political elite – which in sum embodies the neoliberal state, below that we witness the shrinking of the masses that are slowly descending from the 'middle class' into new perilous social strata characterised by insecure, unstable and often part-time labour. Being in paid employment and on an average income is no longer guarantee of being financially secure. Having fewer rights than other social classes, the precariat is taken away from rights, condemned to face the constant precariousness of 'unknown unknowns', and exposed to chronic uncertainty.

While the transformative power of human agency is certainly still present within the different social strata, lower classes seem to no longer have the strength to impose their political agenda. Chronic uncertainty and political powerless then shape the neoliberal subjectivity: the anxious precariat. The anxious subject is then a subject that is essentially forced to accommodate itself to the world. No possibility of change is offered in the permanent exposure to danger. Rather, the anxious subject tends to perceive the necessity of the dangerousness of the world as a condition for participating in it. The neoliberal subject is therefore a *resilient* subject that has to accommodate, and handle with the effects of potentially hazardous events, renouncing any belief in the possibility of change. The anxious subject accepts, instead, life as a permanent adaptation to threats and dangers, which are now presupposed as endemic to the system and outside human control.[40] An ever-menacing future is what essentially informs the political context of this subjectivity, whose proper character is to be worried about alleged future events and perceived threats. In this sense, anxiety – a future-focused disposition and feeling of worry – is the appraisal of a situation as out of control, being threatening and uncertain.[41]

However, resilience can turn into a form of resistance. Paradoxically, anxiety gives birth to apparently divergent political narratives that, on the one hand, lead to the search for (inaccessible) protection and safety and, on the other hand, to practices of subversion. Anxiety, firstly, motivates people to avoid dangers and to seek protection, often putting their trust in political leaders, or private security sources. Yet, anxiety also promotes a different, active form of political engagement, since it opens the path to variegated emotional reactions. Here it is argued that anxiety triggers a specific form of political engagement that is particularly reflective of current democratic trends.

INDIGNATION AS RESISTANCE

Over the last decades, precariousness and vulnerability have represented the ontological consequences of neoliberal practices in the political domain. Primarily in response to these, anti-austerity mobilisations have sprawled around the world since 2011. In the European context, especially the peripheral countries have witnessed the emergence of a series of protests and collective mobilisations that has shaken the political debate and agenda, giving birth to new political parties. The most famous movements include the Spanish *Indignados* movement and the Greek *Aganaktismenoi*. Together with other European mobilisations in countries such as Portugal, Italy and the United Kingdom, and the experience of the *Occupy* movements in the United States, these movements challenged the neoliberal ideology and the concrete policies that various governments have been implementing in the name of austerity. Although each of these movements is clearly shaped by the local political context – which includes the cultural and organisational traditions – they shared numerous elements. They were all massive protests that, particularly through the employment of new social media technologies, involved citizens from different social and political origins, and that created at least partially autonomous spaces for demonstration and political engagement. If their primary economic goals included a fight against the financial system, guilty of creating huge wealth inequalities, the political ambition was also to democratise power in more participatory ways, which could empower the masses bearing the brunt of economic strains. Within this general assumption, two main discursive strands characterised these phenomena: on the one hand an opposition to politicians and the financial elites blamed for corruption and criticised for emptying out the very meaning of democracy; on the other hand, the attempt to counter the naturalised, hegemonic neoliberal discourse, guilty of perpetuating structural inequalities. In this vein, these movements' aim was to shake people out of their routine trust and loyalty towards authorities, and they represent a sign of popular discontent and disaffection towards political representatives and the financial system.[42]

However, what is noteworthy here is that, beyond structural and organisational features, these social movements also share the common perception of political and economic injustice, which soon provoked indignation and anger. Anxiety about economic and political life therefore contributed to the birth of these political mobilisations. In combination with indignation and anger, protests against austerity convert negative and constraining passions into protest. In other words, the anxious neoliberal subject found the ways to publicly express its wide emotional dispositions, imagining a change beyond the oppression the 'necessity' of risks and danger represents. Thus, beyond the concrete demands of policy change expressed during the cycle of mobilisations, the idea of recent protests is to blame the coercing power of governing structures and narratives, as well as to demand for a change.

While some scholars prefer to choose the term 'occupy social movements'[43] – or 'networks of outrage and hope'[44] – over the more widespread 'indignant mobilisations', what is clear is that these phenomena put the emphasis on a greater concern: the political relevance of affective bonds. Although Benjamín Tejerina argues that indignation was not the 'sole, and perhaps not even the most decisive emotion at play in this cycle of contention',[45] indignation, and similar emotional perceptions such as outrage and anger were nonetheless the emotions that ignited these mobilisations, and characterised their political nature. A 'strategic' vision was clearly present within these movements – i.e. their objective was to modify a situation perceived as unjust. Nonetheless, here it is argued that the emotional dynamics and their discursive translations played a key role: not only was the identity formation of protesters at play; rather, emotions were also directly involved in the questioning of current democratic practices that the protests performed.

In the anti-austerity mobilisations we have witnessed the emergence, presence and usage of a variegated number of emotional factors (within rhetoric, discourse, contentious dynamics), obviously related to the economic and political crisis these social movements are embedded in. Wrath, indignation, fear, anger, anxiety, humiliation, pain and so forth are all distinctive emotions of these phenomena. In the specific Spanish case, ¡*Democracia Real Ya!* (DRY) – one of the many platforms that played a key role in organising the protests of 15 May 2011 and the following events – called for an end of citizen apathy, and a facing up to the unjust situation. It called the people to properly feel this unjust context, and to act consequently. In this sense, with slogans such as *Toma la calle* (Spanish for *Take the Square*), DRY strategically 'mobilised' the emotion of indignation to encourage participation in collective action. From an explicative point of view one might argue that these articulated 'constellations of emotions' were among the principal factors driving people to mobilise and participate in anti-austerity protests. Passion and emotions, as much as ideology and interests, impulse people to mobilise and join collective actions.[46]

Anger at Work: Framing Injustice, Identity and Action

Recent literature has particularly pointed out the relevance of the 'mobilising' side of the spectrum of emotions. Anger, especially, has attracted the attention of much scholarship. In Western culture, anger is a Janus-faced emotion, considered to have both socially constructive and disruptive effects, being both a noble passion of rebellion against injustice and feared as a losing of judicious thinking. Recent literature has emphasised the idea that people mobilise to overcome some form of perceived and real injustice. Anger is then conceived as an immediate, spontaneous response to the perception of unjustified harm or pain to the self or to the social contours, and conceptualised as an active affective reaction to a problematic situation of social hierarchy. Therefore anger often leads to mobilisation, activating individual and collective energy in service of goal attainment. Ben-Ze'ev[47] affirms that '[l]ike other emotions, anger is functional when it is in the right proportion, for example, when it is expressed in a socially constructive way without becoming highly aroused'. Although in an era of increased personal and collective sense of insecurity – job insecurity, civil and economic insecurity, etc. – it is difficult to turn the anger towards clear goals, to transform it into a constructive political power; anger is viewed as motivating people to engage in political action, fuelling collective struggle for justice and recognition. Theodore Kemper[48] argues that we experience anger as a 'real emotion' when we are confronted with power that seriously limits our autonomy and we attribute the blame for the loss of autonomy to the power-holder. In a similar context, Martha Nussbaum asks, 'what moral sentiments will be particularly important in such a political-liberal society, based on ideas of capability and functioning? . . . I have frequently suggested that anger and indignation will be such core sentiments because they react to harm or damage.'[49] Thus, if anger is something people feel when they experience injustice, then understanding anger may offer some insight into the nature of injustice itself. If anger motivates political action, then its study may well offer new insights into the character of struggles for power.

In this context, although the collective expression of anger has historically been discouraged – due to its close association with irrationality, aggression or violent excess – recent studies on social movements have demonstrated that anger motivates and fuels activity and collective struggles for justice.[50] As Gamson[51] pointed out long ago, injustice and inequalities may cause demobilising effects on citizens, such as cynicism and resignation. Similarly, social and political injustice may also cause, moral outrage, anger – as well as hope – that are crucial for mobilisation. The political value of anger, along this line, has been seen to lie in its capacity to communicate that an injustice has been committed, and through this anger to question the legitimacy of power.⁵² Here, special attention will be paid on three central ideas linked with this: injustice, identity and action. These factors, it is argued, can also be useful to enhance the theoretical debate about the relationship between social movements and democracy.

Injustice

Mobilisations often occur when a sense of injustice is felt by protesters and, more broadly, by a sector of a given population. A sense of injustice cannot emerge without a new diagnosis of the situation and a conviction that existing conditions are unjust.⁵³ In this sense, the reason people mobilise is to overcome some form of injustice – whether only perceived or effectively real. Events of social injustice can therefore cause indignation, moral shocks and diffuse anger, and thus move citizens to action.

> Different emotions can be stimulated by perceived inequities—cynicism, bemused irony, resignation. But injustice focuses on the righteous anger that puts fire in the belly and iron in the soul. Injustice . . . is a hot cognition, not merely an abstract intellectual judgment about what is equitable. The heat of moral judgement is intimately related to beliefs about what [concrete] acts or conditions have caused people to suffer undeserved hardship or loss.⁵⁴

This means that emotions such as indignation and anger must be seen beyond their being one of the many preconditions of protest. They have to be linked to the broad conception of justice. In this sense, it has been emphasised that the capacity to respond with anger is crucial to a sense of justice.⁵⁵ Within this framework, the unjust situation responds to deep political and economic consequences citizens have suffered as result of the austerity measures implemented by governments. The list of grievances denounced by these anti-austerity mobilisations is long, and mobilisations have blamed both political and economic sectors as responsible for this. Examples of the ways in which the protesters expressed their perception to this unjust situation can be found on both the financial and political sides, seen as strictly linked together: 'We don't understand why we need to pay the bills of a crisis whose authors continue to enjoy record benefits. We are fed up with injustices', as highlighted in the 15M manifesto *How to Cook a Non-Violent Revolution*. Similarly, protesters expressed a sense of political uselessness – hence injustice – claiming a voice:

> We can vote, but we don't have a voice, and we are frustrated by the politicians' lack of will to develop mechanisms of direct participation in decision-making processes. Mechanisms that would put an end to corruption and to the lack of transparency in politics and public institutions, and that would place the citizen before the markets and other private interests.⁵⁶

Similarly, many citizens felt that they were being affected by a crisis and by neoliberal housing practices that others were responsible for causing. In this vein, one of the most popular slogans of the anti-austerity protests perfectly summarises this feeling: 'It's not a crisis, it's a scam.' This is particularly true for one of the most severe problems for a huge amount of the Spanish population: the housing bubble. Here the concern is not simply that the majority of the population is de facto excluded from housing; rather, the problem is the fact that those who have been integrated into the housing market cannot sustainably afford it, nor face loans payment. Supported by current legislation, over the last few years banks have easily begun legal proceedings against insolvents clients, contributing to the proceedings of house evictions. Paradoxically, Spanish legislation has also contributed to lock people into debt with the banks even after they lose their property.

Given this context, neoliberal governing narratives have contributed to spread the idea of personal responsibility for the crisis, blaming the citizens for their large levels of debt they had accumulated. The media climate, along with legal bases, has backed this diffuse discourse, which has been suggesting that those in mortgage debts had 'lived beyond their means'. As recognised by the same activists involved in the mobilisations against evictions, this feeling of responsibility and guilt has deepened the sense of anxiety of people. However, social mobilisation has dealt with this sense of powerlessness, crucially recognising the emotional and affective dimensions involved in the hegemonic neoliberal discourse. Strategically, during the protests in the streets and in the occupation of public spaces, and against evictions, we have witnessed an attempt to transform this sense of defencelessness into a feeling of empowerment, one that could enable political action and struggle. This shared affective disposition, born as a response to injustice, contributed to the identity formation among protesters and to the creation of an alternative political discourse.

Identity

Emotions contribute to identity formation, which is an essential component of collective action. As with many other political phenomena, protest and social movements involve the formation of individual and collective identities. In this vein, building or reproducing identities is one of the processes through which individuals give meaning to their experiences and the political realm. From inside, social movements see the interconnection between individual-based experience and collective experience. Collective identities are based on, among other things, shared values, attitudes, worldviews, rituals and shared performances in collective protests and actions. These factors set a process of trusting connections among individuals, which is an important element in mobilisations.

Within this context, identity can be both a precondition for and a result of collective action. In both cases, collective action needs the presence of a 'we', which supplies the sense of cohesion and solidarity, as well as the identification of the 'others', which is the collective the movement or collective action moves against.[57] A minimal level of moral empathy, among other emotions bonds, is therefore a necessary step in the demarcation of 'us' and 'them'.

Despite outrage and indignation being considered essential emotions during anti-austerity protests, other affective states such as humiliation and hope were clearly involved and played a key role in generating and sustaining collective actions. As has been argued,[58] participants were also experiencing joy and empowerment from their being involved in public 'encounters' with other peers during the protests – the narrative of being together.[59] As such, both cognitive and emotional mechanisms are embedded into networks of relations. A strong sense of connection between protesters was created and various sets of affects were at play: joy, pride, humour and irony also expressed the prefigurative relations taking place during mobilisations. By creating shared social bonds, these emotions can engender trust and solidarity, and thus form a basis for collective identity and more persistent engagement with the movement.

In this sense, building an identity is an essential moment for individuals and for the collective, and this process not only involves strategic agreements but also demands affective or emotional investments. In an intersubjective interplay of attachments, recognition, feelings and meaning creation, collective identities are formed and shared. In the case of the *Indignados* movement, having 'problems' instead of ideologies or a specific political membership is a clear feature of *inclusiveness*, which marked the *transversal* character of the 15M since its inception. Quoting the manifesto of DRY helps us comprehend this issue:

> Some of us consider ourselves progressive, others conservative. Some of us are believers, some not. Some of us have clearly defined ideologies, others are apolitical, but we are all concerned and *angry* about the political, economic, and social outlook, which we see around us: corruption among politicians, businessmen, and bankers leaving us helpless, without a voice.[60]

In this context, it seems plausible to argue that the *Indignados'* political subject is made up of ordinary, outraged and angry people. Their being angry is indeed what unifies heterogeneous individuals, giving them a political nature. As for the people affected by mortgages, their shared emotional reactions might be seen as a proto-class consciousness, which is characterised by a mix of sense of economic and political frustration, and at once hope for a change. Here, politically, one might recognise a double strain: on the one hand, the neoliberal subjectivity tends to be relatively disengaged. Except for occasional days of rage, the lack of opportunity to imagine an appealing life contributes to a sense of relative frustration and powerlessness. On the other hand, sharing common affective experiences during collective actions helps the creation of a different, transformative, political language, in which a sense of an alternative future is essential. While neoliberalism has over the last decades achieved a discursive hegemony, extending its language into all aspects of economic, social and economic life, the challenge today is precisely to recapture the field of 'discursivity'. Mobilising against neoliberal discourse and practice is then a crucial move in order to create an imagined desirable future.

Action

Emotional responses to a situation perceived as unjust can lead individuals and groups to mobilisations. This response involves the move to protest: from framed emotions to action. In this sense, emotions are an essential factor of what keeps a movement moving, as well the lack of emotional dynamics being able to explain the movements' decline. Although all movements are clearly emotional and strategic at the same time, emotions can play a central role in mobilisation and social change. Therefore, emotions are among the mechanisms that drive people to participate in collective action. Especially the affective responses to a situation perceived as unjust can lead individuals and groups to mobilisations. Similarly to ideology and interests, the affective investments of individuals move people to engage politically. Seen as the *feeling side of values*, emotions can perform an important link between political and moral principles and actions. In this vein, contending the status quo, social movements often re-interpret specific aspects of political reality through an emotional, cognitive and normative re-framing of reality.

In the specific case of the Spanish anti-austerity mobilisations, the fact that a variegated array of emotions contributed to the concrete mobilisations of masses is noteworthy. In this vein, the sense of empowerment and joy among protesters allowed the *Indignados* movement to somehow create the spaces for *Real Democracy* – engaging in a horizontal, inclusive and participatory ways of deciding about 'common matters' – in opposition to the 'institutionalised politics' of political parties. A key common ground for anti-austerity mobilisations is, by various means, the rejection of the old political consensus and parties of the centre-right and centre-left. Similarly, other affective dimensions contributed to trigger political horizons and actions. If, on the one hand indignation about political corruption and banks bail out encouraged people to abstain from voting, the emergence of another 'emotional' signifiers such as 'dignity' in subsequent years – on 22 March 2014 a *March of Dignity* was celebrated in Madrid, gathering people from all over Spain – created the political space for autonomous multitude.[61]

Given this context, there is no doubt that the main target during the heterogeneous cycle of mobilisation in the European context has been the economic programme of the troika (the IMF, the EU and the ECB) and the austerity measures that governments have put into place under its pressure. Concerning the case of housing, the formation of a shared identity around the common perception of the unjust situation contributed to the development of a series of counteractions. Among the multiple activities, the main success of the anti-eviction movement has been blocking of expulsions of citizens from their houses. PAH has to date blocked several hundreds of evictions, primarily gathering at the door of the house that is in proceedings of foreclosure to prevent legal and bank officials from accessing it, or through financial support as a solution to the breakdown in mortgage payments. Moreover, within the repertoire of actions that have characterised the PAH, both the occupation of buildings and what are known in Spanish as 'escraches' played a central role. Being a form of protest that consists of gathering at the domicile of politicians considered as responsible for the unjust situation with the objective of exposing them to public condemnation, 'escraches' have symbolised the public emotional reactions to the crisis and housing bubble. Particularly noteworthy is the fact that the targets of 'escraches' were those politicians who objected to a *Iniciativa Legislativa Popular* (ILP; Popular Legislation Initiative), with which the PAH and other organisations claimed for another regulation on mortgage payments and evictions.[62]

All this shows that while the crisis was primarily identified as economic it also permeates the political sphere. It does so through the mobilising power of emotions: anxiety moves people from the paralysing sense uncertainty towards resistance practices expressed by way of indignation and anger. Thus, with economic and political crisis going hand in hand, the mobilisation has led to the demand for real democracy, and a need to address democratic deficit.

CONCLUSION: 'TINA' AND BEYOND

The Great Recession and the age of austerity have had many social and political consequences, such as countries going bankrupt, the diffusion of inequalities, the rise of unemployment rates, the spread of protest movements and the subsequent birth of new political parties, and so forth. Among the multiple grievances suffered by citizens, foreclosures and evictions have been those that have dramatically informed recent developments in the Spanish context. The images of police and law enforcement officers knocking down doors of houses have become the symbol of the tragedy of the crisis. However, the neoliberal housing practices and their material and visual effects have also turned into a powerful emotional tool, and triggered political engagement. Shared affective reactions about the anguish and pain of people have taken part in the process of reframing the political discourse, and brought the problem of evictions into the public agenda.

As argued by Flesher Fominaya[63] the recent cycle of mobilisation, characterised by massive demonstrations and marches, and occupation of public spaces, is to be considered as the social need to highlight the human drama behind individual and collective suffering caused by austerity politics. In this vein, the emotional responses to the crisis acquired visibility and permeated the political domain. However, these reactions do not simply point to economic grievances. Rather, anti-austerity mobilisations are also a symbol of the illegitimacy of the political elite and the need for a reform of the democratic system. What is more, the political engagement as well as the new political parties born in the aftermath of the crisis is representative of the denial of the 'there is no alternative' (TINA) argument, hegemonic in the public discourse of the equilibrium of the economic system. Hence, by linking the economic and the political crisis – which are seen as intertwined – these phenomena show a broader political state of affairs, and fight against the political exhaustion brought by financial dominance over the political domain. In this sense, both antagonistic movements and new political parties rejected the internalisation of a sense of vain and useless of politics – generally linked to negative emotions, such as insecurity, uncertainty, anxiety, fear and so forth. Linking economic crisis to a crisis of democracy, the normative question has been shifted from the equilibrium of the economic system to the survival of democracy itself.

Neoliberalism, considered as a regime of market-centric rule, will probably maintain its hegemonic position for much longer. Nonetheless, anti-austerity mobilisations and subsequent developments represent an attempt at reviving the very idea of *the future*. While the neoliberal anxious subject seems to be trapped in the dystopia of presentism and dangers, indignation turned constraining affective dispositions into political action and offered an idea of alternative politics.

NOTES

1. Ada Colau and Adrià Alemany, *Vidas Hipotecadas* (Barcelona: Angle Editorial. 2012), 65–66.

2. Eduardo Romanos, 'Evictions, Petitions and Escraches: Contentious Housing in Austerity Spain,' *Social Movement Studies* 13 (2014): 296. Nowadays, a huge amount of empty homes characterise the Spanish housing market. The sum of new

stock left unsold because of the crisis as well as evicted homes resulting from foreclosures forms a surplus of somewhere around six million homes.

3. Romanos, 'Evictions, Petitions and Escraches', 296.

4. Isidro López and Emmanuel Rodríguez, 'The Spanish Model,' *New Left Review* 69 (2011).

5. Colau and Alemany *Vidas Hipotecadas*, 34. Interestingly enough, Colau reminds the connection between the last phase of economic development based on housing and the Francoist period in which property ownership could act as a mechanism for social control, converting insubordinate spirits into more disciplined, moral individuals.

6. Tova Benski and Lauren Langman, 'The Effects of Affects: The Place of Emotions in the Mobilizations of 2011', *Current Sociology* 61 (2013): 525–540; James M. Jasper, 'Emotions and Social Movements: Twenty Years of Theory and Research', *Annual Review of Sociology* 37 (2011): 14.1–14.19.

7. Benjamín Tejerina et al., 'From Indignation to Occupation: A New Wave of Global Mobilization', *Current Sociology* 61 (2013): 377–392; Guy Standing, *The Precariat: The New Dangerous Class* (London and New York: Bloomsbury Academic. 2011).

8. Donatella della Porta, *Can Democracy Be Saved? Participation, Deliberation and Social Movements* (Cambridge: Polity Press. 2013); Donatella della Porta, *Social Movements in Times of Austerity: Bringing Capitalism Back into Protest Analysis* (Cambridge: Polity Press. 2015).

9. Yannis Stavrakakis and Giorgos Katsambekis, 'Left-Wing Populism in the European Periphery: The Case of SYRIZA', *Journal of Political Ideologies* 19 (2014): 119–142; Nadia Urbinati, *Democracy Disfigured: Opinion, Truth, and the People* (Cambridge: Harvard University Press. 2014).

10. Simon Tormey, 'Occupy Wall Street: From Representation to Post-Representation', *Journal of Critical Globalisation Studies* 5 (2012): 132–137. Marina Prentoulis and Lasse Thomassen, 'Political Theory in the Square: Protest, Representation and Subjectification', *Contemporary Political Theory* 12 (2013): 166–184.

11. Ignacia Perugorria and Benjamín Tejerina, 'Politics of the Encounter: Cognition, Emotions, and Networks in the Spanish 15M', *Current Sociology* 61 (2013): 426.

12. David Ost, 'Politics as the Mobilization of Anger. Emotions in Movements and in Power', *European Journal of Social Theory* 7 (2004): 231.

13. Stephen Holmes, *Passions and Constraint: On the Theory of Liberal Democracy* (Chicago: Chicago University Press. 1995), 43.

14. António R. Damasio, *Descartes' Error: Emotion, Reason, and the Human Brain* (New York: Putnam. 1994).

15. Joseph P. Forgas, *Feeling and Thinking: The Role of Affect in Social Cognition* (Cambridge: Cambridge University Press. 2000).

16. Jon Elster, *Strong Feelings: Emotion, Addiction, and Human Behaviour* (Cambridge: MIT Press. 1999).

17. Rebecca Kingston and Leonard Ferry, *Bringing the Passions Back In: The Emotions in Political Philosophy* (Vancouver: UBC Press. 2008); Rebecca Kingston, *Public Passion: Rethinking the Grounds for Political Justice* (Montréal: McGill-Queen's

University Press. 2011); Jeff Goodwin et al., *Passionate Politics: Emotions and Social Movements* (Chicago: University of Chicago Press. 2001).

18. Monica Greco and Paul Stenner, *Emotions: A Social Science Reader* (London: Routledge. 2008); Patricia T. Clough and Jean O'Malley Halley, *The Affective Turn: Theorizing the Social* (Durham, NC: Duke University Press. 2007); Patricia T. Clough, 'The Affective Turn. Political Economy, Biomedia and Bodies', *Theory, Culture & Society* 25 (2008): 1–22.

19. Leonie Huddy et al., 'On the Distinct Political Effects of Anxiety and Anger', in *The Affect Effect: Dynamics of Emotion in Political Thinking and Behaviour*, ed. Russell Neuman et al. (Chicago: Chicago University Press. 2007), 202–230. As one might expect, emotions have been defined in many ways, using many epistemological orientations. A frequent definition suggests that emotions are ways in which individuals react to social situations. Frijda, for instance, defines emotions as 'tendencies to establish, maintain, or disrupt a relationship with the environment . . . so that emotions might be defined as action readiness'. Nico H. Frijda, *The Emotions* (Cambridge: Cambridge University Press. 1987), 71.

20. The most common typology operates by dividing emotions into positive and negative ones. Should emotions be associated primarily with the individual or, on the contrary, with the social and cultural context – or both aspects at once? In this sense, some scholars tend to draw a distinction between primary, natural and universal emotions, and secondary, socially constructed emotions.

21. Helena Flam and Debra King, *Emotions and Social Movements* (London: Routledge. 2005).

22. Flam and King, *Emotions and Social Movements*.

23. Judith N. Shklar and Stanley Hoffmann, *Political Thought and Political Thinkers* (Chicago: University of Chicago Press. 1998), 13.

24. Mark Neocleous, 'Security, Liberty and the Myth of Balance: Towards a Critique of Security Politics', *Contemporary Political Theory* 6 (2007): 131–149; Julian Reid, *The Biopolitics of the War on Terror: Life Struggles, Liberal Modernity and Logistical Societies* (Manchester and New York: Manchester University Press. 2006). In this context, 'resilience' is reshaping the framework of security, in so far as it assumes the not-securable character of life in modern politics, while the logic of security tends to consider this aim as achievable.

25. Max Weber, 'Politics as a Vocation', in *From Max Weber: Essays in Sociology*, ed. Hans H. Gerth and Mills C. Wright (London: Routledge & Kegan Paul. 1970), 79.

26. Ulrich Beck, *World Risk Society* (Malden, MA: Polity Press. 1999).

27. Ulrich Beck, 'The Terrorist Threat: World Risk Society Revisited', *Theory, Culture and Society* 19 (2002): 40.

28. Beck, 'The Terrorist Threat,' 41. Original emphasis.

29. Robert Castel, *L'insécurité sociale : qu'est-ce qu'être protégé ?* (Paris: Édition du Seuil. 2003); Frank Furedi, *The Politics of Fear: Beyond Left and Right* (London: Continuum. 2005).

30. Beck, *World Risk Society*.

31. Bauman, Zygmunt, *Liquid Fear* (Cambridge: Polity Press. 2006).

32. Furedi, *The Politics of Fear*.

33. Joanna Bourke, *Fear: A Cultural History* (Emeryville, CA: Shoemaker Hoard. 2006), 10.
34. Engin Isin, 'The Neurotic Citizen', *Citizenship Studies* 8 (2004): 217–235.
35. Isin, 'The neurotic citizen,' 220.
36. Robert W. Cox, *Political Economy of a Plural World: Critical Reflections on Power, Morals and Civilization* (New York, NY: Routledge. 2002); David Harvey, *A Brief History of Neoliberalism* (Oxford: Oxford University Press. 2005).
37. Jessop Peck, 'Neoliberalizing States: Thin Policies/Hard Outcomes', *Progress in Human Geography* 25 (2001): 445–455.
38. Wendy Brown, 'Neo-Liberalism and the End of Liberal Democracy', *Theory & Event* 7 (2003): 37–59.
39. Standing, *The Precariat*.
40. For a critical view on resilience and neoliberalism see, for instance, David Chandler, 'Beyond Neoliberalism: Resilience, the New Art of Governing Complexity', *Resilience* 2 (2014): 47–63.
41. Ira J. Roseman and Andreas Evdokas, 'Appraisals Cause Experienced Emotions: Experimental Evidence', *Cognition and Emotion* 18 (2004): 1–28.
42. Tormey, 'Occupy Wall Street,' 135.
43. Tejerina et al., 'From Indignation to Occupation'.
44. Manuel Castells, *Networks of Outrage and Hope: Social Movements in the Internet Age* (Cambridge: Polity Press. 2012).
45. Tejerina et al., 'From Indignation to Occupation', 378.
46. Goodwin et al., *Passionate Politics*.
47. Aaron Ben-Ze'ev, *The Subtlety of Emotions* (Cambridge: The MIT Press. 2000), 386.
48. Theodor D. Kemper, *A Social Interactional Theory of Emotion* (New York: Wiley. 1978); Theodor D. Kemper, *Research Agendas in the Sociology of Emotions* (Albany: SUNY Press. 1990).
49. Martha Nussbaum, *Hiding from Humanity: Disgust, Shame, and the Law* (Princeton, NJ: Princeton University Press. 2004), 345.
50. Goodwin et al., *Passionate Politics*; Jasper, *Emotions and Social Movements*.
51. William A. Gamson, *Talking Politics* (Cambridge: Cambridge University Press. 1992), 31–32.
52. Peter Lyman, 'The Domestication of Anger: The Use and Abuse of Anger in Politics', *European Journal of Social Theory* 7 (2004): 133.
53. Gamson, *Talking Politics*, 7, 31–32.
54. Gamson, *Talking Politics*, 31–32.
55. Robert C. Solomon and Mark C. Murphy, *What Is Justice? Classic and Contemporary Readings* (New York: Oxford University Press. 1990), 242.
56. Ignacia Perugorria and Benjamín Tejerina, 'Synchronizing Identities: Crafting the Space of Mobilization in the Spanish 15M', in *The Debt Crisis in the Eurozone. Social Impacts*, ed. Nicholas P. Petropoulos and George O. Tsobanoglou (Newcastle: Cambridge Scholars Publishing. 2014), 296.
57. Alberto Melucci, *Challenging Codes* (Cambridge; New York: Cambridge University Press. 1996).

58. Ignacia Perugorria and Benjamín Tejerina, 'Politics of the Encounter: Cognition, Emotions, and Networks in the Spanish 15M', *Current Sociology* 61 (2013): 424–442.

59. Perugorría and Tejerina, 'Politics of the Encounter,' 437.

60. Democracia Real Ya¡, '*Manifesto*'. 2011. Italics emphasis added.

61. Marina Prentoulis and Lasse Thomassen, 'Autonomy and Hegemony in the Squares: The 2011 Protests in Greece and Spain', in *Radical Democracy and Collective Movements Today: The Biopolitics of the Multitude versus the Hegemony of the People*, ed. Alexandros Kioupkiolis and Giorgos Katsambekis (Farnham: Ashgate. 2014), 221.

62. In February 2013 the PAH collected around one and a half million signatures in order to discuss a Popular Legislation Initiative (ILP). This initiative endorsed a system of mortgage payments that could allow householders to pay off their debt by handing their property back to the bank – something that is not currently possible in Spain. With its absolute parliamentary majority, the conservative party (*Partido Popular*) did not approve the initiative proposed by the PAH. On the contrary, a law proposed by their own parliamentary group was approved, but it did not include the core demands of the ILP.

63. Cristina Flesher Fominaya, 'Redefining the Crisis/Redefining Democracy: Mobilising for the Right to Housing in Spain's PAH Movement', *South European Society and Politics* 4 (2015): 465–485.

BIBLIOGRAPHY

Bauman, Zygmunt. *Liquid Fear*. Cambridge: Polity Press, 2006.
Beck, Ulrich. 'The Terrorist Threat: World Risk Society Revisited'. *Theory, Culture and Society* 19 (2002): 39–55.
Beck, Ulrich. *World Risk Society*. Malden, MA: Polity Press, 1999.
Benski, Tova, and Lauren Langman. 'The Effects of Affects: The Place of Emotions in the Mobilizations of 2011'. *Current Sociology* 61 (2013): 525–540.
Ben-Ze'ev, Aaron. *The Subtlety of Emotions*. Cambridge: The MIT Press, 2000.
Bourke, Joanna. *Fear: A Cultural History*. Emeryville, CA: Shoemaker Hoard, 2006.
Brown, Wendy. 'Neo-Liberalism and the End of Liberal Democracy'. *Theory & Event* 7 (2003): 37–59.
Castel, Robert. *L'insécurité sociale : qu'est-ce qu'être protégé ? Social insecurity: What does it mean to be protected?* Paris: Édition du Seuil, 2003.
Castells, Manuel. *Networks of Outrage and Hope: Social Movements in the Internet Age*. Cambridge: Polity Press, 2012.
Chandler, David. 'Beyond Neoliberalism: Resilience, the New Art of Governing Complexity'. *Resilience* 2 (2014): 47–63.
Clough, Patricia Ticineto. 'The Affective Turn. Political Economy, Biomedia and Bodies'. *Theory, Culture & Society* 25 (2008): 1–22.
Clough, Patricia Ticineto, and Jean O'Malley Halley. *The Affective Turn: Theorizing the Social*. Durham, NC: Duke University Press, 2007.
Colau, Ada, and Adriá Alemany. *Vidas Hipotecadas*. Barcelona: Angle Editorial, 2012.

Cox, W. Robert. *Political Economy of a Plural World: Critical Reflections on Power, Morals and Civilization*. New York: Routledge, 2002.
Damasio, António Rosa. *Descartes' Error: Emotion, Reason, and the Human Brain*. New York: Putnam, 1994.
della Porta, Donatella. *Can Democracy Be Saved? Participation, Deliberation and Social Movements*. Cambridge: Polity Press, 2013.
della Porta, Donatella. *Social Movements in Times of Austerity: Bringing Capitalism Back into Protest Analysis*. Cambridge: Polity Press, 2015.
¡Democracia Real Ya¡. '*Manifesto*'. Accessed 1 March 2013, http://www.democraciarealya.es/manifiesto-comun/manifesto-english.
Elster, Jon. *Strong Feelings: Emotion, Addiction, and Human Behaviour*. Cambridge: MIT Press, 1999.
Flam, Helena, and Debra King. *Emotions and Social Movements*. London: Routledge, 2005.
Flesher Fominaya, Cristina. 'Redefining the Crisis/Redefining Democracy: Mobilising for the Right to Housing in Spain's PAH Movement'. *South European Society and Politics* 4 (2015): 465–485.
Forgas, Joseph Paul. *Feeling and Thinking: The Role of Affect in Social Cognition*. Cambridge: Cambridge University Press, 2000.
Furedi, Frank. *The Politics of Fear: Beyond Left and Right*. London: Continuum, 2005.
Frijda, H. Nico. *The Emotions*. Cambridge: Cambridge University Press, 1987.
Gamson, William Anthony. *Talking Politics*. Cambridge: Cambridge University Press, 1992.
Goodwin, Jeff, James M. Jasper and Francesca Polletta. *Passionate Politics: Emotions and Social Movements*. Chicago: University of Chicago Press, 2001.
Greco, Monica, and Paul Stenner. *Emotions: A Social Science Reader*. London: Routledge, 2008.
Harvey, David. *A Brief History of Neoliberalism*. Oxford: Oxford University Press, 2005.
Holmes, Stephen. *Passions and Constraint: On the Theory of Liberal Democracy*. Chicago: Chicago University Press, 1995.
Huddy, Leonie, Stanley Feldman and Erin Cassese. 'On the Distinct Political Effects of Anxiety and Anger'. In *The Affect Effect: Dynamics of Emotion in Political Thinking and Behaviour*, edited by Russell Neuman, George E. Marcus, Michael Mackuen and Ann N. Crigler, 202–230. Chicago: Chicago University Press, 2007.
Isin, Engin. 'The Neurotic Citizen'. *Citizenship Studies* 8 (2004): 217–235.
Jasper, James M. 'Emotions and Social Movements: Twenty Years of Theory and Research'. *Annual Review of Sociology* 37 (2011): 14.1–14.19
Kemper, D. Theodor. *A Social Interactional Theory of Emotion*. New York: Wiley, 1978.
Kemper, D. Theodor. *Research Agendas in the Sociology of Emotions*. Albany: SUNY Press, 1990.
Kingston, Rebecca. *Public Passion: Rethinking the Grounds for Political Justice*. Montréal: McGill-Queen's University Press, 2011.

Kingston, Rebecca, and Leonard Ferry. *Bringing the Passions Back In: The Emotions in Political Philosophy*. Vancouver: UBC Press, 2008.
López, Isidro, and Emmanuel Rodríguez. 'The Spanish Model'. *New Left Review* 69 (2011): 5–29.
Lyman, Peter. 'The Domestication of Anger: The Use and Abuse of Anger in Politics'. *European Journal of Social Theory* 7 (2004): 133–147.
Melucci, Alberto. *Challenging Codes*. Cambridge/New York: Cambridge University Press, 1996.
Neocleous. Mark. 'Security, Liberty and the Myth of Balance: Towards a Critique of Security Politics'. *Contemporary Political Theory* 6 (2007): 131–149.
Nussbaum, Martha. *Hiding from Humanity: Disgust, Shame, and the Law*. Princeton, NJ: Princeton University Press, 2004.
Ost, David. 'Politics as the Mobilization of Anger. Emotions in Movements and in Power'. *European Journal of Social Theory* 7 (2004): 229–244.
Peck, Jessop. 'Neoliberalizing states: Thin Policies/Hard Outcomes'. *Progress in Human Geography* 25 (2001): 445–455.
Perugorria, Ignacia, and Benjamín Tejerina. 'Politics of the Encounter: Cognition, Emotions, and Networks in the Spanish 15M'. *Current Sociology* 61 (2013): 424–442.
Perugorria, Ignacia, and Benjamín Tejerina. 'Synchronizing Identities: Crafting the Space of Mobilization in the Spanish 15M'. In *The Debt Crisis in the Eurozone. Social Impacts*, edited by Nicholas P. Petropoulos, and George O. Tsobanoglou, 282–304. Newcastle: Cambridge Scholars Publishing, 2014.
Prentoulis, Marina, and Lasse Thomassen. 'Political Theory in the Square: Protest, Representation and Subjectification'. *Contemporary Political Theory* 12 (2013): 166–184.
Prentoulis, Marina, and Lasse Thomassen. 'Autonomy and Hegemony in the Squares: The 2011 Protests in Greece and Spain'. In *Radical Democracy and Collective Movements Today: The Biopolitics of the Multitude versus the Hegemony of the People*, edited by Alexandros Kioupkiolis and Giorgos Katsambekis, 213–234. Farnham: Ashgate, 2014.
Reid, Julian. *The Biopolitics of the War on Terror: Life Struggles, Liberal Modernity and Logistical Societies*. Manchester and New York: Manchester University Press, 2006.
Romanos, Eduardo. 'Evictions, Petitions and Escraches: Contentious Housing in Austerity Spain'. *Social Movement Studies* 13 (2014): 296–302.
Roseman, J. Ira, and Andreas Evdokas. 'Appraisals Cause Experienced Emotions: Experimental Evidence'. *Cognition and Emotion* 18 (2004): 1–28.
Shklar, N. Judith, and Stanley Hoffmann. *Political Thought and Political Thinkers*. Chicago: University of Chicago Press, 1998.
Solomon, Robert C., and Mark C. Murphy. *What Is Justice? Classic and Contemporary Readings*. New York: Oxford University Press, 1990.
Standing, Guy. *The Precariat: The New Dangerous Class*. London and New York: Bloomsbury Academic, 2011.

Stavrakakis, Yannis, and Giorgos Katsambekis. 'Left-Wing Populism in the European Periphery: The Case of SYRIZA'. *Journal of Political Ideologies* 19 (2014): 119–142.

Tejerina, Benjamín, Ignacia Perugorría, Tova Benski and Laura Langman. 'From Indignation to Occupation: A New Wave of Global Mobilization'. *Current Sociology* 61 (2013): 377–392.

Tormey, Simon. 'Occupy Wall Street: From Representation to Post-Representation'. *Journal of Critical Globalisation Studies* 5 (2012): 132–137.

Urbinati, Nadia. *Democracy Disfigured: Opinion, Truth, and the People*. Cambridge: Harvard University Press, 2014.

Weber, Max. 'Politics as a Vocation'. In *From Max Weber: Essays in Sociology*, edited by Hans H. Gerth and Mills C. Wright, 77–128. London: Routledge & Kegan Paul, 1970.

Chapter 9

Neurotic Neoliberalism and the Economics of Anxiety

Japhy Wilson

Neoliberalism remains the dominant economic ideology of our times. For over three decades, economic reforms have adhered to the neoliberal principles of privatisation, deregulation and the dismantling of the welfare state. The free market revolution was driven forward by Thatcherism and Reaganomics in the West, and by the World Bank and the International Monetary Fund in the 'structural adjustment' of the so-called developing world. We were told that free competition in all dimensions of economic life would ensure the best of all possible worlds. In contrast to this utopian vision, the outcome has been persistent poverty, economic oligarchy and a whirlwind of financial crises that spiralled around the world before finally entering the heartlands of global capitalism with the financial crash of 2008 and the ensuing 'Great Recession'. Yet in the aftermath of this unprecedented crisis, neoliberalism has once again emerged as the dominant ideology of Western capitalism. This extraordinary resilience has led many to perceive neoliberalism as a forbiddingly self-assured and one-dimensional 'shock doctrine'.[1] But close attention to its evolution reveals it as a contradictory and anxiety-ridden process, which has morphed continuously over the course of its history, while retaining an obsessive commitment to an underlying vision of the world.

According to Jacques Lacan, anxiety is not caused by separation from an object of desire, as is commonly assumed, but by the overwhelming proximity of that object in the Real. And the Real is not reducible to our everyday experience of material reality, but is an unrepresented domain of traumatic elements that our experiential reality is structured to exclude.[2] This chapter draws on the Lacanian critique of ideology in reconceptualising neoliberalism as an anxious social fantasy that structures reality against the traumatic proximity of the Real of Capital, which is most directly confronted in moments of capitalist crisis and global economic breakdown. I argue that the resilience and transformability of neoliberalism can be explained as a form of obsessional neurosis, in which the neoliberal engages in frenetic activity to prevent anything Real from happening. This argument is developed through an analysis of the career of the influential development economist Jeffrey Sachs. From shock therapy to the salvation of 'Africa', Sachs's peculiar trajectory betrays the classic traits of the neoliberal neurosis. I conclude with some reflections on 'zombie neoliberalism' and the perils of resistance.

NEOLIBERALISM AS OBSESSIONAL NEUROSIS

Neoliberalism differs from other utopian ideologies in the way that it understands its own project. For the neoliberal, the acquisitive individual is the essence of human nature, and market society is the natural order of the social world. Neoliberalism does not therefore set out to create a world that never existed, but rather to liberate a pre-existing reality from the bureaucratic undergrowth of the interventionist state. By removing this undergrowth, the neoliberal aims to release 'spontaneous market forces', and 'entrepreneurial zeal', which will guarantee an optimally efficient distribution of goods and services without the need for government planning or 'heavy-handed' regulation. Neoliberalism therefore represents itself as 'pragmatic' and 'non-ideological', in contrast to the failed utopian ideologies of the past. According to Slavoj Žižek, however, 'it is precisely the neutralisation of some features into a spontaneously accepted background that marks out ideology at its purest.'[3] In its deepest and most powerful form, Žižek argues, ideology operates not as an appearance projected onto reality, but as a 'social fantasy' structuring reality itself against what Lacan called the Real – an ominous presence-absence that is excluded from our everyday experience. Without fantasy, reality disintegrates, and the subject confronts the Real as a traumatic and incomprehensible force.[4]

Far from being pragmatic and non-ideological, neoliberalism should be understood as a social fantasy that structures 'reality' against the Real of Capital. Fantasies are formulated through a process of repression and disavowal in response traumatic events, in which the symbolic and imaginary coordinates of 'reality' are ruptured by the chaotic maelstrom of the Real.[5] In repression, the traumatic event is excluded entirely from consciousness, though it remains operative in the unconscious, from which it continues to exert its destabilising influences. In the subtler operation of disavowal, the Real is incorporated into the symbolic universe through a variety of displacements, through which its properly traumatic dimension is at least temporarily diminished.[6] Both of these strategies, however, are doomed to failure, and reality inevitably comes to be plagued by 'symptoms', certain stains upon the symbolic fabric, which mark the indelible presence of the Real.[7] In cases of obsessional neurosis, the recurrent appearance of these symptoms provokes frenetic activity in order to stop the stains from spreading, and to guard against the possibility of a repeat encounter with the Real.[8] Crucial to this process is the construction of ideological fantasies that infuse reality with a sense of stability and order, and which fill out the gaps and voids in the symbolic order. Fantasy is therefore not an escape from reality, but is integral to the structure of reality itself, constituting 'the frame through which we experience the world as consistent and meaningful'.[9]

Žižek defines capital as the Real of our age, in which ' "reality" is the social reality of the actual people involved in the productive process, while the Real is the inexorable "spectral" logic of Capital which determines what goes on in social reality'.[10] The Real of Capital does not exist as a quantitatively measurable inventory of things, or as a static relationship between sociologically defined classes, rather it *ex-sists*[11] as value-in-motion – as the alienated product of human labour which comes to develop a quasi-autonomous, self-expansionary and crisis-ridden dynamic that increasingly imposes itself upon social reality as 'an abstract form of domination'.[12] Capital *ex-sists* as an invisible presence-absence only identifiable by its effects; as the void constituted by the class relation that cleaves the fabric of capitalist society and as the spectral and traumatic law of value that the neoliberal social fantasy operates to disavow.

The neoliberal fantasy is based on Adam Smith's vision of a natural and harmonious market society, in which the self-interested activities of individual entrepreneurs are mediated by the invisible hand of the market to ensure the optimal allocation of resources. This ideology operates at the level of fantasy, to the extent that it is perceived not as a utopia to be constructed, or as a vision to be projected onto an intransigent reality, but rather as a natural reality already immanent in the structures of the social world.[13] The neoliberal fantasy functions to fill out the voids of the bourgeois symbolic universe against the Real of Capital: value is concealed by marginal utility; class relations are obscured by freedom of exchange; the crisis-ridden dynamics of capitalism are nullified by the assumption of perfectly competitive equilibrium and the spectral logic of capital as an abstract form of domination is expressed in disavowed form as the benign operation of the self-regulating market. In the case of neoliberalism, then, as Žižek argues more generally:

> Ideology is not a dreamlike illusion that we build to escape reality; in its basic dimension it is a fantasy-construction which serves as a support for our reality itself: an 'illusion' which structures our effective social relations and thereby masks some insupportable Real. . . . The function of ideology is not to offer us a point of escape from our reality but to offer . . . social reality itself as an escape from some traumatic, Real kernel.[14]

The trajectory of the neoliberal project can be interpreted in precisely these terms, and is marked by repeated attempts to structure reality as an escape from the traumatic Real of Capital. Adam Smith's theory of the invisible hand was itself born in the midst of the violent establishment of capitalist social relations, providing Smith with a reassuring vision that concealed 'the harsh reality of the world around him'.[15] The economists of the Mont Pelerin Society likewise formulated the neoliberal project in the context of the Great Depression, the Second World War and the rise of communism, and have described themselves as 'drawn together by a common sense of crisis', and 'huddled together . . . for warmth on a cold dark night'.[16] In this traumatic moment, the neoliberal fantasy acquired 'an irresistible attraction . . . the almost silent hum of a perfectly running machine; the apparent stillness of the exact balance of counter-acting pressures; the automatic smooth recovery from a chance disturbance'.[17]

Neoliberalism rose to hegemonic status through representing subsequent economic crises as crises of Keynesianism or developmentalism, against which the neoliberal project could be advanced as a return to the natural order of a market society.[18] From the 1980s onwards, however, with the consolidation of neoliberalism as the hegemonic ideology, these crises began to tear through the fabric of the neoliberal fantasy itself. The continuity of the neoliberal project has thus taken the form of an increasingly elaborate process of disavowal, through which the symptoms of the Real of Capital have been incorporated into the symbolic universe of neoliberalism.[19] Hence the proliferation of discourses of 'market failure', 'imperfect competition', 'bad equilibrium' and so on, which have modified the neoliberal imaginary while leaving its fundamental coordinates unchanged, and which have framed the trajectory of the neoliberal project towards increasingly intensive forms of social engineering.[20] In the field of international development, for example, this trend has been embodied in the transition from the Washington Consensus to the Post-Washington Consensus, which retains the basic principles of the former, while augmenting them with multiple social interventions than aim to address the proliferating symptoms of uneven capitalist development in order to maintain the neoliberal ideal of 'rational utility-maximising individuals engaged in harmonious exchange relations'.[21] Despite their divergence from orthodox neoliberalism, the Post-Washington Consensus and other forms of 'roll-out neoliberalism' should therefore be understood as preserving, rather than transforming, the fundamental structures of the neoliberal fantasy.

From this perspective, the evolution of the neoliberal project appears not as the meticulous manipulation of social reality, but as a series of anxiety-ridden attempts to hold the very fabric of reality together, through constant ideological modifications devoted to explaining away the symptoms of the Real of Capital in such a way that the contours of the neoliberal fantasy can be retained. This process typifies the behaviour of the obsessional neurotic, who 'builds up a whole system enabling him to postpone the encounter [with the Real] ad infinitum'.[22] We can therefore conceptualise neoliberalism not as a pragmatic technocratic project, but as a form of obsessional neurosis. The remainder of this chapter develops this argument in the case of Jeffrey Sachs, interpreting the failure of shock therapy in Russia as a traumatic event, in which the neoliberal fantasy was shattered by the Real of Capital, and exploring the strategies of repression and disavowal through which he has sought to reconstruct the coordinates of his fantasy.[23]

FROM SHOCK THERAPY TO CLINICAL ECONOMICS

Jeffrey Sachs was born in Detroit in 1954. For Sachs, as for the members of the Mont Pelerin Society before him, the initial appeal of neoclassical economics was rooted in an obscure dread of communism. Sachs describes a high school trip to Russia and a subsequent visit to East Germany as life-changing experiences, in which he was confronted by the differences between capitalism and communism in ways that caused him to question the inherent superiority of the capitalist system.[24] In 1972, Sachs entered Harvard to read economics, where he was introduced to the work of the key figures of the Mont Pelerin Society – Friedman, Hayek and Von Mises. His initial doubts about capitalism were allayed, and as Sachs recalls, 'I *learned about a way of seeing the world*'.[25] Once immersed in the neoliberal fantasy, Sachs rose rapidly through the academic ranks at Harvard, becoming a tenured professor in 1983 at the age of 28. Two years later, a Bolivian delegation requested his assistance in managing a crisis of hyperinflation. It was here that Sachs first developed the doctrine that became known as 'shock therapy', based on the imposition of a sudden and systematic package of neoliberal reforms, including privatisation, trade liberalisation, macroeconomic stabilisation and the abolition of subsidies and price controls. The speed and comprehensiveness of shock therapy was designed both to shock the economy into health, and to shock the population with its immediacy, in order to avoid effective political contestation.[26]

The implementation of shock therapy in Bolivia seemed to confirm the reality of the neoliberal fantasy, by ending hyperinflation and facilitating a rapid transition to a free market economy, despite being characterised by increased poverty and political repression.[27] Sachs received international acclaim, leading to consultancy roles around the world in which he was invited to repeat his experiment. When communism began to collapse, Sachs returned to Eastern Europe, contributing to shock therapy programmes in Poland and elsewhere. Despite inducing a deep recession with severe social consequences, Sachs's role in Poland was again hailed as a triumph. Sachs was described in the *New York Times* as 'the Indiana Jones of economics',[28] and commentators marvelled at his 'Sachs appeal'.[29]

In November 1991, while still only 37, Sachs was invited to serve as an economic advisor to the Yeltsin administration, with the responsibility of planning Russia's transition from communism to capitalism. Russia was the place where Sachs had first been confronted by an alternative system of economic organisation, against which he had developed a conceptual framework that had affirmed the naturalness and superiority of the capitalist system. This framework had inspired his political interventions around the world, which seemed to offer dramatic confirmation of its validity. Now, riding a wave of elite adulation, Sachs had the opportunity to implement shock therapy in Russia itself, at a truly world-historical moment in the consolidation of global capitalism. As Sachs himself recalls, 'Communism was falling, and I was pinching myself because I was in the centre of this, the absolute epicentre of it.'[30]

At that moment, disaster struck. Russia's shock therapy programme resulted in 'the longest and deepest recession in recorded human history'.[31] Industrial production halved between 1990 and 1999,[32] and the number of people living in poverty increased from 2 million in 1989 to 74 million in 1996.[33] Furthermore, the Russian privatisation process of 1992–1994 – the largest and most rapid privatisation in world history – has been directly correlated with a dramatic increase in mortality rates,[34] while also facilitating the rise of the notorious 'oligarchs'.[35] In 1994, Sachs resigned from the Yeltsin administration, and abandoned Russia to its continued implosion.[36] He has since described Russia's collapse as a 'whirlwind',[37] which generated 'confusion, anxiety, and [a] profound sense of bewilderment about market forces',[38] and which he experienced as 'life in the shock-trauma unit'.[39] This language conveys the profound disorientation of someone whose fantasy frame has disintegrated, and who is suddenly confronted by the Real of Capital, revealed not as a harmonious natural order, but as a formless vortex, a destructive force operating beyond the limits of control:

> Fantasy . . . sustains the subject's 'sense of reality'. When the phantasmatic frame disintegrates, the subject undergoes a 'loss of reality' and starts to perceive reality as an 'unreal' nightmarish universe with no firm ontological foundation; this nightmarish universe is not 'pure fantasy' but, on the contrary, *that which remains of reality after reality is deprived of its support in fantasy*.[40]

As Sarah Kay has argued, the shock of the Real thus 'makes legible . . . what was repressed or rendered invisible by the current order. However, the Event and its truth are unrecognisable within the order of knowledge that is sanctioned by the prevailing ontology'.[41] Despite being confronted by Real of

Capital, Sachs was therefore unable to comprehend the 'truth' of capitalism that Russia had laid bare – its grounding in the production of specific class relations, its generation of poverty and inequality, and its uncontrollable, crisis-ridden dynamics. In the years following his abandonment of Russia, Sachs published a series of papers celebrating the final consolidation of 'a global capitalist world system, with profound benefits for both rich and poor countries',[42] and setting out a vision of capitalism from which all symptoms of the Real had been erased. Marx, he argued, had been correct in his prediction of the triumphant march of globalisation, but had been limited by 'a very crude labour theory of value, according to which . . . the income of capitalists resulted from the exploitation of labour'.[43] Equally, Keynes had been mistaken in his claim that capitalism was inherently unstable, as the Great Depression had proved to be 'a one-time fluke of grotesque proportions' rather than indicating 'an intrinsic feature of industrial capitalism'.[44] Furthermore, colonialism was not the pioneer of capitalism, but was to be ranked alongside communism and developmentalism as examples of failed non-market systems.[45] Capitalism was thus cleansed of exploitation, crisis and past violence. Yet these beatific eulogies were interrupted by incongruous visions of possible social collapse, of 'chronic chaos', 'turbulence and value destruction', 'disease ravaged societies' and 'an orgy of . . . lawlessness and . . . war'.[46]

The seemingly involuntary manifestation of such apocalyptic imagery within Sachs's determinedly Panglossian representation of global capitalism can be interpreted as the return of the repressed – as the intrusion of the Real within a symbolic universe from which it has been forcibly excluded.[47] Over time, however, Sachs's understanding of capitalism has come to be characterised less by repression than by disavowal. Poverty, inequality and other symptoms of the internal contradictions of capitalism are now increasingly acknowledged, but are explained in terms of external pathologies threatening the natural health of the capitalist social body. Sachs's work in this regard includes a revival of environmental determinism, in which uneven geographical development is attributed to inherent environmental differences rather than political-economic processes.[48] He has also sought to reframe the relationship between poverty and health, arguing that poor health is a cause of poverty rather than vice versa, and reducing the value of health care to its quantifiable contribution to labour productivity.[49] Continuing the medical metaphors of shock therapy, Sachs now describes his approach as 'clinical economics',[50] according to which multiple 'infectious agents' can contribute to the crisis of a normally healthy system, provoking 'a downward spiral of catastrophe'.[51] These external agents include 'urgent problems involving poverty traps, agronomy, climate, disease, transport, gender and a host of other pathologies that undermine economic development'.[52]

From this perspective, capitalism appears not as a social order to be constructed, but as a natural body to be returned to health.[53] Yet if actually existing capitalism is so chronically 'diseased', what grounds Sachs's belief in its natural health? Here we reach the level of the 'fundamental fantasy', which for Žižek is always a 'fantasy of origins'.[54] Žižek identifies Adam Smith's mythical prehistory of capitalism as the quintessential fantasy of origins,[55] and it is precisely this fantasy that grounds Sachs's faith in the natural health of capitalism. Following the Russian crisis, Sachs began to increasingly invoke the name of Adam Smith as the 'subject supposed to know' – the figure whose knowledge the subject typically appeals to in the generation of new meaning.[56] The attraction of Smith for Sachs is clear. As discussed previously, Smith himself was concerned with providing an account of capitalism that removed all traces of internal antagonism. Central to this account was an imagined history of the original accumulation of capital as a natural and inevitable process. According to Smith, the origins of capitalism lay in private smallholding farmers accumulating capital by dint of their own frugality, and putting it to work in the process of further accumulation, leading to the division of labour and the growth of trade, and resulting in the peaceful emergence of a commercial society of small-scale entrepreneurs.[57] In setting out his own account of economic development, Sachs reproduces this Smithian fantasy of origins, telling a story of the emergence of capitalism through the accumulative activities of 'a single farm household',[58] which 'exemplifies Smith's insight'.[59] Through hard work the household acquires some savings, moves from subsistence to cash crops, upgrades its capital inputs and acquires more land.[60] Capitalism, Sachs concludes, is the aggregate outcome of this process operating 'through the interactions of thousands or millions of households linked together by markets'.[61] This, then, is the naturally healthy capitalist social body that clinical economics endeavours to cure and protect.

Adam Smith's fantasy of origins can thus be identified as the fundamental fantasy upon which Sachs has structured his system of disavowal, through which symptoms of the Real of Capital appear as external pathologies, rather than internal contradictions. Yet as Marx has argued in his critique of Smith's account of original accumulation, this 'paradise lost of the bourgeoisie' functioned precisely to obscure the inherent violence of capitalism as a social system founded upon primitive accumulation – the separation of the peasantry from the land through which capitalist social relations were historically established.[62] This founding violence was implicit in the rapid privatisation programmes so central to shock therapy, but it was only in Russia that Sachs was confronted with the full material force of its social implications. Smith's fantasy of origins is therefore a screen that shields Sachs not only from the Real of Capital but also from his own instrumentality in the violence of its production. As Žižek insists, 'There is no order of being as a positive ontologically consistent whole: the false semblance of such an order relies on the self-obliteration of the [violent foundational] Act.'[63] The following section interprets the Millennium Villages Project as a further attempt at 'obliteration' in this sense, through which Sachs has sought to realise his fantasy of origins within the supposedly abject space of 'Africa'.

THE SUBLIME OBJECT OF NEOLIBERAL IDEOLOGY

Since the start of the new millennium, Jeffrey Sachs has successfully reinvented himself as a development guru. His work on clinical economics discussed in the previous section led to his appointment in 2002 as the UN secretary general's Special Advisor on the Millennium Development Goals, and in the same year he was appointed director of the Earth Institute at Columbia University. He has made high-profile journeys to sub-Saharan Africa with celebrities such as Bono, Madonna and Angelina Jolie, and was listed among *Time* magazine's 100 most influential people in the world in 2004 and 2005. In his best-selling anti-poverty manifesto, *The End of Poverty*, Sachs distances himself from shock therapy, and argues for an increased role for state intervention and international aid in providing the 'big push' necessary for poor countries to 'gain a foothold on the bottom rung [of] the ladder of development'.[64] Influential critics of neoliberalism, including David Harvey[65] and Naomi Klein,[66] have suggested that Sachs's new agenda indicates an abandonment of neoliberalism. Equally, unreconstructed neoliberals such as the development economist William Easterly have attacked Sachs for betraying the fundamental tenets of neoliberalism by engaging in 'utopian social engineering'.[67] Here I suggest that, on the contrary, Sachs's newfound concern with poverty in sub-Saharan Africa continues to betray the anxious compulsions of the neoliberal neurosis.

Žižek argues that when the Real of Capital 'is disavowed, when its key structuring role is suspended, other factors. . . . may come to bear an inordinate weight; indeed, they may bear all the weight of the sufferings produced by capitalism'.[68] For Sachs, it is 'Africa' that has come to bear this weight. Following his abandonment of Russia in 1994, Sachs became fixated on sub-Saharan Africa, making his first journey there in 1995.[69] Sachs recalls experiencing Africa as a 'horrific catastrophe',[70] 'collapsing from social and economic disorder',[71] and characterised by the 'omnipresence of disease and death',[72] and he persistently depicts the continent as the land of 'the voiceless dying',[73] in which 'people have nothing and are not even successful enough to stay alive'.[74] Sub-Saharan Africa is of course confronted by very severe socio-economic problems. Nevertheless, the apocalyptic imagery with which 'Africa' is relentlessly portrayed by Sachs, and his sudden shift of attention from Russia to Africa, together suggest that the disturbing symptoms of the former may have been displaced onto the latter. Writing in 1994, only months after leaving Russia, Sachs contrasted Russia's circumstances to those of Africa, arguing that 'If its reforms are given a chance, Russia will prove not merely viable economically, but highly promising. The same cannot be said of . . . Africa, where misrule, disease, and civil strife have left hundreds of millions untouched by the forces of global economic integration.'[75] For Sachs, then, the discovery of Africa allowed the symptoms of shock therapy's failure in Russia to be displaced into an abject space in which they could be attributed not to global capitalism, but rather to its absence, appearing as grotesque aberrations of poverty, crisis and death, in relation to which Sachs has been able to reconstruct his own identity as an economic doctor administering emergency treatment.

Within the symbolic universe of Jeffrey Sachs, Africa has thus come to function as what Žižek would call a 'sublime object of ideology'.[76] A sublime object is a common material object which acquires a peculiar fascination for the subject, due not to some inherent essence, but to its symbolic location as an object that both obscures and embodies the repressed presence of the Real. The sublime object provides stability to the symbolic structure by concealing the traumatic Real within it, yet at the same time, the Real 'shines through' this object, illuminating it with an uncanny allure that is both terrifying and compelling.[77] For Sachs, 'Africa' can be understood as a sublime object in this sense, concealing the void in his symbolic universe that the Russian crisis had revealed, but bathed in the light of the Real of Capital that shines behind it, leading Sachs to recoil in horror – as demonstrated by his apocalyptic descriptions of the continent – but also drawing him towards it as site for intervention in which the Real can be meaningfully engaged with, if only in disavowed form. As Sachs himself says of his experience of Africa, in terms that capture this unsettling mixture of horror and fascination, 'The dominant experience is disease and death; *it was shocking and riveting on an emotional level.*'[78]

In 2005, Sachs published *The End of Poverty*, in which he set out his strategy for ending extreme poverty in Africa. In the same year the United Nations' Millennium Project published an influential report, which was produced by a 250-strong task force chaired by Sachs himself. The report provided the policy detail to accompany the messianic vision of *The End of Poverty*, and proposed a comprehensive approach to the achievement of the Millennium Development Goals.[79] The fundamental assumption underpinning the Millennium Project is that 'If every village has a road, access to transport, a clinic, electricity, safe drinking water, education, and other essential inputs, *the villagers in poor countries will show the same determination and entrepreneurial zeal of people all over the world.*'[80] This appeal to the universal human nature of *homo economicus* is combined with a Dickensian fantasy of the deserving poor, who are 'hard working, prepared to struggle to stay afloat and to get ahead . . . They are also ready to govern themselves responsibly, ensuring that any help they receive is used for the benefit of the group rather than pocketed by powerful individuals'.[81]

Here we can see the outlines of the Smithian fantasy of origins discussed in the previous section – the imagined history of capitalist development based on the entrepreneurialism and community spirit of the smallholder village. Sachs has sought to realise this fantasy in the Millennium Villages Project (MVP), which he launched in 2006 to demonstrate the efficacy of his development strategy. The MVP applied his agenda in clusters of villages across ten countries in sub-Saharan Africa, with the aim of achieving the Millennium Development Goals by their deadline at the end of 2015.[82] Funded by his own Millennium Promise philanthropic organisation, and drawing on the scientific expertise of the Earth Institute, the MVP constituted Sachs's first direct engagement in policy implementation since his abandonment of Russia. As such, the project can be interpreted as a further step in the reconstitution of his social fantasy, through which he sought to reveal the immanence of a harmonious market society within the abject space of 'Africa'. According to Sachs, this social order was already latent in African reality, and would spontaneously emerge as soon as the right conditions were in place:

> Almost all of Africa is the private sector. Farmers, that's the private sector. . . . But private sector doesn't mean you just leave them alone. . . . They can't get started because they're so impoverished. So we should help a private sector-led development by helping these farmers use inputs, boost their productivity. . . . Bring in microfinance and let them rip. And that's basically the model.[83]

The irony, however, is that far from demonstrating the natural order of a market society, the MVP demonstrates the extent to which this society must be socially produced. The first five-year phase of the project included a comprehensive and integrated set of interventions targeting all dimensions of everyday life, and focused on raising the inhabitants' human, social, physical, natural and financial capital to 'the threshold level, above which the villages can move towards self-sustaining growth'.[84] Beginning in 2011, the second five-year phase was focused primarily on 'business development'.[85] Subsidies were replaced by microcredits for farm inputs, links were established with private sector agribusinesses and peasant farmers were encouraged to 'diversify to off-farm employment', and to make the shift 'from sub-subsistence to small-scale entrepreneurs'.[86] Having begun his career with shock therapy, which assumed that the removal of state impediments would be sufficient to reveal the spontaneous order of a market society, Sachs was thus finally forced to engineer that society in its entirety in the form of the Millennium Villages.

The success of this paradoxical utopia would have allowed Sachs to finally reconstitute his social fantasy in the face of the Real of Capital revealed by the crisis in Russia. Yet instead of embodying the fairy-tale story imagined by Sachs, the MVP has become another site of controversy and failure. In 2010, the project published a progress report that made dramatic claims of success.[87] These claims, however, were called into question by evaluation experts who argued that the project's research methodology had been fundamentally compromised by its failure to establish control villages against which to judge the relative progress of the Millennium Villages themselves. Without such control villages, it was impossible to determine the extent to which progress over time within the Millennium Villages could be attributed to the project, as opposed to broader national and regional trends.[88] Sachs rejected control villages as 'unethical', and the MVP continued to report impressive results based on the same methodology, which continued to be disputed.[89] The issue came to a head in 2012, when the MVP was forced to retract claims regarding the reduction of child mortality that it had published in *The Lancet*.[90] This was followed by a highly critical editorial in *Nature*.[91] As an article in *Foreign Policy* concluded, 'No-one takes the Millennium Villages seriously . . . no-one in development economics.'[92]

Once again, Sachs's fantasy frame was disintegrating under the weight of the Real. Having lost the argument on the terrain of research methodology, Sachs sought to hold his fantasy together by appealing to the direct experience of empirical reality, dismissing the evaluation experts as 'critics who don't seem to ever leave their offices, don't know what's happening in the field, don't really see it'.[93] In 2013, however, *Vanity Fair* journalist Nina Munk published a damning account of her first-hand experiences of the Millennium Villages in northern Kenya and southern Uganda, which William Easterly cited as proof that Sachs's 'idea that aid could rapidly bring the end of poverty was wrong'.[94] Further research on the Millennium Villages in Uganda revealed that the project was functioning to deepen existing relations of inequality,[95] while research on the project in Ghana demonstrated that its fantasy of harmonious capitalist development had been shattered by a gold mining boom driven in part by mining corporations financing the project as an element of their corporate social responsibility programmes.[96] Just as had happened in the aftermath of the Russian debacle, Sachs once again found himself abandoned by the global elite who had previously endorsed him. Bill Gates, one of his philanthropic supporters, published an article distancing himself from the MVP, and accusing Sachs of 'wearing blinders' in his determined rejection of all criticism of the project.[97] This phrase precisely captures the function of the fantasy frame in structuring 'reality' in relation to the Real. Far from holding these blinders in place, the MVP has confronted Sachs with the 'return of the repressed' that it was supposed to protect him from, by once again exposing both the Real of Capital and his own instrumentality in its social production.

CONCLUSION: THE DEATH DRIVE OF ZOMBIE NEOLIBERALISM

This chapter has drawn on the case of Jeffrey Sachs in conceptualising neoliberalism as an anxious form of crisis management, which operates less as a utopian ideal to be constructed within reality than as a social fantasy structuring reality itself. The persistence and transformability of the neoliberal project can accordingly be explained, not as the calculative manipulation of social reality, but as an increasingly desperate struggle to hold reality together, against the traumatic incursions of the Real of Capital. It is this continual struggle, advancing through multiple processes of repression and disavowal, which has driven the neoliberal project towards ever-more intensive forms of social engineering, resulting in the social production of the supposedly natural order of a market society. This constant anxious activity, directed towards ensuring the stability of the subject's symbolic universe against encounters with the Real, is the definitive characteristic of obsessional neurosis. For this reason, I have suggested that the neoliberal project can be conceptualised in terms of a 'neoliberal neurosis'. This is not to claim that all neoliberals are neurotic. On the contrary, the parameters of mainstream debate are increasingly defined by neurotic neoliberals like Sachs on one side, and unreconstructed neoliberals like William Easterly on the other. As we have seen, Easterly accuses Sachs of compromising his commitment to the market. Yet it is precisely through their willingness to compromise certain ideological precepts that Sachs and his fellow neurotic neoliberals have succeeded in sustaining the basic symbolic coordinates of neoliberalism as the foundation of mainstream development policy. It is therefore the neurotic neoliberals, as opposed to their more orthodox counterparts, who have ensured the continuity of the neoliberal project.[98]

As we have seen, the neoliberal neurosis is characterised by repeated attempts to maintain the coherence of the neoliberal fantasy against the Real of Capital. Yet because neoliberalism is premised on removing all barriers to the movement of value, and on extending capitalist social relations to the ends of the earth, it paradoxically intensifies the very contradictions of capitalism that it is shielding its protagonists from. The predicament of the neurotic neoliberal thus recalls that of the private investigator Harry Angel in Alan Parker's *Angel Heart*, who fruitlessly pursues a serial killer through numerous false leads, only to make the final discovery that he himself is the murderer. In a similar way, the neoliberal neurosis compels its agents to engage with the symptoms of the Real of Capital, but in a disavowed form that prevents them from identifying themselves as those responsible for the exacerbation of the very symptoms that they are attempting to address. Angel's final realisation results in psychotic breakdown, the moment at which the distance between the Imaginary and the Real has finally collapsed, and the subject is gripped by what Freud called 'death drive' – a 'blind insistence that follows its course with utter disregard for the requirements of our concrete life-world'.[99] This definition of death drive resonates with an understanding of the Real of Capital as 'blind, processual, and quasi-organic . . . an alienated, abstract, self-moving Other, characterised by a constant directional movement with no external goal'.[100] It also recalls Jamie Peck's definition of the post-crash economic order as 'zombie neoliberalism', in which 'The living dead of the free-market revolution continue to walk the earth'.[101] Deprived of their social fantasy, the zombie neoliberals stagger forward into the ruins of a crisis-ridden future, driven by the death drive of the Real of Capital.

Jeffrey Sachs would appear to have escaped the clutches of these lurching zombie hordes. Since the onset of the Great Recession, Sachs has launched outspoken tirades against 'the mad pursuit of corporate profits'[102] and 'the avarice of globally mobile capital'.[103] He even appeared at Occupy Wall Street, where he gave an angry speech denouncing bankers, corporations and the business press.[104] Yet this seemingly radical discourse continues to be underpinned by a faith in a benign and ethical capitalism. In his writings on the crisis, Sachs persists in his belief that 'Self-interest, operating through markets, leads to the common good', while gently warning that 'Self-interest, without morals, leads to capitalism's self-destruction'.[105] The neoliberal fantasy is thus retained, and corrupt bankers and corporate lawbreakers are only the latest symptoms through which the Real of Capital is disavowed. Once again, the solution to the pathologies of global capitalism is to be found in capitalism itself. Indeed, it is capitalism that is to be defended against its own potential 'self-destruction'. In this way, the transformative potential of Occupy Wall Street is sublimated into a reaffirmation of the status quo. If there is a lesson for those struggling against zombie neoliberalism, it must be to keep a close eye on those who appear to be fighting alongside you. As Žižek warned during his own appearance at Occupy, 'Beware not only of enemies, but also of false friends who pretend to support us, but who are working hard to dilute our protest'.[106] In other words, *Jeffrey Sachs wants to eat your brain*!

NOTES

1. Klein, N., *The Shock Doctrine* (London: Penguin, 2007).
2. Fink, Bruce, *The Lacanian Subject: Between Language and Jouissance* (Princeton, NJ: Princeton University Press, 1995).

3. Žižek, Slavoj, *Violence* (London: Profile, 2008), 31.
4. Žižek, S., *The Sublime Object of Ideology* (London: Verso, 1989); Žižek S., *The Ticklish Subject: The Absent Centre of Political Ontology* (London: Verso, 1999).
5. Žižek, S., *Welcome to the Desert of the Real* (London: Verso, 2002).
6. McMillan, C., Symptomatic Readings: Žižekian Theory as a Discursive Strategy. *International Journal of Žižek Studies* 2(1) (2008), http://zizekstudies.org/index.php/ijzs/article/view/91/157, (accessed 22 January 2013).
7. Žižek, *The Sublime Object*, 78; Žižek, *The Ticklish Subject*, 331.
8. Žižek, *The Sublime Object*, 191.
9. Ibid., 123.
10. Žižek, *The Ticklish Subject*, 331.
11. Fink, *The Lacanian Subject*, 25.
12. Postone, M., *Time, Labour, and Social Domination* (Cambridge: Cambridge University Press, 1993).
13. It is important to distinguish here between the ordoliberal and neoliberal strands of the neoliberal project, the former of which originated in Germany, with the latter being most closely associated with Milton Friedman and the Chicago School. Whereas for the ordoliberals, neoliberalism was a self-consciously constructivist project, the Chicago School neoliberals understood market society as a spontaneous order to be revealed rather than produced; see Lemke, Thomas, 'The Birth of Bio-Politics: Michel Foucault's Lecture at the College de France on Neo-Liberal Governmentality'. *Economy and Society* 30(2) (2001), 190–207; Peck J., *Constructions of Neoliberal Reason* (Oxford: Oxford University Press, 2010a), 65–68. It was the latter strand of the project that became hegemonic, hence my privileging of it here.
14. Žižek, *The Sublime Object*, 45.
15. Perelman, M., *The Invention of Capitalism: Classical Political Economy and the Secret History of Primitive Accumulation* (Durham, NC: Duke University Press, 2000), 208.
16. Cited in Peck, *Constructions of Neoliberal Reason*, 50, 66.
17. Robinson, J., *Economic Philosophy* (London: Penguin, 1962), 77–78.
18. Peck, *Constructions of Neoliberal Reason*, 83, 106.
19. In the words of one neoclassical economist, 'It's as if there is a very pretty but highly complex picture out there, which is perfectly harmonious within itself . . . and if there's a speck where it isn't supposed to be, well, that's just awful . . . it is a flaw that mars the beauty', quoted in Klein, *The Shock Doctrine*, 53. This comment captures the experience of the symptom as 'a stain. . . which colours the alleged neutral universality of the symbolic frame', in Žižek, *The Ticklish Subject*, 331.
20. Peck, J. and A. Tickell, 'Neoliberalizing Space'. *Antipode* 34 (2002), 380–404; Fine, B., 'The New Development Economics'. In Jomo, K. S. and Fine, B. (eds) *The New Development Economics: After the Washington Consensus* (London: Zed, 2006), 1–21.
21. Taylor, Marcus, 'Responding to Neoliberalism in Crisis: Discipline and Empowerment in the World Bank's New Development Agenda'. *Research in Political Economy* 21 (2004), 17.
22. Žižek, *The Sublime Object*, 192.

23. My engagement with Sachs's work in this chapter is necessarily brief and impressionistic. For a more detailed and sustained critique of Sachs, see Wilson, J., *Jeffrey Sachs: The Strange Case of Dr Shock and Mr Aid* (London: Verso, 2014a), which builds on the theoretical approach taken in this chapter, and Wilson, J., 'The Shock of the Real: The Neoliberal Neurosis in the Life and Times of Jeffrey Sachs'. *Antipode* 46 (2014b), 301–321, which develops this theoretical approach in greater detail.

24. Sachs, in Richardson, J., *Society: Jeffrey Sachs*. *Esquire*, 1 December 2003, http://www.esquire.com/features/best-n-brightest-2003/ESQ1203-DEC_SACHS (accessed 22 January 2013).

25. Sachs, J., 'Testimonial: Abram Bergson'. *Comparative Economic Studies* 47 (2005b), 495, emphasis in original.

26. Sachs, J., 'Twentieth Century Political Economy: A Brief History of Global Capitalism'. *Oxford Review of Economic Policy* 15 (1999), 90–101; Sachs, J., 'Life in the Economic Emergency Room'. In Williamson, J. (ed) *The Political Economy of Policy Reform* (Washington: Institute for International Economics, 1994b), 503–523; Murrell, P., 'What Is Shock Therapy? What Did It Do in Poland and Russia?' *Post-Soviet Affairs* 9 (1993), 111–115.

27. Green, D., *Silent Revolution: The Rise and Crisis of Market Economics in Latin America* (New York: Monthly Review Press, 2003), 74–75; Klein, *The Shock Doctrine*, 153.

28. Wayne, L., 'A Doctor for Struggling Economies'. *New York Times*, 1 October 1989.

29. Holstrom, L., 'Sachs Appeal'. *Euromoney*, February 1992, 32–38.

30. Quoted in Richardson, *Society: Jeffrey Sachs*.

31. Clarke, S., 'Globalization and the Subsumption of the Soviet Mode of Production under Capital'. In Saad-Filho, A. (ed) *Anti-Capitalism: A Marxist Introduction* (London: Pluto, 2002), 187.

32. Ibid., 196–197.

33. Klein, *The Shock Doctrine*, 237–238.

34. Stuckler, D., L. King and M. McKee, 'Mass Privatization and the Post-Communist Mortality Crisis: A Cross-National Analysis'. *The Lancet*, 15 January 2009.

35. Holmstrom, N. and R. Smith, 'The Necessity of Gangster Capitalism: Primitive Accumulation in Russia and China'. *Monthly Review* 51 (2000), http://monthlyreview.org/2000/02/01/the-necessity-of-gangster-capitalism (accessed 22 January 2013).

36. Erlanger, S., 'Two Western Economists Quit Russia Posts'. *New York Times*, 22 January 1994.

37. Sachs, J., *The End of Poverty: How We Can Make It Happen in Our Lifetime* (London: Penguin 2005a), 131.

38. Sachs, *Life in the Economic Emergency Room*, 507.

39. Ibid., 503.

40. Žižek, *The Ticklish Subject*, 57.

41. Kay, S., *Žižek: A Critical Introduction* (Cambridge: Polity, 2003), 118.

42. Sachs, J., 'Consolidating Capitalism'. *Foreign Policy*, Spring 1995, 50.

43. Sachs, *Twentieth Century*, 91.
44. Ibid., 96, 100.
45. Sachs, J., 'Notes on a New Sociology of Economic Development'. In Harrison, L. and Huntingdon, S. (eds) *Culture Matters: How Values Shape Human Progress* (New York: Basic, 2000).
46. Sachs, 'Notes of a New Sociology', 36; Sachs, J., 'Global Capitalism: Making It Work'. *The Economist*, 10 September 1998, 7, 2; Sachs, *Consolidating Capitalism*, 64.
47. Žižek, *The Sublime Object*, 55, 169.
48. Gallup, J. L. and J. Sachs with A. D. Mellinger, 'Geography and Economic Development'. In Pleskovic, B. and Stiglitz, J. (eds) *Annual World Bank Conference on Development Economics 1998* (Washington: World Bank, 1999), 127–170.
49. Commission on Macroeconomics and Health, *Macroeconomics and Health: Investing in Health for Economic Development* (Geneva: World Health Organisation, 2001).
50. Sachs, *The End of Poverty*, 74–89.
51. Sachs, *The End of Poverty*, 76.
52. Ibid., 79.
53. Discussing the politics of disavowal, Žižek notes the appeal of 'the medical model: society is a corporate body, an organism; social divisions are like illnesses of this organism', which must be cured if 'the health of the social body is to be established' (Žižek, *The Ticklish Subject*, 226). The implicit assumption of a healthy social body underpinning Sachs's metaphors of pathology and disease typifies this medical model.
54. Sharpe, M., *Slavoj Žižek: A Little Piece of the Real* (Aldershot: Ashgate, 2004), 154.
55. Žižek, S., *The Plague of Fantasies* (London: Verso, 1997), 11.
56. Žižek, *The Sublime Object*, 185. Sachs appeals to Adam Smith as an unquestionable source of authority on innumerable occasions, including his writings on geography (Sachs, *The End of Poverty*, 34), his theory of value (Sachs, *Twentieth Century*, 91) and his account of human nature (Gallup, Sachs and Mellinger, 'Geography and Economic Development', 166). In Sachs's own words, 'It's all in Adam Smith!' (Sachs, in Snowdon, B. 'A Global Compact to End Poverty: Jeffrey Sachs on Stabilisation, Transition, and Weapons of Mass Salvation'. *World Economics* 6 (2005), 37).
57. Perelman, *The Invention of Capitalism*, 171–228.
58. Sachs, *The End of Poverty*, 51.
59. Ibid., 53.
60. Ibid., 52–53.
61. Ibid., 54.
62. Marx, K., *A Contribution to the Critique of Political Economy* (London: Beekman, 1972), 59; Marx, K., *Capital, Vol. I* (New York: Random House, 1977), 873–940.
63. Žižek, *The Ticklish Subject*, 287.
64. Sachs, *The End of Poverty*, 2.
65. Harvey, D., *A Brief History of Neoliberalism* (Oxford: Oxford University Press, 2005), 221.
66. *Shock Doctrine*, 247.

67. Easterly, W., 'The Big Push Déjà Vu: A Review of Jeffrey Sachs's *The End of Poverty: Economic Possibilities for Our Time*'. *Journal of Economic Literature* XLIV (2006), 96.

68. Žižek, S., 'Class Struggle or Postmodernism? Yes, Please!' In Butler, J., Laclau, E. and Žižek, S. (eds) *Contingency, Hegemony, Universality* (London: Verso 2000), 97.

69. Sachs, *The End of Poverty*, 188.

70. Ibid., 7.

71. Sachs, *Consolidating Capitalism*, 59.

72. Sachs, *The End of Poverty*, 194.

73. Ibid., 188.

74. Sachs, J., *The Millennium Villages Project: A New Approach to Ending Poverty* (Washington: Centre for Global Development, 2006).

75. Sachs, J., 'Beyond Bretton Woods: A New Blueprint'. *The Economist*, 1 October 1994a, 28.

76. Žižek, *The Sublime Object*.

77. Žižek, S., 'The Rhetorics of Power'. *Diacritics* 31 (2001), 100.

78. Cited in McClellan, F., 'Jeffrey Sachs'. *The Lancet* 362(672) (2003), emphasis added.

79. Millennium Project, *Investing in Development: A Practical Plan to Achieve the Millennium Development Goals* (New York: United Nations Development Programme, 2005).

80. Ibid., 15, emphasis added.

81. Sachs, *The End of Poverty*, 242.

82. The countries participating in the Millennium Villages Project are Ethiopia, Ghana, Kenya, Malawi, Mali, Nigeria, Rwanda, Senegal, Tanzania and Uganda. These countries were selected for their established records of 'good governance', and the Millennium Villages are thus embedded within neoliberal policy landscapes at the national level. The total population of the Millennium Villages is approximately 500,000; see Millennium Villages Project, *Millennium Villages Project: The Next Five Years, 2011–2015* (New York: Millennium Villages Project, 2011).

83. Sachs, *The Millennium Villages Project*.

84. Sanchez, P., J. Sachs et al., 'The African Millennium Villages'. *PNAS* 104 (2007), 16775–16780.

85. Millennium Villages Project, *Millennium Villages Project: The Next Five Years, 2011–2015*.

86. Sanchez, P., J. Sachs et al., 'The African Millennium Villages'.

87. Millennium Villages Project, *Harvests of Development in Rural Africa: The Millennium Villages after Three Years* (New York: Earth Institute, 2010).

88. Clemens, M. and G. Demombynes, 'When Does Rigorous Impact Evaluation Make a Difference? The Case of the Millennium Villages'. *World Bank Policy Research Working Paper No. 5477* (2010).

89. Clemens, M. and G. Demombynes, 'The New Transparency in Development Economics: Lessons from the Millennium Villages Controversy'. *Center for Global Development Working Paper 342* (Washington, DC: Center for Global Development, 2013).

90. Pronyk, P., 'Errors in a Paper on the Millennium Villages Project'. *The Lancet* 379 (2012), 1946.

91. *Nature*, 'With Transparency Comes Trust'. *Nature* 485, 10 May 2012, http://www.nature.com/nature/journal/v485/n7397/full/485147a.html (accessed 5 June 2013).

92. Starobin, P. 'Does It Take a Village?' *Foreign Policy*, July/August 2013. Available at http://www.foreignpolicy.com/articles/2013/06/24/does_it_take_a_village (accessed 1 July 2013).

93. Quoted in Mulholland, J. 'Aid: We're Not Arguing for a Culture of Dependency. We're Arguing to End It'. *The Observer*, 15 January 2012, http://www.theguardian.com/world/2012/jan/15/ghana-aid-jeffrey-sachs-bono (accessed 9 April 2012).

94. Easterly, W., 'The Aid Debate Is Over'. *Reason*, 26 December 2013, http://reason.com/archives/2013/12/26/theaid-debate-is-over (accessed 18 June 2014).

95. Wilson, J., 'A Strange Kind of Science: Making Sense of the Millennium Villages Project'. *Globalizations* 12(4) (2015), 641–659.

96. Wilson, J., 'The Village That Turned to Gold: A Parable of Philanthrocapitalism'. *Development and Change* 46(1) (2016), 3–28.

97. Gates, B., 'Why Jeffrey Sachs Matters'. *Project Syndicate*, 21 May 2014, http://www.project-syndicate.org/commentary/bill-gates-explains-why-the-millennium-villages-project – though-a-failure – was-worth-the-risk (accessed 27 July 2014).

98. Other examples of neurotic neoliberals could arguably include Joseph Stiglitz and Paul Krugman. Like Sachs, Stiglitz has made a name for himself as a critic of the neoliberal project, but has remained wedded to its fundamentals. Stiglitz served as chief economist of the World Bank from 1997 to 2000, and masterminded its transition from Washington to Post-Washington Consensus; see Cammack, P., 'What the World Bank Means by Poverty Reduction and Why It Matters'. *New Political Economy* 9(2) (2004), 189–211. In contrast to his current status as a reborn Keynesian, Krugman served as an economic advisor in the Reagan administration, and then played a key role in the shift to the Post-Washington Consensus, through the development of his 'new economic geography'; see Wilson, J., 'Colonising Space: The New Economic Geography in Theory and Practice'. *New Political Economy* 16(3) (2011), 373–397.

99. Žižek, S., 'Actual Politics'. *Theory and Event* 14 (4) (2011), http://muse.jhu.edu/journals/theory_and_event/v014/14.4S.zizek.html (accessed 17 February 2012), 98.

100. Postone, *Time, Labour, and Social Domination*, 270, 278.

101. Peck, J., 'Zombie Neoliberalism and the Ambidextrous State'. *Theoretical Criminology* 14 (2010b), 109.

102. Sachs, J., 'The Economics of Happiness'. *Project Syndicate*, 29 August 2011, http://www.project-syndicate.org/commentary/the-economics-of-happiness (accessed 14 September 2012).

103. Sachs, J., 'A Manifesto for the Fund's New Supremo'. *Financial Times*, 31 May 2011.

104. The speech can be seen at http://www.youtube.com/watch?v=mB_eoUqbKDw (accessed 15 May 2012).

105. Sachs, J., 'Self-Interest, without Morals, Leads to Capitalism's Self-Destruction'. *Financial Times*, 18 January 2012.

106. Žižek, 'Actual Politics'.

BIBLIOGRAPHY

Cammack, P. (2004). 'What the World Bank Means by Poverty Reduction and Why It Matters'. *New Political Economy* 9(2):189–211.

Clarke, S. (2002). 'Globalization and the Subsumption of the Soviet Mode of Production under Capital'. In Saad-Filho A. (ed), *Anti-Capitalism: A Marxist Introduction* (187–198). London: Pluto.

Clemens, M. and G. Demombynes. (2010). 'When Does Rigorous Impact Evaluation Make a Difference? The Case of the Millennium Villages'. *World Bank Policy Research Working Paper No. 5477*.

Clemens, M. and G. Demombynes. (2013). 'The New Transparency in Development Economics: Lessons from the Millennium Villages Controversy'. *Center for Global Development Working Paper 342*. Washington, DC: Center for Global Development.

Commission on Macroeconomics and Health. (2001). *Macroeconomics and Health: Investing in Health for Economic Development*. Geneva: World Health Organisation.

Easterly, W. (2006). The Big Push *Déjà Vu*: A Review of Jeffrey Sachs's *The End of Poverty: Economic Possibilities for Our Time*. *Journal of Economic Literature* XLIV:96–1057.

Easterly, W. (2013). 'The Aid Debate Is Over'. *Reason*, 26 December, http://reason.com/archives/2013/12/26/theaid-debate-is-over (accessed 18 June 2014).

Erlanger, S. (1994). 'Two Western Economists Quit Russia Posts'. *New York Times*, 22 January.

Fink, B. (1995). *The Lacanian Subject: Between Language and Jouissance*. Princeton, NJ: Princeton University Press.

Fine, B. (2006). 'The New Development Economics'. In Jomo, K. S. and Fine, B. (eds), *The New Development Economics: After the Washington Consensus* (1–21). London: Zed.

Gallup, J. L. and J. Sachs with Mellinger, A. D. (1999). 'Geography and Economic Development'. In Pleskovic, B. and Stiglitz, J. (eds), *Annual World Bank Conference on Development Economics 1998* (127–170). Washington: World Bank.

Gates, B. (2014). 'Why Jeffrey Sachs Matters'. *Project Syndicate*, 21 May, http://www.project-syndicate.org/commentary/bill-gates-explains-why-the-millennium-villages-project – though-a-failure – was-worth-the-risk (accessed 27 July 2014).

Green, D. (2003). *Silent Revolution: The Rise and Crisis of Market Economics in Latin America*. New York: Monthly Review Press.

Harvey, D. (2005). *A Brief History of Neoliberalism*. Oxford: Oxford University Press.

Holstrom, L. (1992). 'Sachs Appeal'. *Euromoney*, February, 32–38.

Holmstrom, N. and R. Smith. (2000). 'The Necessity of Gangster Capitalism: Primitive Accumulation in Russia and China'. *Monthly Review* 51(9), http://monthlyreview.org/2000/02/01/the-necessity-of-gangster-capitalism (accessed 22 January 2013).

Kay, S. (2003). *Žižek: A Critical Introduction*. Cambridge: Polity.

Klein, N. (2007). *The Shock Doctrine*. London: Penguin.

Lemke, Thomas. (2001). 'The Birth of Bio-Politics: Michel Foucault's Lecture at the College de France on Neo-Liberal Governmentality', *Economy and Society* 30(2):190–207.

Marx, K. (1972). *A Contribution to the Critique of Political Economy*. London: Beekman.
Marx, K. (1977). *Capital, Vol. I*. New York: Random House.
McClellan, F. (2003). 'Jeffrey Sachs'. *The Lancet* 362:672.
McMillan, C. (2008). 'Symptomatic Readings: Žižekian Theory as a Discursive Strategy'. *International Journal of Žižek Studies* 2(1), http://zizekstudies.org/index.php/ijzs/article/view/91/157 (accessed 22 January 2013).
Millennium Project. (2005). *Investing in Development: A Practical Plan to Achieve the Millennium Development Goals*. New York: United Nations Development Programme.
Millennium Villages Project. (2010). *Harvests of Development in Rural Africa: The Millennium Villages after Three Years*. New York: Earth Institute.
Millennium Villages Project. (2011). *Millennium Villages Project: The Next Five Years, 2011–2015*. New York: Millennium Villages Project.
Mulholland, J. (2012). Aid: 'We're Not Arguing for a Culture of Dependency. We're Arguing to End It'. *The Observer*, 15 January, http://www.theguardian.com/world/2012/jan/15/ghana-aid-jeffrey-sachs-bono (accessed 9 April 2012).
Munk, N. (2013). *The Idealist: Jeffrey Sachs and the Quest to End Poverty*. New York: Doubleday.
Murrell, P. (1993). What Is Shock Therapy? What Did It Do in Poland and Russia? *Post-Soviet Affairs* 9(2):111–140.
Nature. (2012). 'With Transparency Comes Trust'. *Nature* 485, 10 May, http://www.nature.com/nature/journal/v485/n7397/full/485147a.html (accessed 5 June 2013).
Peck, J. (2010a). *Constructions of Neoliberal Reason*. Oxford: Oxford University Press.
Peck, J. (2010b). 'Zombie Neoliberalism and the Ambidextrous State'. *Theoretical Criminology* 14:104–110.
Peck, J. and A. Tickell. (2002). 'Neoliberalizing Space'. *Antipode* 34:380–404.
Perelman, M. (2000). *The Invention of Capitalism: Classical Political Economy and the Secret History of Primitive Accumulation*. Durham, NC: Duke University Press.
Postone, M. (1993). *Time, Labour, and Social Domination*. Cambridge: Cambridge University Press.
Pronyk, P. (2012). 'Errors in a Paper on the Millennium Villages Project'. *The Lancet* 379:1946.
Richardson, J. (2003). 'Society: Jeffrey Sachs'. *Esquire*, 1 December, http://www.esquire.com/features/best-n-brightest-2003/ESQ1203-DEC_SACHS (accessed 22 January 2013).
Robinson, J. (1962). *Economic Philosophy*. London: Penguin.
Sachs, J. (1994a). 'Beyond Bretton Woods: A New Blueprint'. *The Economist*, 1 October.
Sachs, J. (1994b). 'Life in the Economic Emergency Room'. In Williamson, J. (ed), *The Political Economy of Policy Reform* (503–523). Washington: Institute for International Economics.
Sachs, J. (1995). 'Consolidating Capitalism'. *Foreign Policy*, Spring: 50–64.
Sachs, J. (1998). Global Capitalism: Making It Work. *The Economist*, 10 September.
Sachs, J. (1999). 'Twentieth Century Political Economy: A Brief History of Global Capitalism'. *Oxford Review of Economic Policy* 15(4):90–101.

Sachs, J. (2000). 'Notes on a New Sociology of Economic Development'. In Harrison, L. and Huntingdon, S. (eds), *Culture Matters: How Values Shape Human Progress* (30–43). New York: Basic.
Sachs, J. (2005a). *The End of Poverty: How We Can Make It Happen in Our Lifetime*. London: Penguin.
Sachs, J. (2005b). 'Testimonial: Abram Bergson'. *Comparative Economic Studies* 47:492–502.
Sachs, J. (2006). *The Millennium Villages Project: A New Approach to Ending Poverty*. Washington: Centre for Global Development.
Sachs, J. (2011a). 'The Economics of Happiness'. *Project Syndicate*, 29 August, http://www.project-syndicate.org/commentary/the-economics-of-happiness (accessed 14 September 2012).
Sachs, J. (2011b). 'A Manifesto for the Fund's New Supremo'. *Financial Times*, 31 May.
Sachs, J. (2012). 'Self-Interest, without Morals, Leads to Capitalism's Self-Destruction'. *Financial Times*, 18 January.
Sanchez, P., J. Sachs et al. (2007). 'The African Millennium Villages'. *PNAS* 104:16775–16780.
Sharpe, M. (2004). *Slavoj Žižek: A Little Piece of the Real*. Aldershot: Ashgate.
Snowdon, B. (2005). 'A Global Compact to End Poverty: Jeffrey Sachs on Stabilisation, Transition, and Weapons of Mass Salvation'. *World Economics* 6(4):11–67.
Starobin, P. (2013). 'Does It Take a Village?' *Foreign Policy*, July/August, http://www.foreignpolicy.com/articles/2013/06/24/does_it_take_a_village (accessed 1 July 2013).
Stuckler, D., L. King and M. McKee. (2009). 'Mass Privatization and the Post-Communist Mortality Crisis: A Cross-National Analysis'. *The Lancet*, 15 January.
Taylor, Marcus. (2004). 'Responding to Neoliberalism in Crisis: Discipline and Empowerment in the World Bank's New Development Agenda'. *Research in Political Economy* 21:3–30.
Wayne, L. (1989). 'A Doctor for Struggling Economies'. *New York Times*, 1 October.
Wilson, J. (2011). 'Colonising Space: The New Economic Geography in Theory and Practice'. *New Political Economy* 16(3):373–397.
Wilson, J. (2014a). *Jeffrey Sachs: The Strange Case of Dr Shock and Mr Aid*. London: Verso.
Wilson, J. (2014b). 'The Shock of the Real: The Neoliberal Neurosis in the Life and Times of Jeffrey Sachs'. *Antipode* 46(1):301–321.
Wilson, J. (2015). 'A Strange Kind of Science: Making Sense of the Millennium Villages Project'. *Globalizations* 12(4):641–659.
Wilson, J. (2016). 'The Village That Turned to Gold: A Parable of Philanthrocapitalism'. *Development and Change* 46(1):3–28.
Žižek, S. (1989). *The Sublime Object of Ideology*. London: Verso.
Žižek, S. (1997). *The Plague of Fantasies*. London: Verso.
Žižek, S. (1999). *The Ticklish Subject: The Absent Centre of Political Ontology*. London: Verso.
Žižek, S. (2000). 'Class Struggle or Postmodernism? Yes, Please!' In Butler, J., Laclau, E. and Žižek, S. (eds), *Contingency, Hegemony, Universality* (90–135). London: Verso.

Žižek, S. (2001). 'The Rhetorics of Power'. *Diacritics* 31(1): 91–104.
Žižek, S. (2002). *Welcome to the Desert of the Real*. London: Verso.
Žižek, Slavoj. (2008). *Violence*. London: Profile.
Žižek, S. (2011). 'Actual Politics'. *Theory and Event* 14(4), http://muse.jhu.edu/journals/theory_and_event/v014/14.4S.zizek.html (accessed 17 February 2012).

Part IV

EPILOGUE

Chapter 10

Sovereign Anxiety and Baroque Politics

Michael Dillon

> We kill people based on metadata.
> (Michael Hayden: Former Director CIA and
> US National Security Agency[1])

This chapter concerns how modern sovereignty, seeking escape from the aporetic anxiety and terror posed by the prospect of sovereign decision, and through the ever more baroque and militarised architecture of modern power relations, mourns the catastrophic outcomes of its decision making in equally baroque self-justifications. It is the way in which sovereign machination and criminality characteristically also wraps itself in the faux religiosity of baroque self-pitying, that especially intrigues me here; the most notable contemporary democratic examples include Richard Nixon and Tony Blair.

The baroque in this chapter does not refer simply, however, to an aesthetic, nor is it limited to a period defined by art historians. It refers, instead, to a generative field of formation and problematisation that emerged when Christian eternity metamorphosed into modern infinity, which novel differentiation of the finite from the infinite, in turn re-specifying each, has mutated through many different forms. Forms that do not simply help to define what it is to be modern, but also specify how it 'feels' to be modern, or, rather, how being modern casts us into a changing affective as much as geopolitical, local territorial or urban spaces.[2]

Politically speaking, the temporal horizon within which politics, truth and rule as well as knowledge were then problematised became that of the infinity of finitely knowable things, and of their government without end. The baroque thus found its first expression in politics, government and rule, including of course the theorisation of politics, as much as it did in science, religion, theatre and art.³ It was not confined to Southern Catholic Europe, a popular misconception; neither was it a mere instrument of the Catholic Counter-Reformation. It found its expression in Northern and Eastern as much as Southern Europe, and within Protestant as well as Catholic cultures. It was also, and it remains, a formative influence throughout the Americas, North and South. Even within the Europe, in relation especially to baroque drama, for example, there was considerable diversity and variation: the Catholic Spanish court drama of Calderón, and Shakespearean English 'tragedy', differing significantly in style and form from each other as well as from German Protestant *Trauerspiel*,⁴ to which I will return later. The baroque is, then, at least as much a mood as an epoch; the mood, politically, of modern factical finitude itself.

What I, therefore, call 'factical finitude' institutes the modern political imagination in terms of a changing manifold of ways in which the modern differentiation of the finite and the infinite sets the horizons of possibility and operability for modern finitude politically; its moods as well as its tactics and strategies, newly allying specular imagination and technical artifice. It is in this way, and as such, that the very vernacular of modern politics – of wealth as well as of truth, rule and techno-scientific knowledge – as well as its affective sensibilities, became baroque. Global from its very emergence, modern existence continues to pursue the material life of this finitudinally facticity through molecular and digital as well as analogue and allegorical terms.⁵

But politics is not simply a temporal phenomenon. It takes place. In consequence it is not only a spatio-temporal but also a performative phenomenon. If the temporality of our modern baroque politics is, therefore, set by novel accounts of infinity, its spatiality is comprised of 'affect' as much as it has been comprised of urbanisation, territorialisation and geopoliticisation. We inhabit 'mood' as much as we inhabit physical space; indeed, of course, we only ever inhabit physical space affectively. Land and territory may be positively surveyed, assayed and mapped, but such activities are never divorced from the political, social and cultural 'affects' that do not simply adhere to them after the event, so to speak. Affect precedes and orients them from the very beginning: Homeland; *La Patrie*, The West.⁶ As contemporary cultural and political geographers now also teach us, within its changing spatial parameters, modern urbanisation is, of course, also inextricably saturated with 'affectivity'.⁷ Sjoerd van Tuinen has noted, as well, that there has been an 'affective' turn more generally in the human, social and neurosciences in recent years. That turn has been unthinkable, he says, without the pioneering work of Gilles Deleuze.⁸ He is correct. But the influence here is more Martin Heidegger.

'Affectivity' and Mood' are placed in scare quotes because both are so deeply invested with the subjective and the psychic. But the subject, especially, is itself the expression of a 'mood'. To be a subject is to inhabit a continuously crafted and variable locale, itself expressing a *Stimmung*. I thus wish instead to invoke Heidegger's ontological conception of *Stimmung*.[9] Closely related to another Heideggerian term *Befindlichkeit* – to find one self – these terms indicate that we are not blank subjects, however supposedly rational, and that neither are we simply thrown into the iron cage of a given world. We are always already in the position of 'finding ourselves', taking our bearings and assuming whatever corporeal bearing may distinguish us, within and through worlds that are never anything but settings, which settings change as we interpret and enact them. We thus start out founded, perhaps even foundering, but also having to find ourselves, and we never cease having to take and assume our bearings. How we find ourselves thus oriented – disposed, indisposed and ill-disposed – shapes what we are and do. Baroque politics is how we currently show ourselves as moderns, through bearings that are as much corporeal as they are subjectivist and psychic; directional and intentional as much as they are also vectoral and veridical.

FATAL STRATEGIES

The core argument of the chapter is, therefore, as follows. The modern conception, practices and pursuit of sovereignty comprise a complex baroque artifice. Its inventions were a response to the problematisation of politics, truth and rule in terms of the infinity of finitely knowable things, and their endless government. This arose as the temporal horizon within which truth and rule became problematised mutated from the eternity of revealed religion into that of the positivised, later to be probabilised, infinity of baroque times. Baroque times are a project, not an accomplishment. They call modern sovereignty forth, and they do so affectively as much as they do so philosophically and politically. But, they set impossible conditions for it. Sovereigns cannot in fact do, or be, what the modern conception of sovereignty demands that they must do and be. Sovereign decision making can, therefore, only ever simulate and dissimulate what it can never actualise. That is why spectacle and show – 'shit shows' to use Barack Obama's pointed description of the disastrous Franco-British intervention in Libya in 2011 – in which democratic as much as tyrannical demagoguery is also rife – is essential to the exercise of sovereign power relations.

Whereas the definitive practical questions that once defined sovereignty – irresolvably onto-theological, as they were practical – revolved around the appointment of magistrates and the passing of legislation,[10] they progressively moved towards 'the monopoly of the legitimate use of physical force in a given territory'.[11] *Pace* Carl Schmitt, among others, monopolising the lethal use of force, including, specifically, knowing who to kill and when to kill, are not themselves, however, the politically definitive questions for the exercise of modern sovereignty.

Sovereigns must instead be in possession of a strategic calculus of necessary killing. If they are not, then their killing becomes murder, a sovereign contradiction since sovereignty is said to be necessary for the suppression of the killing that, from individual murder to private war, threatens the sovereign ordering of things. A strategic calculus of necessary killing is necessary for the institution and maintenance of modern political order, otherwise known as sovereign peace. It is, then, the exercise of a strategic calculus of necessary killing that poses the politically definitive question for modern sovereignty. And that question comes down to this: How much killing is enough?

This is **not** an exclusively existential question in the way that Carl Schmitt maintains. It never has been, and it never will be. It is always already, and inescapably also, a matter of lethal political economies: political economies widely preoccupied now with the infinite monetisation of finitude as a principal means of regulating the infinity of finite things scientifically as well as politically.

Sovereignty's fatal strategies are therefore 'fatal, but only fatal for now'.[12] Which 'now' is, of course, the factical finitude of an infinity of finite 'nows' that sovereignty promotes temporally as it governs infinitely. However, if the sovereign cannot determine how much killing is enough – that is, for the institution and maintenance of sovereign peace – then the sovereign order of things becomes gangsterism and the generalisation of murder and private warfare. To be a modern sovereign therefore means to be in possession of a strategic calculus that does not simply teach you who to kill and when to kill; neither is emergency is its only point, and perhaps not even its essential point. It must teach when to stop, something that modern securitisation has not been able to do, and for good reason. Such a calculus does not exist, and one can never be securely formulated. Its absence is not a function of inadequate intelligence, strategic savvy or miscalculation. It cannot be conjured by more calculated knowing. The very conditions of possibility and operability that found modern calculation and knowing forbid it; for modern epistemology's condition of possibility is the *infinity* of finitely knowable things. The point is not simply their finite positive knowability. It is that infinitely contingent coming and going which engenders the infinity of more things to be finitely known. More things to be finitely known include an infinity of finitely knowable threats to which positivised entities are necessarily also exposed by their very ontological and epistemological status as finite entities – they never last. They are, therefore, less expressions of a divine plan than the radical contingency of their unconditional giveness, and of the modern struggle to bring this aporia of infinity (infinities) under some kind of scientific, ultimately mathematical, control.

Who to kill? When to kill? How to kill? These and other such subsidiary questions are subordinate to the politically definitive question of how much killing is enough. If you know how much killing is enough, for the preservation of modern sovereign order and the securing of its peace, you might be able to derive answers to these secondary questions. Since no such strategic calculus of necessary killing is possible, the attempt to provide one only ever engendering an infinity of finite threats requiring more killing – My Lai in 1968, Aleppo in 2016 – confronted by the question how much killing is enough, modern sovereigns and their strategic advisors can only ever answer 'more'. Thus does modern baroque sovereignty subvert its very own raison d'être.

Instituted to stop private killing, sovereignty can only ever therefore simulate more killing as that which is politically calculable and juridically necessary. Sovereigns must consequently know how much killing is enough if the modern conception of sovereign power and politics is to be actualised. That it never has been, because it simply cannot be, helps account for the sovereign anxiety and political horror into which modern times descend. Modern sovereignty is, therefore, more a fatal predicament than a universal political solution.

I am not claiming that this is the only explanation for the political anxieties and horrors of modern times, simply that this definitive account of modern sovereigntist politics of security is itself inescapably implicated in them, not an escape from, or an amelioration of, them. Sovereignty is not simply confronted by irresolvable problems. It is itself an aporia. Aporias are not philosophical abstractions; they are material enactments: practical – political, economic and ethical – predicaments, finding expressions as much in political moods as they do in the decisionist vernacular of modern government and rule.

If we understand that decisionism is itself a mode of being in the world, sovereignty's mode of being is to simulate decision while bloodily dissimulating the undecidability of which it is comprised. As such it is comprised of political 'mood' as much as it is comprised of rational calculation. It is often said that where calculative decision attains its limits, mood decides. In fact, calculative decision making always already *is* the expression of a *Stimmung*, an encountering of the world in a certain, technically 'affective', ways. Herein, then, is a key source of modern sovereign anxiety. Pursuing solutions to how much killing is enough, via phantasmagorical as well as technoscientific political economies of mass killing, upon which much of global wealth and knowledge production also depends, they become immersed in anxiety-filled aporias characteristic now of much of modern national and international politics.

There are, of course, different Lacanian as well as Heideggerian readings of this *Stimmung*, or 'political mood', of 'Anxiety'. My gloss is to note that the modern infinity of finite things – its ontology or spatio-temporal setting – poses the endless securitisation and government of knowable things. And that is why, to adapt Heidegger, in claiming that security is the *Politische Grundstimmung* (the key setting, or politically founding mood) of the modern age, I am in fact doing no more than rephrasing what modern political theorists of the state have long maintained. But, some proclaim it as the essence of politics. Others, more circumspectly, only proclaim it as the essence of the politics of the modern sovereign state. I describe it as a changing setting that emerged in response to the advent of factical finitude's problematisation of politics, truth and rule as the infinite governmental securitisation of finite things. Aporetic: democratic sovereigns, especially, often frankly experience it aporetically. My examples – Nixon and Blair especially – suggest as much.

Thus modern sovereigns are characterised by endlessly dissimulating what they cannot realise. Seeking to make sovereignty their own, they are inducted into a play that is not of their own scripting. Thus trapped, they duck, dive and cheat since, more than any others, it is sovereigns that know how impossible is the warrant to which they are all in thrall. Dissimulation, machination and intrigue are the affective games that surround them, and their courts. Their political knowing – their *arcana imperii* – is modern knowing premised upon the infinity of finitely knowable things. Such things are, however, finite. They come and go, and, in sovereign politics, they do so murderously.

POLITICAL TRUTH AND KNOWLEDGE

The differentiation of truth (*aletheia*) and knowledge (*episteme*) is a classic one, but it found novel expression from the sixteenth and seventeenth centuries onwards. Each evolved in the context of, as well as giving changing expression to, the problematisation of time as infinity rather than as eternity. Intimately connected, therefore, it should also be noted that there is a profound difference between the affective and technical practices comprising knowledge and truth. These differences compound the aporetic anxiety that characterises modern sovereignty.

Knowing is an epistemological game. Truth telling is a veridical one. The former went positivistic from the sixteenth to seventeenth centuries onwards, as the latter lost its 'secure' apophantic grounding in a previously dominant onto-theology comprised of a monotheistic faith in revelation. Although the two continually flow in and out of one another, folding and unfolding in an interpretative political dance, modern knowing is an epistemological game founded in experimentation and positivity, albeit latterly also in probability, rather than veracity. It is not only inspired by the infinity of finitely knowable things. Practically speaking, especially in mathematics, changing accounts of infinity is its operational mode. That is how and why modern political science also became pursuit of what is needed for the endless government of finitely knowable things. As it claims to demarcate what is not to be governed, and how to govern according to the properties of whatever is to be governed, baroque political science has nonetheless also followed the exponential growth and transformation in knowing and governing as the infinity of threats to finite orders of things became ever more evident, demanding more power/knowledge to have them governed, especially securely self-governed, accordingly.

Two standard responses to this predicament concern truth instead of positive knowledge. The first is that politics should become an expression of the truth. The second is that some means of speaking truth back to the bio- and geo-power relations instituted by the requirement to secure the infinite government of finite things. Neither works unproblematically in the ways proclaimed, because truth, including the truth of revealed religion, is ultimately opaque even to the veridical apparatuses and professional truth tellers proclaiming it. The philosophical grounds to which such truth claims frequently appeal rely on a dogmatism and moralism that is more or less complicit with what they seek to attack.[13] As Geoffrey Bennington noted recently, this complacency, or failure, of thought:

> stems from an unwarranted assurance as to the relations between politics and truth (or even Truth) and more especially from an assumption of being in possession of the latter, or at least being able to call us all sternly back to it from our supposedly skeptical and irresponsibly complicit postmodern play and revelry.[14]

Which is very much *not* to say that there is, therefore, no truth to be told, and that truth telling is a fruitless activity.

It simply means that while it is certain that there is a manifold of truths to be told, there is no certainty to be had in truth telling beyond that upon which dogmatic force, violence and aggression insist as they pursue their untruthful ways. In our age of baroque politics the infinite government of finite things cannot therefore be definitively contested by critique alone, since, founded upon the infinity of finitely knowable things, our baroque politics systematically absorbs critique while its veridical shows are explicitly crafted to persuade and deceive. Such epistemological and veridical artifice is integral to the very artfulness of our baroque drama of politics, truth and rule. In such circumstances, wanting in definitive truth, we become in want of truths more than ever.

Ultimately, the truth of our political condition can only be illuminated and contested by counter-political truths. That itself requires a further philosophical interrogation of truth and untruth for which there is no space here, but such a thing is essential to a political interrogation of our political condition. No one escapes the demand to tell the truth, and there is no end of truths to be told. It is not so much the paucity of truth, or the blatant suppression of truth, that is ultimately responsible for the opacity of political truth writhing self-destructively at the epicentre of modern sovereign politics. Exceeding all finite expression of it, truth is founded in a supplementarity that exceeds critical knowledge, veridical political dramas or pronouncements by the religiously self-elected.

Telling the truth politically also demands courage (*parrhesia*). Foucault's reflections on the courage of truth inspire this thought even if those reflections are no more than a fallible beginning, along, differently of course, with those of Derrida, Heidegger and Walter Benjamin, to take three other challenging philosophical reflections on truth.[15] Mortal life struggles to live out the supplement of truth. Pursuit of such knowing does not aim to tell the truth, and positivist knowing does not resolve the problematic of truth. Its ambitions are more instrumental, utilitarian and fungible than veridical. Epistemological dispositifs and veridical apparatuses are thus baroquely infolded and enfolded in the theory and practice of modern politics. No more so than in the baroque courtly politics of sovereign power, and the neurotic behaviour of modern sovereigns executing their definitive warrants; death dealing conducted as much through biopolitical as geopolitical power relations.[16]

One final point: knowledge making and truth telling are not confined to speech, logos or discourse. These things also take place. Thus they are also irredeemably performative. Spectacle and show are as integral to them as they are to sovereignty. If truth has to be made manifest, knowledge of it has to be gathered, disseminated and taught, publicised and applied. None of this has ever relied exclusively on purely philosophical, theological or epistemological techniques alone, because they cannot. Reasoning is an art form. Techno-science is a corporately dominated performative. We thus live in the midst of theatrical political economies of truth and techno-scientific spectacles of knowledge production.

Little wonder, then, that modern sovereigns are saturated with an anxiety expressing a *Stimmung* that their epistemological and veridical apparatuses compound rather than resolve. The target of my refection is not their insatiable demand for new forms of truth, knowledge and policy-oriented pedagogy. It is, instead, the very onto-political setting in which they find themselves posited, and the conceptions of politics, truth and rule that follow from it.

I move on to clarifying some of the foundational conceptual assumptions I draw from this predicament. These concern the opacity of truth, the chiasmic relation of truth and rule, and the deeply riven nature of sovereignty. My chapter then seeks to illustrate and elaborate these and other related points by visiting the scenes of two judicial executions, those of the execution of Damiens for attempted regicide in France in 1715 (famously described by Foucault at the beginning of *Discipline and Punish*), and the botched execution of Clayton Crockett in the United States in 2014. I then recall the classic account of sovereign anxiety in the Nixon White House exposed by the Watergate tapes before moving on to Blair. In other words I move across diverse theatrical settings: those of the gallows, the execution chamber and, finally, the theatre of war.

THE OPACITY OF TRUTH, RULES OF TRUTH AND TRUTHS OF RULE, AND THE STASIS OF SOVEREIGNTY

' . . . il faut la vérité.' (. . . wanting in truth.)

(Derrida, *Positions*)

THE OPACITY OF POLITICAL TRUTH

No prophet, theologian or philosopher ever proclaimed the transparency of truth, and human beings have never been granted unmediated access to the truth. Anything that exists takes place. Consequently, when it takes place, truth is as performative as it is historical. Hence, there are different truths, different veridical apparatuses for truth telling and different kinds of truth tellers, but also different dramatic enactments of truth telling.

Like all else, truth also exceeds the historicality and the idiomaticity of its taking place. A transcendental gesture of some description therefore also haunts every scriptural and literal as well as epistemological and veridical expression of truth. In Derrida's terms there is always not only a veridical supplement – an excess of truth over its expression – but a wider ontological supplement in which expressions of truth also arise, the excess of the giveness of existence as such. There is truth, then, a kind of ontological claim. But truth telling is also idiomatic, an historical claim. Truth is never transparent and immediately accessible, never liberated from the mystery of existence in which it arises and never cleansed of the idioms through which it finds historical expression. For those reasons, Truth is a scandal. It is a scandal because transcendence and history cannot be reconciled. This is not a problem for positive history alone. Salvation history has never escaped it either. Little wonder truth remains opaque to those who make sovereign claims upon it, and that any attempt to exercise sovereign control over it should be wracked by anxiety and lethal violence in relation to it, as well as confessions of faith in it, and mourning for it. For these, and other reasons, we are condemned to struggle with, for and against truth. As Derrida observed, we are always wanting in truth. Wanting only ever reinstalls our desire for it, our need of it, and the compulsion to escape the dogmatic forces that distinguish its diverse historical expressions.

However, as my mother used to say, 'wanting doesn't get.' Working on and through critique, the will to truth nonetheless incites a striving that exceeds the positivistic knowing upon which so much critique remains reliant. Inspired by Foucault, I am going to call this struggle the politics of truth. The politics of truth is not only integral to sovereign anxiety and the politics of politics. Disturbingly, it exceeds the politics of critique and the critique of politics vainly promised by critique.

I think our age of political anxiety, at least in these respects, emanates from the sovereign anxieties that pervade our rulers as much as it does the apparatuses of government, and the subject positions through which they seek to dominate and domesticate those that they rule. Quite evidently, also, sovereign anxiety is closely bound up with the fact that truth in general, political truth in particular, is as opaque to our masters as it is to us. *Arcana imperii* mystify the governors as much as the governed, and when such mystifications are punctured, or fail to work, a change of affect follows; regularly comprising mourning and melancholia, self-pitying expressions of political ressentiment and sovereign bathos (c.f., especially, Blair and Nixon). This brings me to an additional supposition of the paper, and the chiastic formula that it deploys throughout.

CHIASMUS: RULES OF TRUTH AND TRUTHS OF RULE

There is no truth that does not simultaneously also tell you how to conduct yourself, or how others should also be so conducted. Foucault calls this the imperative of truth. Similarly, however, there is no rule of truth that does not invoke some truth of rule. No rule of truth, then, without its corresponding truth of rule, no truth of rule without its corresponding rule of truth.

This does not mean that truth and rule are the same thing. They are not. There is truth and there is rule. Nor can they ever be made to add up. They are radically heterogeneous entities. Locked in an ineradicable, mutually disclosing as well as reversible, relationship, they continually intersect one another. Their relationship is irretrievably chiastic.[17]

Recall, by way of clarification, Paul de Man's observation: 'Chiasmus . . . can only come into being as the result of a void, of a lack that allows for the rotating motion of the polarities.'[18] The lack at the centre of truth is its very scandalous supplementarity. That void in relation to the politics of both truth and knowledge revolves around a centre that proves to be empty of final determination because it is characterised by ineliminable supplementarity. It ultimately consists in a space suitable only for political crossing or, rather, the very possibility and necessity of something called 'politics'.

Here, then, is that supplementarity which accounts for the very opacity of truth, specifically, when dealing with the sovereign as well as wider political anxieties of our age, the opacity of rules of political truth and truths of political rule to rulers and ruled alike. Traversing it entails wider political challenges; indeed, a politics of politics beyond those posed sovereign by government, its decisionistic instrumental impulses and fatal imperatives.

Part of the anxiety that stalks modern baroque politics is the very rarity, therefore, of the courage of truth that politics requires, and the very many ways in which the courage of truth – the honour and dignity of which it also may be comprised – has been marginalised within, even systematically driven out of, democratically governing institutions wherein 'interest' vies irreconcilably with truth, especially in pluralist accounts of the demos, engendering an ethos which threatens the very institutions – pedagogic as well as religious – cherished vocation is said to be the pursuit of truth as such. Be that as it may, through what features does sovereign anxiety display itself, and why is it so dangerous as well as pathetic and bathetic, continually haunted with the undecidability of the decision said to be definitive of it?

RIVEN SOVEREIGNS

> If every unity implies a duality and therefore the possibility of uproar, or stasis, is immanent, then theology seems to become 'stasiology'.[19]
>
> (Carl Schmitt, *Political Theology* 2: 126)

Sovereign anxiety derives from the very conceptualisation and practice of sovereign power itself. Here, I rely on Carl Schmitt's definitive account of sovereignty in the modern age.

One objection might immediately be raised against this choice, however. Modern power relations are diverse and heterogeneous. They are comprised of many different forms of power relations according to how the objects and subjects of power are conceived and constituted. It has often been said that these additional forms of power, especially disciplinary power and the biopower that takes species existence as its referent object, have superseded sovereign power over death. Species, for example, are quite differently conceived from sovereigns; comprised of quite different properties. Biopower thereby seeks to exercise power over life through manipulation of the biological and behavioural properties of whatever is currently described as species existence. Its practices have been undergoing dramatic change particularly in response to the impact of the molecular and digital revolutions on the very conceptualisation of both life and death.

There is no space to deal with this important objection in detail here. I have argued extensively elsewhere, however, that modern power relations do not supersede one another. Diverse forms of modern power do not compete in a zero-sum game. They are folded in the complex matrices of modern power relations. Sovereign power is very much alive and part of that modern palimpsestuous matrix of power relations. Suffice to say, also, that from their very inception, in the sixteenth and seventeenth centuries, modern sovereigns have always availed themselves of power over life, not least when exercising power over death. It turns out also that the distinction between life and death was never as distinct as we have been taught to think, no more so now than in the age of molecular biology and the digital sciences of animation and artificial intelligence.[20] Derrida's deconstruction of theologico-political absolutisation of the differentiation of life from death is no more compelling when dealing with sovereignty, and the sovereign execution of the death penalty.[21]

Schmitt's political theology provides us with a political theorisation of the modern sovereign conception of power and its genealogical dependence upon the theological absolutism of Christianity's *via moderna*. That theorisation exposes how sovereignty – comprised of an originary and ineliminable fracture – institutes the very idea of politics, government and rule as a political stasiology. Whereas the stasiology to which Schmitt refers arises in respect of his argument against Petersen's invocation of Christology and the Trinity (2011), as that which defeats the very possibility of political theology, the fracture to which I am referring is different, but it nonetheless haunts Schmitt's texts, notably *The Concept of the Political* (2007), *Political Theology* (2006) and *Political Theology 2* (2008).

This fracture lies within the component parts of the sovereign conception of power itself. Only by dividing time into the temporality of the instant (of decision) and the temporality of succession (of the unproblematic legislation of sovereign will into the historical actuality of a juridico-political order) can the sovereign myth that sovereigns reign and governments rule be posited and sustained. This artifice elides every problematic binary distinction that it institutes, upon which it relies, and with which historical orders of sovereign power have struggled since time immemorial: metaphysics versus mechanics; essence versus existence; homogeneity versus heterogeneity; hierarchy versus heterarchy; reigning versus ruling; sovereignty versus government; strategy versus tactics; policy versus administration; friend versus enemy; contingency versus necessity; inequality versus equality and so on. Sovereignty's stasiological fracture is thus as compound as it is constitutive.

It runs, first, between these binaries. Their fractures cannot, however, arise sequentially, as if it were possible to have sovereignty and then government, or to have metaphysics and then mechanics, or essence and then existence. Technicity, Bernard Stiegler reminds us, is originary.[22] There can be no essence without its existence; no principle without its process; no emanation without its liturgical acclamation; no spectacle without its impresarios, stage managers, set designers, producers, directors, script writers, play actors and spectators. No reigning, in short, without ruling; no sovereignty without government. Sovereignty poses these fractures as things to be violently overcome in spectacles of oneness between rulers and ruled, engineered to subordinate and recruit the ruled into the endless war of normalising exception required for the continuous re-institution of the very conception of sovereignty itself. Anxiety seams the entire ensemble of sovereign rule.

Second, it also runs, however, between rulers and ruled. But I am less interested in that fracture, and the anxieties that it engenders, for the moment. What I want to draw attention to, here, is the critical fracture that arises within the very order of the sovereign itself. For if the sovereign is not a homogeneous unity, if the sovereign is instead an unstable heterogeneity – its hierarchy a heterarchy – comprised of elements that do not add up, then an entirely different problematisation of politics, government and rule arises than that offered by the stasiology of modern theologico-political sovereignty; whose principal effect is to install war as the foundation of political order, and to require political order to make war if it is continually to reinstall itself. Sovereign anxiety thus regularly finds its expression in violent martial forms driven by an impetus towards totalisation. The spectacular, indeed specular, nature of such a regime of governance, what Agamben calls glorification[23] (Agamben, 2011), finds its paradigmatic expression in the theory and practice of war – not least 'the war in heaven' whose significance, unaccountably overlooked by Agamben, is so integral to the institution of the sovereign imaginary that dominates the modern theologico-political imagination gone baroque.[24]

I do not, therefore, dissent from the view that Schmitt captures something essential about the character of modern sovereignty. I do dissent from the view that in doing so he captures something essential about politics. He doesn't. And in the process he misses the congenital anxiety that attends sovereign power. What he misses is, I think, captured better by Michel Foucault on the one hand and Walter Benjamin on the other.

To drive home the point, and to finesse the tiresome charge that this is postmodern 'bull', consider also Rheinhart Koselleck's summary of the early modern institution of sovereignty.[25] It supplements Schmitt by recalling that it was no mere juridical abstraction but, to use a favourite Schmittean expression, a concrete historical formation: 'The absolute ruler recognised no authority over himself than God, whose attributes in the political and historical field he appropriated.'[26] Other operational entailments followed logically from the conceptualisation and institutionalisation of modern sovereignty, and these compounded the inability of Schmitt's fractured sovereign to act the sovereign in the way demanded of it. 'To meet his all-encompassing responsibility,' observes Koselleck, 'the prince had to seek the measure of his actions in their calculable effect on everyone else. The compulsion to act thus provoked a need for heightened foresight. A rational calculation of all possible consequences came to be the first political commandment.'[27]

Schmitt's decisionist sovereign has to be a miracle worker – the analogy of the decision with the miracle is not an analogy at all. It is the logical corollary – a necessary entailment – of Schmitt's theologico-political account of human existence as such. Albeit Schmitt elides the entire serpentine history of the Church's adjudication of what is to be miraculous and what is not, the condition of miraculous possibility – the instant of decision – sets conditions of operability that oblige the sovereign to strategise as well. No miracle outwith a divine strategy, within which the miracle and the miracle worker must fit. Whichever way you cut it, there is no escaping the originary co-belonging of *phusis* and *technē* (even for the divine planner).

Specification of the state of emergency, differentiation of friend from enemy and the execution of public killing are therefore said to be the expression of a single, unified and immediate political will. But how can that be? How is the friend/enemy distinction to be drawn? How does one know that one is existentially threatened? What does it take? How is the existential enemy to be securely identified? Will any enemy do? What happens if you get it wrong? How would you know? Conversely, what if you get that wrong as well? Again, how would you know? Will any friend suffice to determine your existential belonging? Is it possible for sovereigns to mistake the enemy? Is it possible for sovereigns to misconceive the friend, or be deceived by them? What if more than one existential threat exists? Is anyone and everyone a potential existential threat? Which one is more existentially threatening than another? Again, how would you now? Assuming that existential threats are intelligent and therefore may be capable of deceiving you, on what evidence or whose advice – counter-intelligence – would you rely? How is the allocation of resources between more than one existential threat to be decided? What if your existential condition is one of radical uncertainty and undecidability? How do you cope with that? How and when would a decision acquire the *imprimatur* 'miraculous'? It wouldn't do for it to come after the event. Since it is supposed to constitute the event itself, you would be buggered if it came afterwards rather than before or at precisely the right moment. (The sexual connotations of sovereignty are rampant throughout sovereign discourse, not least Schmitt's.) Even the Church required some forensic and juridical process for an 'event' to receive the accolade 'miracle'. It takes years, usually centuries, and the ground rules continually change. The analogy that Schmitt draws, draws his account into a minefield, one that he dextrously (rhetorically) avoids. But it doesn't take a jurist, philosopher or theologian to point it out. It stares you in the face. It is the abyss into which all sovereigns *manqué* look. And there is no sovereign that isn't manqué.

And so, if the sovereign is to be a miracle worker the sovereign cannot misconceive the friend or mistake the enemy, and the response to multiple threats must always be equally decidable. To be sovereign is to be God. Well, not any God, not every God, but the One God. However, according to legend and revelation, the One God emerged out of a war in heaven – a kind of primordial stasiology extending the war between good and evil required for its very emergence into the post-war triumph of the One. Albeit, thereafter, there is always already also hell. And hell has not only to be policed for all eternity, since there seems to be no parole from it, although divine pardon cannot be ruled out, the sufferings of the damned have also to be displayed for the delectation of the saved. They are integral to the rewards of salvation and the delights of heaven (Forsyth, 1989).

Forget the difficulties of positivistically posing, let alone answering, such questions. How is sovereign command over one's creation to be retained after the act of creation ex nihilio? Forget also the warning issued by the tale of the *Sorcerer's Apprentice*, who let loose all manner of things beyond his command. What if the relationship between friend and enemy and the miracle of decision for which it calls is altogether and radically undecidable? But, let us pass by this Derridean challenge, and stay with the one posed to the modern miracle worker simply by its unrealisable positivistic will to know.

To be sovereign. To become sovereign, requires the exercise of a strategic calculus of necessary killing to resolve these and other related issues, not least those to do with timing and interpreting what Machiavelli called the signs of the times.[28] This definitive political question cannot be elided. Schmitt's analytic cannot avoid having it posed. How much killing is enough to satisfy the strategic calculus for which the sovereign differentiation of friend from enemy and the institution of a stable juridico-political order calls? The sovereign's strategic calculus of necessary killing cannot arise before the decision is made. It cannot arise after the decision is made. It has, miraculously in Schmitt's terms, to be the decision itself. How much killing is enough may or may not be explicitly included as part of the strategic calculus of necessary killing. But it is directly posed, and it has to be answered somehow, if the regimes of modern sovereigns *manqué* are not to become those of the abattoir.

These are precisely the problems to which Koselleck refers. And they were recognised from the very beginning of the institution of the concepts and practices of modern sovereigns. They were, for example, the very problems explored in the German *Trauerspiel* of the late seventeenth century that Walter Benjamin analysed in a book whose title is translated as *The Origins of German Tragic Drama* (1998), and on which I draw towards the end of the paper.

Charged not only with exercising a strategic calculus of necessary killing but also with answering the question how much killing is enough, every human sovereign is condemned to fail the test of sovereignty itself. Forget the rational pursuit of strategic ends. For all it has had impact, forget, also, the strategist's condemnation of Bush and Blair. Strategists do not have the answer either. For no such strategic calculus of necessary killing is humanly available, and none is thereby capable of specifying how much killing is enough to realise the sovereign ends that such a calculus presupposes. When asked how much killing is enough, the sovereign always answers more (trapped as he or she remains within a sovereigntist understanding of politics, government and truth, c.f. Tony Blair's call for military intervention against 'Islamic extremism' in general and into the Syrian civil war in particular).

Again, Koselleck references, historically, a point that is a logical entailment of the very conceptualisation of political power as sovereign. The modern sovereign, he says, 'accumulated all responsibility . . . but to maintain it he had to remain aware of the augmented responsibility it entailed. . . . Then, and only then, was he in possession of the authority that guaranteed his power . . . [and] came to feel a compulsion to act which continually conjured up new decisions . . . the consequences of inaction could be as serious as those of its opposite. One risk matched and constantly challenged the other. Indeed the danger of falling from one extreme into the other was the very source of the evidence of sovereign decisions'.[29] However, he concludes: 'In order to keep the consequences of his actions (which once committed were not humanly alterable) under his own control as long as possible, the prince was driven to augment his power, which in turn increased the sources of danger, the risk of abusing or failing to use the accumulated power.'[30] The miracle of sovereign decision is therefore also comprised of an escalatory 'logic of absolute responsibility',[31] the discharge of which can only ever be humanly simulated rather than exercised: hence its totalising impulse.

Reigning and ruling therefore comprise no sequence. Theirs is also a reversible relationship. Just as Foucault reminds us of the continuing significance of coup d'état so also does coup d'état reminds us of this crucial point. To reign is to rule and to rule is to reign. However conceptually heterogeneous they may be, and they are, reigning and ruling are also locked in a chiasmic relationship. They are not only reversible – praetorians, janissaries, mamluks, military chiefs and cameralist administrators having done so for millennia in ways that continually haunt fearful sovereigns – they are also subject to the mediation of a third term. That third term, I suggest, is politics. A politics unthought by Schmitt because it is the unthought of the very rules of truth and truths of rule of theological absolutism from which the modern account of sovereignty derives.

Schmitt's sovereign – one might say the classical theo-logico-political conception of sovereignty – is thus constitutively incapable of doing what it is supposed to do and remaining what it is supposed to be. Here the sovereign's rule of truth and truth of rule must ultimately be rendered also as the positivistic knowing (*connaissance*) of modern strategic thought. The burgeoning of strategic thinking and its will to positivistic knowledge promises an escape from this aporia, but singularly fails, of course, to deliver the sovereign from it. It becomes an integral part of that great spectacle of simulation and dissimulation that the apparatus of modern sovereignty demands in order to maintain the fiction of sovereign power. The appetite for strategic *connaissance* – how else is the existential enemy to be specified, its properties positivistically mapped and its threat exposed so that it can be securely overcome? – is endlessly fed by the appetite for miraculous decision making. The one stimulates and services the other in resonances as sexual as they are political. Inevitably, each condemns the other for failing to deliver.

My excursus into the originary political stasiology of the sovereign conception of power is therefore designed to reinforce this central point. The modern baroque sovereignty of which Schmitt speaks is a fractured compound comprised of heterogeneous terms. That very heterogeneity must be construed as an originary state of emergency, the violent resolution of which is always already in play before any sovereign gets started on its mortal counterparts. Sovereignty is fatally compromised conceptually by the stasiology of which it is conceptually comprised. Schmitt comes close to admitting as much in *Political Theology 2* when trying to contest Petersen[32] and Blumenberg[33]: Petersen for his Christological and Trinitarian dismissal of the very possibility of political theology and its theologico-political sovereign; Blumenberg for his dismissal of the secularisation of the modern age, of which Schmitt was of course a principal exponent. The pluralisation of the Godhead, he noted, threatens to institute the uproar or stasis of heterarchy rather than the peace of the One.

So, sovereigns must fail. They fail serially. For, when exercising the very power over death of which they are said to be uniquely comprised, bound to executing the penalty of death against murderers and alien others alike, they fail utterly. Recall this early modern and notorious example.

Bourbon Shock and Awe

Let's revisit baroque France and the execution of Robert-Francois Damiens, convicted of attempted regicide. Recounting that event, Foucault famously introduces *Discipline and Punish*.[34] Re-staging Damiens' execution to re-direct our gaze to the analytics of disciplinary power relations – for which we remain indebted to him – might cause us, however, to overlook something about the baroque figure of modern sovereignty that Damiens' execution exposes: specifically, the ways in which the violent self-glorifying exaltation of sovereign power – the ways in which it exults reproductively in its own bloody spectacles – simultaneously also finds its expression in the bathetic, inept and corrupt banality of its everyday existence. For the incompetently brutal excess of imperial majesty camping itself as *arcana imperii* proceeds by warranting rule in the name of political truths as opaque to modern sovereigns as they are to their subject/citizens, warrants operationalised also by contingently contrived governmental mechanics whose outcomes sovereigns and governments alike are equally unable to predict or control. *L'état c'est moi*, says the eighteenth century boy with halitosis and a perfumed wig. 'Mission accomplished', says the twenty-first century boy in the bomber jacket.

The *mise en scène* is Pythonesque. On 1 March 1757 Damiens was condemned 'to make the *amende honorable* before the main door of the Church of Paris,' from whence, according to a man, Bouton, Officer of the Watch, he was to be, 'taken and conveyed in a cart, wearing nothing but a shirt, holding a torch of burning wax weighing two hundred pounds . . . to the Place de Grève where, on a scaffold that will be erected there, the flesh will be torn from his breasts, arms thighs and calves with red-hot pincers, his right hand holding the knife with which he committed the said parricide, burnt with sulphur, and, on those places where the flesh will be torn away, poured molten lead, boiling oil, burning resin, wax and sulphur melted together and then his body drawn and quartered by four horses and his limbs and body consumed by fire, reduced to ashes and his ashes thrown to the winds'.[35]

Why a torch of 200 pounds? Why the specific combination of lead, oil and resin? From what archive were these and other specifications drawn? Who first recorded them? Who dug them out for this event? And, if there was nothing in the archive to go on, what curious imagination drew up this agenda? The king? Possibly. Sometimes likely, since the historical record is full of sovereign beasts fully hands-on screwing their opponents. Equally also, however, one can imagine Louis, silk pantalooned and lace-cuffed tottering away on high heels, waving a scented linen handkerchief over the dirty work busying his boys. All the mucky microcosmic material staging necessary for the conjuring of spectacle always threatens to distract from it.

Just as the truth of metaphysics requires its mechanics, so also does the sovereign require government. The monarch has thus declared that Damiens must die the death of a regicide. All deaths are idiomatic, and this sovereign killing is designed, as is all sovereign killing, notably that of modern warfare, to have sovereign mechanics inscribe sovereign metaphysics on the body; body politic as much as individual corporeal being. The sovereign is nothing if not incarnated in and through the dead bodies of its subjects. The word is made flesh in a terroristic and terrorising display of sovereign transcendence become immanent in one deliberate terroristic and terrorising mode of killing.

The king has decreed Damiens' death. However much they are royally commissioned to draw out the dying, the executioners also intend that he should die the death pronounced upon him. Damiens, himself, will, in fact, also wish to die. Expressly designed to inscribe the sovereign's power on the victim's body, the body nonetheless proves unaccountably resistant to it. For a time at least – no one could predict how long it would take – the body will defy Damiens as much as it will defy the king and his torturers. It will resist, and it will not quite die to order.

The king ordained that Damiens should die, and the executioners will eventually kill him. But, as is often the case, the execution of sovereign willing turns into banal butchering as the execution proceeds. Consider the record of many judicial executions in the United States. Glorification of the mystery of state symbolised in sovereign majesty is bathetically banalised by the incompetent dismembering that begins to take its place. The chaotic horror of the battlefield repeated in the clinically modern execution chamber as much as on the scaffold, or in the squares of 18th-century Paris.

Damiens' executioners were in fact spectacularly incompetent. Perhaps they were in need of more anatomical learning. Perhaps they required more experience, since unlike their modern equivalents they had nothing like as much form in the game of individual and mass execution. Who knows? Yet it can hardly be the case that they were totally without experience since the butchery of execution as a paradigm of modern sovereign power has been a constant of modern sovereign politics since its inauguration in the 17th century.

In any event, Bouton left us his account. More Monty Python. 'The sulphur was lit, but the flame was so poor that only the top skin of the hand was burnt. Then the executioner with his sleeves rolled up took the steel pincers that had been specially made for the occasion and pulled first at the calf of the right leg and then at the thigh, and, from there at the two fleshy parts of the right arm, then at the breasts. Although reportedly a "strong and sturdy fellow" . . . [he] found it so difficult to tear away the pieces of flesh that he set about the same spot two or three times, twisting the [custom made; but who made them and to what specifications?] pincers as he did so.'[36] The 'same executioner dipped an iron spoon in the pot containing the boiling potion, which he poured liberally over each wound.'

Things went from bad to worse, however, with the quartering. It was clearly made up as it went along. 'This last operation was very long,' reported the *Gazette D'Amsterdam* of 1 April 1775: 'The horses were not accustomed to drawing; consequently, instead of four, six were needed; and when that did not suffice, they were forced, in order to cut off the wretches thighs, to sever the sinews and hack at the joints.'[37] You could not blame the horses. These 'tugged hard, each pulling straight on a limb, each horse held by an executioner.' 'After a quarter of an hour, the same ceremony was repeated and finally, after several attempts, the direction of the horses had to be changed, thus: those at the arms were made to pull towards the head, those at the thighs towards the arms, which broke the arms at the joints. This was repeated several times without success. . . . Two more horses had to be added to those harnessed to the thighs, which made six horses in all. Without success . . . the horses gave up and one of those harnessed to the thighs fell to the ground.'[38] The horses were not alone in giving out. Damiens had asked to be kissed. The chronicle reports that 'The Parish Priest of St Paul's [whose professional responsibilities seemed to dictate that he should]' also lost his (spiritual) bottle and reportedly 'did not dare to.'

The final act entailed the executioners drawing their knives to 'cut the body at the thighs instead of severing the legs at the joints; the four horses gave a tug and carried off the two thighs after them . . . then the same was done with the arms, the shoulders, the arm pits, and the four limbs; the flesh had to be cut almost to the bone, the horses pulling hard carried off the right arm first and the other afterwards.'[39]

Damiens' remains were as a troublesome in death, however, as his body had been alive: 'The pieces of flesh and trunk had taken about four hours to burn,' it was reported. Having commenced the execution in the early morning, 'The last piece to be found in the embers was still burning at half-past ten in the evening.'[40] And thus did sovereign spectacle became a fuck up from beginning to end. Recall the lying, deceit and mercurial machination, the shock, awe and sheer wilful bloody ignorance that characterised the Western conquest and occupation of Iraq.

A more contemporary example of how sovereigns fail entails a shift of scene from Bourbon Shock and Awe to modern Capital Punishment.

A Clinical Strike

On the 29 April 2014, Clayton Lockett, condemned to death for rape and murder in the United States, was subject to death by lethal injection in Oklahoma. The injections didn't work – they rarely seem to do so – and while what precisely happened remains unclear, the outcome here was also a bloody mess.

Lockett was administered an untested mixture of drugs that had not previously been used for executions in the United States. According to reports, when the state proceeded to execute Lockett he did not fall unconscious for ten minutes.

Three minutes after he was declared unconscious, he lurched forward against his restraints, writhing and attempting to speak. He strained and struggled violently, his body twisting and his head reaching up from the gurney as if trying to escape from the execution table. Sixteen minutes after the execution began, Lockett said 'Man' and warden Anita Trammell ordered that the blinds be lowered to shield the witnesses from the execution. The artery used for the injection had apparently burst, the cocktail of drugs injected into his groin failing to kill him and the Corrections director declared that he died of a heart attack forty-three minutes after the execution had begun.

It was not an instant of decision that matched the requirements of sovereign power. Perhaps a firing squad would be more effective, mused a Republican senator? No doubt? But then there would be the issue of the gunmen, the issue of the gun, the calibre of the bullets. These would be overcome, after a fashion. Recall the British execution of Irish Republican revolutionaries in 1916, one of whom, previously wounded, had to be carried out and tied to a chair in order for the execution to take place. So, look more closely at Lockett's execution. It presages no easy resolution of the business of execution, for the time of execution exceeds the instant so-called of death, introducing an altogether more troublesome and extended time line:[41]

0506 hours: The Correctional Emergency Response Team arrived at Lockett's cell to escort him to medical for X-rays as part of the execution protocol. Lockett refused orders to be restrained.

0509: CERT team left unit in preparation for cell entry.

0550: CERT team and medical personnel on unit to conduct planned use of force. After giving a verbal order to be restrained, offender Lockett refused, and an electronic shock (taser) was administered.

0553: Offender Lockett was taken to H Unit Medical room where it was found he had a self-inflicted laceration to his right arm. Treatment was administered. Offender Lockett was then transported by vehicle to the medical facility, Intermediate Health Care Center at Oklahoma State Penitentiary.

0635: Offender Lockett arrives at IHCC for treatment of self-inflicted injuries, which were observed during the cell extradition at 0550 hours.

0645: Offender Lockett was moved to an observation cell in IHCC. Medical personnel examined Offender Lockett's self-inflicted wounds. Three officers were assigned for continuous observation until 1719 hours.

0700–0815: Offender Lockett was checked by the cell watch team, accompanied by medical personnel, every 15 minutes.

0815: Physician Assistant examined offender Lockett and determined that sutures were not needed.

0840: Offender Lockett was returned to an observation cell in IHCC.

0850–0935: Offender Lockett was checked by the cell watch team every 15 minutes.
0915 (approx.): Offender Lockett refused visits from his attorneys.
0942: Offender Lockett was offered a food tray and refused the food tray.
0955–1045: Cell watch team checked Offender Lockett every 15 minutes.
1025 (approx.): Offender Lockett confirmed his refusal to visit with attorneys.
1111: Offender Lockett was offered a food tray and refused the food tray.
1135–1450: Cell watch team checked Offender Lockett every 15 minutes.
1510–1555: Cell watch team checked Offender Lockett every 15 minutes.
1610–1640: Restraint team escorts offender Lockett from IHCC to H-Unit SW shower (final holding cell prior to execution).
1655–1710: Offender Lockett visits with mental health personnel.
1719: Offender Lockett was escorted from SW shower to the execution chamber by Warden Trammell and the restraint team.
1722: Offender Lockett was placed and restrained on the execution table.
1727–1818: Phlebotomist enters execution chamber to determine appropriate placement for IV. The phlebotomist examined offender Lockett's left and right arms, left and right legs, and both feet to locate a viable insertion point. No viable point of entry was located. The doctor then examined the offender's neck and then went to the groin area.
1818: The IV insertion process was completed. Insertion point was covered with a sheet to prevent witness viewing of the groin area.
1820: Phlebotomist left execution chamber.

Watergate

Recall, now, the three baroque political archetypes (sovereign, tyrant and martyr) and of the properties, in particular, of sovereign anxiety, explored by Walter Benjamin in his analysis of the German *Trauerspiele* of the late 17th century; anxieties manifested by two contemporary democratic sovereigns, Nixon and Blair. I begin first with that classic account of sovereign anxiety that unfolded as Nixon's Whitehouse disintegrated into the criminality that was to be exposed by the Watergate tapes.

We expect vituperation and banal blasphemies from tyrants that we would not countenance in the martyr. However much he was inclined to depict himself as such, Nixon was, however, no martyr. Neither was he a tyrant. It seems as if we need another category for sovereign democratic wannabees. One more attuned to the small-time *Trauerspiele* of democratic leaders gone hubristic or just plain bad. There is the vast forgotten wealth of the Watergate tapes to remind us of what goes on back stage in the courts of contemporary democratic sovereigns. Let's first remind ourselves of the descent of sovereign transcendence into bathos and disgrace before turning to Blair and the Baroque. Two examples, two moments, in the Watergate affair will suffice.

Consider first this conversation between Richard Nixon and his senior advisor, Charles Colson, on 13 February 1973. Colson had just confided in Nixon that he had always had what he coyly described as 'a little prejudice'. Nixon replied in comradely fashion that he was not prejudiced either but that nonetheless also: 'I've just recognized that, you know, all people have certain traits. . . . The Jews have certain traits. The Irish have certain – for example, the Irish can't drink. What you always have to remember with the Irish is they get mean. Virtually every Irish I've known gets mean when he drinks. Particularly the real Irish.' Warming to his theme: 'The Italians, of course, those people of course don't have their heads screwed on tight. They are wonderful people, but. . . .' His voice trails off and then returns a moment later to Jews: 'The Jews are just a very aggressive and abrasive and obnoxious personality.'

Thanks to those two professional parrhesiastes Woodward and Bernstein, we hear the bathos of the Nixon presidency climax at the height of the Watergate crisis. Consider secondly, then, Nixon's Oval Office confessional as Watergate reaches its climax, invoking God's grace and seeking a companion in prayer.[42]

APRIL 22, 1973:

THE PRESIDENT, H.R. "BOB" HALDEMAN, AND HENRY KISSINGER, 9:50–10:50 A.M., OVAL OFFICE.

President Nixon: Where is . . . where is that kike, Kissinger?

Kissinger: I'm right here, Mr. President.

President Nixon: Oh . . . uh, Henry, good, I'm glad you're here . . . I want you to get down on your knees, Henry, and pray for me . . . I'm up shit creek without a paddle. I've got the damn Jew press on me like a "kick me" sign taped to my ass.

Kissinger: Of course, Mr. President.

Haldeman: You can kneel over here, Henry.

President Nixon: Never mind that . . . just get me some support from those sons-of-bitches in the cabinet. Tell them I've got stuff on them . . . pictures.

Kissinger: But, Mr. President, you have these things?

President Nixon: We've got tons of stuff . . . tons . . .

Kissinger: All right, Mr. President, but it would help me if I could . . . see the pictures.

Haldeman: We'll get some for you, Henry.

Kissinger: Good. Now, sir, I want to discuss the latest operation in Camb— (cuts off).

Sadly, there are no Downing Street tapes to afford an insight into the grubbiness of sovereign intrigue and decision making in 10 Downing Street, albeit I think some intimation of it can be gleaned from the diaries of its key actors; Alastair Campbell, for example.[43] Detailed, if sanitised, documentary evidence will be available in the evidence submitted to the British Chilcot Inquiry, published in July 2016.[44]

And so to war.

'Yo! Blair!'

One month after Clayton Lockett's execution, the conservative British think tank The Royal United Services Institute issued a report that roundly condemned the Bush/Blair conspiracy to wage war on Iraq and Afghanistan as a comprehensive strategic failure – radicalising British Muslim youth and increasing the terrorist threat to the UK, all for the cost of £29 billion to the British Exchequer and hundreds of thousands of deaths in Iraq and Afghanistan. Precisely one day later, the shamefully delayed Chilcot Inquiry into Britain's participation in the Iraq war announced that it would not release the Bush/Blair correspondence that was instrumental to the deceit and misinformation on the basis of which Blair and his court marshalled the Cabinet and the House of Commons into supporting British participation in the war. It would provide a 'gist' only of the correspondence together with some selected quotations.

A classic case of the failure of representative and accountable government. Sure. A classic case of gross political incompetence at the very highest levels of sovereign power as well? Of course. Out with the fantasies of regime change and emancipation, Bush and Blair made no serious attempt to consider the impact of their war on Iraq's social and political order. But a classic instance also of the failure to which sovereign power is condemned.

We do not know if King Luis spent much time reflecting on Damiens' death, or on excusing himself for the work done that day as contemporary figures now do in a blizzard of diaries, taped conversations, self-saving testimonies before tribunals of enquiry, media interviews and political autobiographies. Curiously, despite the volume of political biography and autobiography, such material escapes political critique. There is a genre here that is itself also a contribution to the simulation and dissimulation of sovereignty.

Suspended in a vicious aporia instituted by having to ally a metaphysics of creative power as decisional will with a mechanics of rule capable of translating will into policy designed to render the world governable – creating a world is one thing, governing it is another – *Trauerspiel* teaches how sovereign sorrow at its decisional predicament is one of the prevailing tropes of the spectacle of sovereign terror (hence the *Trauerspiel* or mourning play). Constituted by an aporia from which there is no escape, sovereigns are themselves terrorised by having to will the sovereign abyss rather than be devoid of sovereign will. In the process they regularly invoke a God now pre-empted by sovereign command as much as overcome by an overrated decline in religious faith and credulity.

The radical undecidability posed by sovereignty's aporia massively elevates the imperative to decide as it threatens to overwhelm the sovereign with indecision. Fear of indecision the complement to the wreaking of bloody terror. Bush's greeting 'Yo! Blair!' seems to have been as much a locker room injunction to act, as it was the 'Little Bro' recognition of a partner in crime. The burden of undecidability clearly also disposes the sovereign to treat events as the proving ground of their capacity to be sovereign.

'There is,' however, Walter Benjamin observes, 'this one thing to be said in favor of the Caesar as he loses himself in the ecstasy of power: he falls victim to the disproportion between the unlimited hierarchical dignity, with which he is divinely invested and the humble estate of his humanity.'[45] In the process he invokes his God, models himself on Christ's passion and renews his kinship with the divine through martyrdom on the cross of decision.

Recall the attempt at sovereign pathos Blair gave in his post-war interview with the TV talk show host Michael Parkinson. Answering yes when asked on ITV1 chat show *Parkinson* if he had sought holy intervention on the decision to participate in the invasion of Iraq. He went on: 'Of course, you struggle with your own conscience about it . . . and it's one of these situations that, I suppose, very few people ever find themselves in.' 'In the end, there is a judgement that, I think if you have faith about these things, you realise that judgement is made by other people . . . and if you believe in God, it's made by God as well.' 'When you're faced with a decision like that, some of those decisions have been very, very difficult, most of all because you know these are people's lives and, in some case, their deaths.' 'The only way you can take a decision like that is to do the right thing according to your conscience.'. . . . 'My Father, if it is possible, may this cup be taken from me. Yet not as I will, but as you will.'[46]

CONCLUSION

The most important thing about acting is honesty. If you fake that you've got it made.

(George Burns)

What inspired these reflections and what do I now take away from them, since our baroque politics has been nothing if not a transformation in the politics of the politics of truth. I will be brief and schematic

First is the importance of distinguishing between truth (*alētheia*) and knowing (*epistēme*). Second is the veridical deficit integral to modern knowing. Third is the requirement for an analytic of veridiction as distinct from critique. Fourth is an analytic of spectacle integral to the analytic of veridiction, since truth takes place – must be made manifest – and is ultimately therefore a matter of showing. Such showing is dramatically impacted and transformed by modern techno-science not least the sciences of digitalisation and its algorithmic as well as geometric power. Fifth, the politics of truth embraces an extensive long-standing and deeply problematic debate within and between politics, philosophy, language, reason and rhetoric. The resources that fuel it are ancient as well as modern, and they are subject to fundamental reappraised. That reappraisal cannot be elided by the claim that since we are in want of truth we must have truth and that only one truth will do.

There are many reasons for being deeply suspicious of this claim and for rejecting it. Not least of those reasons is this. It poses the most difficult challenge of all. The very possibility of truth always already contains the possibility of untruth (*pseudos*). This is no relativistic claim. It is a logical entailment of the possibility of truth itself and its consequences for political thought as much as political practice cannot be avoided. Tyranny lies at the heart of any philosophy or theology that fails to address this aporetic condition. Failure to acknowledge and address it lies at the heart, also, of political tyranny.

It is sovereign anxiety confronted by the aporia of truth perhaps even more than knowing; sovereigns have always known that that they can never know enough, that is perhaps the greatest of current dangers, since it is one from which we can never in fact be secured by sovereigns and from which sovereigns can never secure themselves.

NOTES

1. Mathias Schwartz, 'More Than a Million Names,' *London Review of Books*, 38(12) (16 June 2016): 39.

2. The differentiation of the finite from the infinite has posed problems since the Greeks. It comprises fields of formation and problematisaton in which the differentiation not only of 'good infinity' from 'bad infinity', but also of the good from the bad as such, are always also at issue. Thus infinity has a diverse and changing history from Pythagoras and Aristotle onwards. It is one, in addition, that has always been deeply implicated in the changing politics of truth and rule as well. I am not concerned, then, with saying what infinity is, or of tracing its much-needed pre-modern genealogy, so much as preoccupied with exploring the modern status and functions of infinity including, especially, its role in the positivisation of modern factical life, and of the institution of a politics of truth and rule in which the infinite government of finite things via their indefinite securitsation has become foundational. For an excellent history of 'the infinite', from which its genealogy may be extracted, see

Moore, A.W., *The Infinite* (London: Routledge, 2001), 2nd Edition; and for comprehensive account of David Hume's classic critique of infinity, see Dale Jacquette, *David Hume's Critique of Infinity* (Leiden: Brill, 2001). See also Maravall, José, *Culture of the Baroque: Analysis of a Historical Culture* (Minneapolis: Minnesota University Press, 1986); Deleuze, Gilles, *The Fold* (London: Bloomsbury, 1993); Hills, Helen, *Rethinking the Baroque* (London: Routledge, 2016b); Hills, Helen, *The Matter of Miracles: Neapolitan Baroque Architecture and Sanctity* (Manchester: Manchester University Press, 2016b); Kaplan, Robert and Kaplan, Ellen, *The Art of the Infinite* (Oxford: Oxford University Press, 2003); and, Clegg, Brian, *A Short History of Infinity* (London: Robinson, 2003).

3. Maravall, *Culture of the Baroque*; Gal, Offer and Chen-Morris, Raz, *Baroque Science* (Chicago: Chicago University Press, 2013a); Gal, Offer and Chen-Morris, Raz, eds., *Science in the Age of the Baroque* (Dordrecht: Springer, 2013b); Lambert, Gregg, *On the New Baroque* (Aurora, CO: The Davies Press, 2008); Eggington, William, *The Theater of Truth* (Stanford, CA: Stanford University Press, 2010).

4. Benjamin, Walter, *The Origins of German Tragic Drama* (London: Verso, 1998).

5. Murray, Timothy, *Digital Baroque. New Media and Cinematic Folds* (Minneapolis: Minnesota University Press, 2008).

6. Elden, Stuart, *The Birth of Territory* (Chicago: University of Chicago Press, 2013).

7. Barnett, Clive, 'Political Affects in Public Space: Normative Blind-Spots in Non-Representational Ontologies,' *Transactions of the Institute of Geographers*, 32(2) (2008): 186–200; Thrift, Nigel, *Non-Representational Theory* (SAGE: London, 2007); McCormack, D.P., 'Molecular Affects in Human Geographies,' *Environment and Planning A*, 39(2) (2007): 359–377; Carter, S. and McCormack, D.P., 'Film, Geopolitics and the Affective Logics of Intervention', *Political Geography*, 25(2) (2006): 228–245.

8. Sjoerd van Tuinen, *Elasticity and Plasticity, Unabridged, final author's version*. Forthcoming in: Arie Graafland, Andrej Radman & Heidi Sohn (eds., 2016). *Critical and Clinical Cartographies*. Edinburgh: Edinburgh University Press, and in French translation in Erik Bordeleau & Dalie Giroux (eds., 2016). Aux limites de l'empire: Grandeurs de Sloterdijk, Paris: éditions Dehors.

9. Heidegger, Martin, *Being and Time* (Oxford: Basil Blackwell, 1978); Flatley, Jonathan, *Affective Mapping: Melancholia and the Politics of Modernism* (Cambridge, MA: Harvard University Press, 2008); Mullaney, Steven, *The Reformation of Emotions in the Age of Shakespeare* (Chicago: University of Chicago Press, 2015); Karant-Nunn, Susan C., *The Reformation Feeling. Shaping the Religious Emotions in Early Modern Germany* (Oxford: Oxford University Press, 2010).

10. Tuck, Richard, *The Sleeping Sovereign: The Invention of Modern Democracy* (Cambridge: Cambridge University Press, 2016).

11. Weber, Max, 'Politics as a Vocation,' in H.H. Gerth and C. Wright Mills eds., *From Max Weber: Essays in Sociology* (New York: Oxford University Press, 1946).

12. I take this pungent one-liner from a wonderful new play (*The Ockerbys on Ice*) written by playwright Debbie Oakes, produced by Joe Sumsion, at The Dukes Theatre Lancaster. My subtitle gestures to Jean Baudrillard, *Fatal Strategies* (New York: Semiotext(e), 2007), 2nd Rev. Edition.

13. Bennington, Geoffrey, *Scatter 1. The Politics of Politics in Foucault Heidegger and Derrida* (New York: Fordham University Press, 2016), 2.
14. Ibid.
15. Bennington, *Scatter 1*.
16. Dillon, Michael, *Biopolitics of Security: A Political Analytic of Finitude* (London: Routledge, 2015).
17. Wiseman, Boris and Paul, Anthony, eds., *Chiasmus and Culture* (Oxford: Berghahn Books, 2014).
18. De Man, Paul, *Allegories of Reading* (New Haven: Yale University Press, 1979), 49.
19. Stasis/Stasiology: From the Greek στάσις 'a standing still'. As defined by Thucydides: a set of symptoms indicating an internal disturbance in both individuals and states. 'The one—*to hen*—is always in uproar *stasiazon- against itself—prosheauton*.' (Gregory of Nizianzanus)
20. Palladino, Paolo, *Biopolitics and the Philosophy of Death* (London: Bloomsbury, 2016).
21. Derrida, Jacques, *The Death Penalty: v. 1 (Seminars of Jacques Derrida)* (Chicago: Chicago University Press, 2014).
22. Stiegler, Bernard, *Technics and Time; The Fault of Epimetheus* (Stanford, CA: Stanford University Press, 1998).
23. Agamben, Giorgio, *The Kingdom and the Glory* (Stanford, CA: Stanford University Press, 2011).
24. Forsyth, Neil, *The Old Enemy: Satan and the Combat Myth* (Princeton, NJ: Princeton University Press, 1989).
25. Koselleck, Reinhart, *Critique and Crisis: The Pathogenesis of the Modern Age* (Cambridge, MA: The MIT Press, 1988).
26. Ibid., 17.
27. Ibid., 20.
28. Dillon, Michael, 'Lethal Freedom: Divine Violence and the Machiavellian Moment', *Theory and Event*, 11(2) (2008): 1–22.
29. Koselleck, *Critique and Crisis*, 20.
30. Ibid.
31. Ibid.
32. Petersen, Erik, *Theological Tractates* (Stanford, CA: Stanford University Press, 2011).
33. Blumenberg, Hans, *The Legitimacy of the Modern Age* (Cambridge: The MIT Press, 1983).
34. Foucault, Michel, *Discipline and Punish* (London: Peregrine Books, 1982).
35. Foucault, Michel, *Discipline and Punish* (London: Peregrine Books, 1982), 3.
36. Foucault, Michel, *Discipline and Punish* (London: Peregrine Books, 1982), 4.
37. Ibid., 3.
38. Ibid., 4.
39. Ibid., 5.
40. Ibid.
41. http://www.theatlantic.com/national/archive/2014/05/oklahoma-releases-a-timeline-of-clayton-locketts-botched-execution/361544/.

42. Further details concerning Nixon's deep anti-Semitism are also evident here http://www.theatlantic.com/national/archive/2014/05/oklahoma-releases-a-timeline-of-clayton-locketts-botched-execution/361544/.
43. Campbell, Alastair, *The Blair Years* (London: Arrow, 2008).
44. Chilcot, Sir John, *The Iraq Inquiry*, http://www.iraqinquiry.org.uk/the-report/ (accessed: 6 July 2016).
45. Benjamin, *The Origins of German Tragic Drama*, 70.
46. Ratcliffe, Mathew, *Feelings of Being: Phenomenology, Psychiatry and the Sense of Reality* (Oxford: Oxford University Press, 2008), 26, 36–46.

BIBLIOGRAPHY

Agamben, Giorgio. (2011). *The Kingdom and the Glory*, Stanford: Stanford University Press.
Barnett, Clive. (2008). 'Political Affects in Public Space: Normative Blind-Spots in Non-Representational Ontologies,' *Transactions of the Institute of Geographers*, 32(2): 186–200.
Baudrillard, Jean. (2007). *Fatal Strategies*, New York: Semiotext(e), 2nd Revised Edition.
Benjamin, Walter. (1998). *The Origins of German Tragic Drama*, London: Verso.
Bennington, Geoffrey. (2016). *Scatter 1. The Politics of Politics in Foucault Heidegger and Derrida*, New York: Fordham University Press.
Blumenberg, Hans. (1983). *The Legitimacy of the Modern Age*, Cambridge: The MIT Press.
Campbell, Alastair. (2008). *The Blair Years*, London: Arrow.
Carter, S. and McCormack, D. P. (2006). 'Film, Geopolitics and the Affective Logics of Intervention,' *Political Geography*, 25(2): 228–245.
Chilcot, Sir John. (6 July 2016). *The Iraq Inquiry*, http://www.iraqinquiry.org.uk/the-report/.
Clegg, Brian. (2003). *A Short History of Infinity*, London: Robinson.
De Man, Paul. (1979). *Allegories of Reading*, New Haven, CT: Yale University Press.
Deleuze, Gilles. (1993). *The Fold*, London: Bloomsbury.
Derrida, Jacques. (2014). *The Death Penalty: v. 1 (Seminars of Jacques Derrida)*, Chicago: Chicago University Press.
Dillon, Michael. (2008). 'Lethal Freedom: Divine Violence and the Machiavellian Moment,' *Theory and Event*, 11(2): 1–22.
Dillon, Michael. (2015). *Biopolitics of Security: A Political Analytic of Finitude*, London: Routledge.
Eggington, William. (2010). *The Theater of Truth*, Stanford, CA: Stanford University Press.
Elden, Stuart. (2013). *The Birth of Territory*, Chicago: University of Chicago Press.
Flatley, Jonathan. (2008). *Affective Mapping: Melancholia and the Politics of Modernism*, Cambridge, MA: Harvard University Press.
Forsyth, Neil. (1989). *The Old Enemy: Satan and the Combat Myth*, Princeton, NJ: Princeton University Press.

Foucault, Michel. (1982). *Discipline and Punish*, London: Peregrine Books.
Gal, Offer and Chen-Morris, Raz. (2013a). *Baroque Science*, Chicago: Chicago University Press.
Gal, Offer and Chen-Morris, Raz, eds. (2013b). *Science in the Age of the Baroque*, Dordrecht: Springer.
Heidegger, Martin. (1978). *Being and Time*, Oxford: Basil Blackwell.
Hills, Helen. (2016a). *The Matter of Miracles: Neapolitan Baroque Architecture and Sanctity*, Manchester: Manchester University Press.
Hills, Helen. (2016b). *Rethinking the Baroque*, London: Routledge.
Jacquette, Dale. (2001). *David Hume's Critique of Infinity*, Leiden: Brill.
Kaplan, Robert and Kaplan, Ellen. (2003). *The Art of the Infinite*, Oxford: Oxford University Press.
Karant-Nunn, Susan C. (2010). *The Reformation Feeling. Shaping the Religious Emotions in Early Modern Germany*, Oxford: Oxford University Press.
Koselleck, Reinhart. (1988). *Critique and Crisis: The Pathogenesis of the Modern Age*, Cambridge: The MIT Press.
Lambert, Gregg. (2008). *On the New Baroque*, Aurora, CO: The Davies Press.
Maravall, José. (1986). *Culture of the Baroque: Analysis of a Historical Culture*, Minneapolis: Minnesota University Press.
McCormack, D.P. (2007). 'Molecular Affects in Human Geographies', *Environment and Planning A*, 39(2): 359–377.
Moore, A.W. (2001). *The Infinite*, London: Routledge, 2nd Edition.
Mullaney, Steven. (2015). *The Reformation of Emotions in the Age of Shakespeare*, Chicago: University of Chicago Press.
Murray, Timothy. (2008). *Digital Baroque. New Media and Cinematic Folds*, Minneapolis: Minnesota University Press.
Palladino, Paolo. (2016). *Biopolitics and the Philosophy of Death*, London: Bloomsbury.
Petersen, Erik. (2011). *Theological Tractates*, Stanford, CA: Stanford University Press.
Ratcliffe, Mathew. (2008). *Feelings of Being: Phenomenology, Psychiatry and the Sense of Reality*, Oxford: Oxford University Press.
Stiegler, Bernard. (1998). *Technics and Time; The Fault of Epimetheus*, Stanford, CA: Stanford University Press.
Thrift, Nigel. (2007). *Non-Representational Theory*, London: SAGE.
Tuck, Richard. (2016). *The Sleeping Sovereign: The Invention of Modern Democracy*, Cambridge: Cambridge University Press.
Weber, Max. (1946). 'Politics as a Vocation,' in H.H. Gerth and C. Wright Mills eds., *From Max Weber: Essays in Sociology*, New York: Oxford University Press, 77–128.
Wiseman, Boris and Paul, Anthony, eds. (2014). *Chiasmus and Culture*, Oxford: Berghahn Books.

Index

action, 154–55. *See also* anti-austerity mobilisations; emotions
advertising campaigns, for suspicious activities, 79–80, 83. *See also* suspicion
affectivity, 192–93
affects, 21–23, 28, 153. *See also* emotions
Afghanistan, 214
Africa: ending poverty in, 174–75; Sachs on, 173–75; as sublime object, 174. *See also* Millennium Villages Project (MVP)
Agamben, Giorgio, 41, 203
Aganaktismenoi, 148
Age of Suspicion (Sarraute), 84
Agoraphobia Society, 62
Ahmed, Sarah, 134
Alleanza Nazionale. *See* Movimento Sociale Italiano (MSI)
Alternative Fur Deutschland Party, Germany, 123
American Psychiatric Association (APA), 61
American Psychological Association (APA): multi-media approach, 71; 'Road to Resilience' campaign, 71–72
Andrejevic, Mark, 84

Andreotti, Giulio, 129
Angel Heart, 177
anger, 150–51
anti-austerity mobilisations: aim of, 148; anger and, 150–51; demand for change, 149; emotional factors in, 149; heterogeneous cycle of, 155; identities and, 152–54; injustice and, 149, 151–52; local political context and, 148; social media technologies and, 148; strategic vision, 149
anti-capitalist approaches, 2
anticipation: logics and consequences of, 81–84. *See also* suspicion
anti-establishment parties, 1
anti-terror campaigns, 83, 84
anxiety, 37–39, 61; affect and, 21–23, 28; Bourke on, 6; Freudian approach to, 19–21; Lacanian concept of, 21–31; logics of, 6–7; materiality and immateriality, 2–4; pathological interpretation, 22; philosophical interpretations, 22; resistance and, 8–9; security logic of. *See also* security; World Health Organization
'Anxiety' (Freud), 19
anxious subject, 147
aporias, 195. *See also* sovereignty
Arab Spring, 6

221

Aradau, Claudia, 65
arcana imperii, 196, 200, 208
Argentina, 48
Asia, 109, 111
Australia, 83
authoritarian mobilisations, 63
avoidance of situations, 62
awareness campaigns, 112

Balibar, Etienne, 50
Barcelona, 141
Barcelona en Comú (Barcelona in Common), 141
Barnes, Judith, 41
baroque, 191–92
Beck, Ulrich, 4, 146
Befindlichkeit, 193
Behavioral Health Management, 72
behaviours, 62
Belgium, 79; de-radicalisation strategy, 85–86, 87; extremist inmates categorised in, 87; *Ministerial Circular on Terrorism and Violent Radicalisation*, 88; *Plan R*, 85–86; social workers, 91; STRESAVIORA I, 86
Benjamin, Walter, 203
Bennington, Geoffrey, 197
Ben-Ze'ev, Aaron, 150
Bettelheim, Bruno, 69
Beyond the Pleasure Principle (Freud), 67
biopower, 201–2
bird flu, 101, 111, 114
Blair, Tony, 191, 196, 206, 214–15
blind spot, 27
Bolivia, 169
Bonelli, Laurent, 91–92
Bounce, 81
Bounce[along], 86
Bounce[up], 86
Bounce[young], 86
Bourke, Joanna, 146
Bowie, M., 127
Breen-Smyth, Marie, 86
Bush, George W., 214, 215

Calais, 79
Cameron, David, 124, 125, 132
Campbell, Alastair, 214
Canada, 88
capital: bourgeois subjectivity, 66; generating uncertainty in subjectivity, 66; Žižek on, 167
capitalism, 2; communism, 169, 170; crisis-ridden dynamics, 167; natural health of, 172; Russia's transition to, 170; self-destruction, 178
capitalist class, 2
Caruth, Cathy, 39, 40–43, 44, 47, 48
castration anxiety, 19
Centre for the Prevention of Radicalisation Leading to Violence (CPRLV), 88
centre-left and centre-right parties, 134
Chan, Janet, 84
Channel schemes, 85, 89
Cheaters (TV show), 79
Chilcot Inquiry, 214
child mortality, 176
children: castration anxiety and, 19; trauma, 70
Christianity, 202
chronic uncertainty, 147
Civil Contingencies Act 2004 (UK), 65
civil protection, 106–7
classical literature/novel, Sarraute on, 84
clinical economics, 171
clock boy. *See* Mohamed, Ahmed
Colau, Ada, 141, 142
Cold War, 106
colour-coded terror alerts, 4–5
Colson, Charles, 213
communication: corporate, 114; crisis, 112–14; expertise in, 114; risk, 113; speaking, 43, 44; timing for, 114
communism, 169
concentration camp survivors, 68, 69
The Concept of the Political (Schmitt), 202
conflicts, 1
consumerism, 66

Contest (British programme), 85, 89
contingency planning, 64
corporate communication departments, 114
cosmopolitan culture, 8
Counter-Terrorism Act (UK), 89
courage of truth, 198
CPRLV. *See* Centre for the Prevention of Radicalisation Leading to Violence (CPRLV)
Crank, John P., 80
crisis communication, 112–14
crisis management, 104
critical infrastructure: protection of, 106–7; regulations for, 107
cultural-political conflict, 17

Damiens, Robert-Francois, 199, 207–10
dangers, 64–67; disasters, 64–65; Freudian approach to perceptions of, 20; perceived/imagined, 18, 20; phenomenology of, 21; real, 20; risk *vs.*, 105; subjectivity and, 21; as threat to itself, 21. *See also* resilience; risk(s); trauma
death drive, 178
decisionism, 195
decisions: miracle and, 204; risk *vs.* danger, 105
delegation of responsibility, 106–8
DeLillo, Don, 70
¡*Democracia Real Ya!* (DRY), 149
Department of Homeland Security, 72, 83
de-radicalisation programmes/strategies, 85–90. *See also* radicalisation
Derrida, Jacques, 70, 199, 200, 202; Freud and, 46–47; metaphysics of presence, 43–44
deserving poor, 174–75
desire: dialectical *vs.* analytical logic of, 25; frustrated satisfaction, 24; Hegelian schema of, 25–26; Lacanian notion of, 23–26; need *vs.*, 23–24
desire for desire, 25
developing world, 165

de Vos, Bernard, 90
Diagnostic and Statistical Manual of Mental Disorders (DSM), 61–62; DSM-II, 61, 67; DSM-III, 62, 68; DSM-IV, 62; DSM-V, 62
Di Donato, Giulio, 129
disasters, 64–65, 91, 101; natural, 64; political, 64
disciplinary power, 201
Discipline and Punish (Foucault), 207
'Discourse of Rome.' *See* 'The Function and Field of Speech and Language in Psychoanalysis' (Lacan)
distant traumatic effects, 69. *See also* trauma
dreams: scientific theory of interpretation, 44–46; wish-fulfilling theory, 45–46
DSM. *See Diagnostic and Statistical Manual of Mental Disorders* (DSM)

Earth Institute, Columbia University, 175
Easterly, William, 173, 176, 177
ecology, 65
economic inequality, 2
economic reforms, 165
ego, threat to, 20
The Ego and the Id (Freud), 19, 32
emergency preparedness, 64
emotional suffering, 18
emotions, 3; action and, 154–55; anger, 150–51; disciplines on, 144; identity and, 152–54; marginalisation of, 144; politics and, 126, 144–48
employment, 2
The End of Poverty (Sachs), 173, 174–75
environmental determinism, 171
escalation model of pandemics, 109–11
Europe: far-right parties in, 123–34
European Commission Prevention of and Fight against Crime programme, 86
European Commission's Radicalisation Awareness Network, 89

events, traumatic. *See* traumatic events
evictions, Spanish mobilisation against, 141, 142
expertise, in handling communication, 114
extremist inmates categories, in Belgium, 87

face masks, 112
face-to-face interaction, 43
factical finitude, 192, 194, 196
Falling Man (DeLillo), 70
Fallon, Michael, 125
Fanon, Frantz, 51
far-right parties, 123–34; assumption, 125; as insurgency, 124, 125, 133; Italian case, 128–30; leadership of, 124; mainstream parties and, 123, 124; overview, 123–24; understanding of, 124
fascism, 63, 129; as 'the other', 125
Fassin, Didier, 68
fear, 37; effects of, creating fearful masses, 146; patterns of, 146; risk society, 146; of situations, 62; Weber on, 145–46
Fear: A Cultural History (Bourke), 146
financial crisis, 2, 165
the First World War, 63, 67
Flam, Helena, 145
FOIA. *See* Freedom of Information Act (FOIA)
Foreign Policy, 176
Foucault, Michel, 198, 199, 200, 203, 206, 207
France: attempted regicide in, 199, 207–10; Paris attacks, 41–42, 87
Franco-British intervention in Libya, 193
free competition, 165
Freedom of Information Act (FOIA), 89–90
free market revolution, 165
Freud, Sigmund, 17, 18; on anxiety, 19–21; Derrida and, 46–47; incomprehensible phobias for, 37; on shattered subject, 46; theory of dreams' interpretations, 44–46; unconscious repression, 37, 38, 45–46
Front National, France, 123
frustrated satisfaction, 24. *See also* desire
F section (foreign fighters), 87
Fukushima disaster, 101
'The Function and Field of Speech and Language in Psychoanalysis' (Lacan), 28
Furedi, Frank, 70, 146
future, trauma of, 70

Gamson, William Anthony, 150
Gates, Bill, 176
gaze, 27
Gazette D'Amsterdam, 209
generalised anxiety disorder (GAD), 62
German Influenza Pandemic Preparedness Plan, 108
Germany, 102, 103; critical infrastructure and services in, 107; pandemic wave in, 108; private sector in, 107, 108
Ghana, MVP in, 176
Giddens, Antony, 4
Goede, De, 82
government agencies, security of population and assets, 106
Great Depression, 171
Great Recession, 165
Greer, Steven, 86
gross stress reaction, 67–68
'gufo', 134

H1N1 pandemic, 114
Harvey, David, 2, 173
health and poverty, 171
Hegel, G. W. F., 25–26
Heidegger, Martin, 192–93, 196, 198
Hillyard, Paddy, 86
Holocaust, 41
hope, 153
housing in Spain, 141–42; economic recession, 142

humiliation, 153
hygienic measures, against pandemics, 111–12

identity: affective/emotional investments, 153; collective action, 152, 153; emotions and, 152–54
immateriality, materiality and, 2–4
Independence Party, UK, 123, 124
Indignados movement, 141, 148
indignation, as resistance, 148–55. *See also* anti-austerity mobilisations
Industrial Revolution, 42
'Infantile Sexuality' (Freud), 19
influenza, 109
'Inhibitions, Symptoms and Anxiety' (Freud), 19, 20, 67
Iniciativa Legislativa Popular (ILP), 155
insecurity: imminent, 19–21; sense of, 150
insurance: premium, 105; risk, 105
International Consortium for Organizational Resilience, 65
International Monetary Fund, 165
International Society for Traumatic Stress Studies, 70
The Interpretation of Dreams (Freud), 49
Introduction to the Reading of Hegel (Kojève), 25
Iraqis, 69
Iraq war: Britain's participation in, 214–15
Irène (patient), analysis of, 40–41
Irish community, 86
Isin, Engin, 146
ISIS, 125
Islam: radicalisation and, 85
Italy, 128–30; MSI, 129–30, 132–33

Janet, Pierre, 39, 40
Janus-faced emotion, 150. *See also* anger
Jews, 41
Journal of Traumatic Stress, 70

Kay, Sarah, 170
Kemper, Theodore, 150
Keynes, J. M., 171
killing and sovereignty, 194–95, 205, 206
'killjoy', 134
Klein, Naomi, 173
knowledge: Cartesian rationality of, 30; linear life cycle of, 30; and truth, 196–99
Kojève, Alexander, 25
Koselleck, Rheinhart, 203–4

Lacan, Jacques, 165; on anxiety, 21–31, 126, 165; on desire, 23–26; objet a, 26–29; Symbolic-Imaginary-Real, 28
The Lancet, 176
language of trauma, 39–42; appropriation of, 46–49
Lanzmann, Claude, 41
Left: double death of, 134
Leys, Ruth, 3
liberalism: authoritarian tendencies, 128; neoliberal security policies, 128; as radical security project, 145
liberal political subjectivity, 63
Libya, 193
Lindekilde, Lasse, 90
Local Integrated Security Cells (LIVC), 85–86, 89
Lockett, Clayton, 210–12
logocentrism, 43–44; fallacy of, 47
lower classes, 147
loyalty, 145
Luckhurst, Roger, 42
Luhmann, Niklas, 105

Machiavelli, Niccolò, 205
mainstream parties, 123, 124; centre-left and centre-right, 134; Žižek on, 133
Mann, Heinrich, 17
Mann, Thomas, 17
March of Dignity (Spain), 154–55
Marx, Karl, 66
Marxism, 2
mass surveillance, 82

materiality and immateriality, 2–4
meaning, 3
medicines, 110–11. *See also* pandemics
Medicine san Frontieres, 51
mental illness, 18
metaphysics of presence, 43–44
Michel, Charles, 87
middle class, 147
Middle East, 1
Millennium Development Goals, 175
Millennium Promise, 175
Millennium Villages Project (MVP), 175–77
Mills, Wright, 91
Ministerial Circular on Terrorism and Violent Radicalisation (Circulaire GPI 78), 88
mitigation of risks, 104, 105
mobilisations. *See* anti-austerity mobilisations
Mohamed, Ahmed, 79
Mont Pelerin Society, 169
mood, 192–93
Movimento Sociale Italiano (MSI), 129–30, 132–33
MSI. *See* Movimento Sociale Italiano (MSI)
multinational company, 105. *See also* organisations
Munk, Nina, 176
Muslims, 79; counter-terror measures and, 86; as suspect community, 86–87
MVP. *See* Millennium Villages Project (MVP)
Mythen, G., 84

nachträglich, 48
National Phobics Society. *See* Agoraphobia Society
National Police Chiefs' Council, UK, 90
National Resilience Development Act (US), 72
National Security Strategy, 72
natural disasters, 64

necessary killing, strategic calculus of, 194–95, 205, 206
need *vs.* desire, 23–24
neoliberal authenticity: resilience and, 66–67; trauma and, 70
neoliberal citizenship, 66
neoliberalism: contemporary politics and, 146–47; critics of, 173; discursive hegemony, 154; economic reforms, 165; emotions–politics nexus, 144–48; obsessional neurosis, 166–69; overview, 165–66; shock therapy, 169–73; Western capitalism, 165; zombie, 178
neoliberal subjectivity, 145–48
nervous trauma, 63
networks of outrage and hope, 149
Neumann, Franz, 63
neurosis, 19, 68, 166–69
New York Metropolitan Transportation Authority, 79, 83
Nice, attack in, 90
9/11, 38, 101, 128; as collective trauma, 70; colour-coded terror alerts after, 4; Derrida on, 47; testimony of, 41
Nixon, Richard, 212–13
Nougayrède, Natalie, 41–42
Nussbaum, Martha, 150

Obama, Barack, 79, 193
obsessional neurosis, 166–69
obsessive insecurity, 18
occupational medicine, 111
occupy social movements, 149
Occupy Wall Street, 178
OECD, 65
Oklahoma City bombings, 38
O'Malley, Pat, 71
opacity of truth, 199–200
organisations: crisis preparedness, 114; delegation of responsibility, 106–8; pandemics, 109–14; resilient, 101, 103–5; risk insurance, 105
The Origins of German Tragic Drama (Benjamin), 206

Osborne, George, 124
the Other, 24–25; 'objet a', 26–29; the other *vs.*, 26; primordial affect, 25; structure of, 25; subject's experience of the world as, 27–28

pandemics, 109–14; communication, 112–14; definition of, 109–11; escalation model, 109–11; in Germany, 108; hygienic measures, 111–12; response actions, 111–12
Pantazis, Christina, 86
Paris attacks, 41–42, 87
Parker, Alan, 177
Parkinson, Michael, 215
party system, 1. *See also* far-right parties; mainstream parties
passions, 144
Peck, Jamie, 178
Pemberton, Simon, 86
penis envy, 19
Petersen, Erik, 202, 207
Peterson, Jan, 71
phonocentrism, 43
physiology, 65
Plan M (Belgian programme), 85
Plataforma de Afectados por la Hipoteca (PAH), 141, 155
police power, 66–67
political disaster, 64
political science, 144
political subjectivity, 3–4
Political Theology (Schmitt), 202
Political Theology 2 (Schmitt), 202, 207
politics, 1; emotions and, 126, 144–48; performative phenomenon, 192; reasonable, 133–34. *See also* anti-austerity mobilisations; trauma
politics of anticipation, 65–66
politics of exceptionalism, 132
Politische Grundstimmung, 196
positivistic knowing *(connaissance)*, 198, 207
post-traumatic stress disorder (PTSD), 68–69. *See also* trauma

Post-Washington Consensus, 168
poverty and health, 171
power: modern relations, 201–2; sovereign, 202; zero-sum game, 202
precariat, 2, 142, 147
pre-emptive action, 64
presence, metaphysics of, 43–44
Prevent (British programme), 85, 86–87
private sector: crisis preparedness, 101; national action plans and, 108; resilient organisations, 101, 103–5
privatisation of public enterprises, 107
'Providing Direction on the Road to Resilience' (Newman), 71–72
psychic disorders, 18; perceived dangers and, 20; war and, 67. *See also* trauma
psychic wounding, 69. *See also* trauma
psychoanalysis, 17–18; early history of, 17; emergence of, 17. *See also* Freud, Sigmund; Lacan, Jacques; trauma
psychology, 65
PTSD. *See* post-traumatic stress disorder (PTSD)

radicalisation: causes of terrorism, 88; de Vos' declarations about, 90; as optical machine, 88; preventive measures and tools, 85–90; violence and, 88
Ragazzi, Francesco, 91–92
rationalism, 144
Reaganomics, 165
real dangers, 20
Rechtman, Richard, 68
regicide in France, 199. *See also* Damiens, Robert-Francois
Renzi, Matteo, 134
representation: hierarchy, 43–44; repression and, 42–46; as reproduction, 43; 'wanting to say', 44, 46, 47; Western philosophy, 44
representational act, 43
repression, 19; fundamental act of, 47; potential agent of, 49; psychoanalytical interpretation

of, 48; representation and, 42–46; self-act of, 46; self-concealing, 45; unconscious, 37, 38, 45–46
reputational risk, 112
resilience, 64–67; APA's campaign, 71–72; concept, 103–4; elements of, 104; official documentation, 65; organisational, 65; as personal attribute, 66; political, 65–66; as resistance, 148–55; strategy options and planning, 104; systemic, 65; training, 66, 72; trauma and, 71–72. *See also* anti-austerity mobilisations
resilient organisation: description, 101; risk and, 103–5
resistance, 8–9; indignation as, 148–55. *See also* anti-austerity mobilisations
responsibility, delegation of, 106–8
right to suspicion, 84
right-wing extremism, 123
risk(s), 4; allocation of, 81; concept of, 146; consequences of, 146; cultural prevalence of, 82; danger *vs.*, 105; decisions and, 105; insurance, 105; logic of, 4; pandemics, 109–14; quantification of, 4; resilient organisation and, 103–5
risk communication, 113–14; *vs.* crisis communication, 113; defined, 113
risk displacement, strategy of, 91
risk society, 4, 146
'Road to Resilience' campaign (APA), 71–72
The Royal United Services Institute, 214
rules of truth, 200–201
Russia, 169

Sachs, Jeffrey: Africa and, 173–75; Easterly on, 173, 176, 177; *The End of Poverty,* 173, 174–75; Gates on, 176; MVP, 175–77; Occupy Wall Street, 178; shock therapy, 169–73
Sarraute, Nathalie, 84
SARS pandemic, 109
scandal, truth as, 199

Schmitt, Carl, 193–94, 201–7
Screening Passengers by Observation Techniques, 80
the Second World War, 67
security, 7–8; anthropological need for, 105; government agencies, 106; logic of, 127; meaning-making process of, 126; measures, 64; neoliberal policies, 128; temporalities of, 4–6; threats, 18. *See also* resilience; risk(s); suspicion
self, trauma and, 70
self-concealing, 45
self-consciousness, 30
shell shock, 63, 67
Shklar, Judith, 145
shock therapy, 175
Sicilian Mafia, 128–30
'Sicilian Vespers' Operation, 128
smartphone app, 83
Smith, Adam, 172
Snowden, Edward, 82
social anxiety disorder, 62
social movements. *See* anti-austerity mobilisations
social organisation, 147
social phobia, 62
social strata, 147
Socrates, 23
Sorcerer's Apprentice, 205
Sospiri, Nino, 133
sovereignty: as aporias, 195; decision making, 193; fatal strategies of, 193–96; fracture, 202–3; Koselleck on, 203–4, 205, 206; as miracle worker, 204–5; mode of being, 195; modern conception of, 193, 194; political theorisation of, 202; power and, 201–2; Schmitt on, 193–94, 201–7; stasiology of, 202, 203; strategic calculus of necessary killing, 194–95, 205, 206
Spanish Land Registry, 142
speaking, 43, 44
Standing, Guy, 2, 147

state: and public security, 106–8; responsibility of, 108. *See also* sovereignty
The State of the World's Children (UNICEF), 70
Stiegler, Bernard, 203
Stimmung, 193, 195
Strachey, James, 19
strategic calculus of necessary killing, 194–95, 205, 206
strategy of risk displacement, 91
Strengthening Resilience against Violent Radicalisation (STRESAVIORA), 86
STRESAVIORA. *See* Strengthening Resilience against Violent Radicalisation (STRESAVIORA)
subjectivity, 21
sublime object: Africa as, 174; concept of, 174
sub-Saharan Africa, 173
super objective, 50
surveillance, 82–83; logic of maximisation of, 83; mass, 82; suspicion and, 83; technologies, 83, 84
suspicion: advertising campaigns, 79–80, 83; anticipation, 81–84; modern scientific endeavour, 80; overview, 79–81; police and intelligence services, 80; right to, 84; as technique of governance, 90–92. *See also* radicalisation
swine flu, 101, 109, 114; crisis plans, 110
Symbolic-Imaginary-Real, 28
Syria, 80

Tamiflu, 110
technocratic politics, 6
Tejerina, Benjamín, 149
Tempora, 82
terra infidelium, 129
terrorism: risk of, 83–84; Žižek on, 38. *See also* risk(s); trauma
Thatcherism, 165
threat: construction of, 127; to ego, 20; existential, 204. *See also* dangers; risk(s); security

'Three Essays on the Theory of Sexuality' (Freud), 19
Toma la calle (Spanish), 149
Transportation Security Administration (TSA), 79–80
Trauerspiel, 205–6
trauma, 63, 67–72; APA's campaign, 71–72; atrocities and, 68; Caruth on, 39, 40–43, 44, 47, 48; consciousness of, 69; Derrida on, 70; of future, 70; horror of, 42; incomprehensible notion, 40–42; Iraqis, 69; language of, 39–42; medical literature, 39; neoliberal authenticity and, 70; psychiatry and, 69; resilience and, 71–72; self and, 70; terminology, 68; TV watching and, 69; victims, 68; warfare and, 68; working-class soldiers and, 68
trauma and memory, 70
trauma talk, 38, 46; Furedi on, 70; implications of, 47
traumatic events, 46–49. *See also* trauma
traumatic memory, 69
traumatism, 70
troika, economic programme of, 155
truth: counter-political truths, 197–98; courage of, 198; knowledge and, 196–99; opacity of, 199–200; rules of, 200–201; as scandal, 199
T section (terrorists), 87
TV watching, trauma and, 69

Uganda, MVP in, 176
uncertainty, 1; delegation of responsibility, 106–8; effects of, 101–14; pandemics, 109–14; resilient organisation, 103–5. *See also* resilience
unconscious repression, 37, 38, 45–46
unemployment, 1
United Kingdom (UK): *Channel* schemes, 85, 89; Civil Contingencies Act 2004, 65; Counter-Terrorism Act, 89; de-radicalisation strategy,

85; distrust for refugees, 79; extremist parties, 124; FOIA, 89–90; immigration, 124, 132; National Police Chiefs' Council, 90; *National Security Strategy,* 72; Tempora, 82; West Midland Police force, 80
United Nations: disaster management document, 65
United States: Department of Homeland Security, 72; National Resilience Development Act, 72; Transportation Security Administration (TSA), 79–80; Watergate crisis, 212–14

value chain, interruption of, 105
van der Hart, Onno, 40
van der Kolk, Bessel, 40
Vanity Fair, 176
van Munster, Rens, 65
van Tuinen, Sjoerd, 192
Vietnam Veterans Working Group, 68
Vietnam War, veterans of, 39, 67–68
violence, 1, 21; metaphysical, 49; political, 38; of psychic life, 18; transnational forms of, 84; unpredictability of, 82. *See also* repression; trauma
violent extremism, 85. *See also* radicalisation
viral infections, 109

Walklate, S., 84
war, 63; contemporary, 69; psychiatric disorder and, 67. *See also* trauma; *specific war*
war neuroses, 67
war on terror, 71
Washington Consensus, 168
Watergate crisis, 212–14
Weber, Max, 145; on fear, 145–46; on loyalty, 145
welfare state, 147
Western societies: anger in, 150; campaigns for suspicious activity, 83; transformation into police states, 84; viral infections in, 109
wish-fulfilling theory, 45–46
working class, 2
working conditions, 2
working poor, 2
World Bank, 165
World Health Organization: on anxiety, 62; pandemic escalation model, 109–11
world risk society. *See* risk society

Young, Allan, 68

Žižek, Slavoj, 166; on capital, 167; on Left, 134; on mainstream parties, 133; Occupy Wall Street, 178; on terrorism, 38
zombie neoliberalism, 178

Author Biographies

Andreja Zevnik is a lecturer in international politics at the University of Manchester. Her research is inspired by psychoanalysis, continental philosophy and aesthetic politics and mainly focuses on the production of subjectivity in acts of resistance. Her most recent project examines how the experience of anxiety alters forms of political participation, produces different political/resisting subjectivities and moulds new political realities. She is particularly interested in the various struggles associated with the civil rights movement in the United States and the various *BlackLivesMatter* initiatives. She recently published a monograph entitled *Lacan, Deleuze and World Politics: Rethinking the Ontology of the Political Subject* and is a co-editor of *Jacques Lacan between Psychoanalysis and Politics* (with Samo Tomsic, 2015) and of *Lacan and Deleuze: A Disjunctive Synthesis* (with Bostjan Nedoh, 2017).

Carsten Baran studied political science at LMU Munich and is currently a doctoral candidate at the University of Erfurt. His main research focus is risk perception in organisations, as well as threats and opportunities of digitalisation, analysing the role of internal risk management and risk mitigation in a digital era.

Emmanuel-Pierre Guittet is Professor in International Relations at the Université Saint-Louis (Brussels – Belgium) and associate researcher at the Research Centre in Political Science (CReSPo, Brussels – Belgium) and at the Centre for Research on Conflict, Liberty and Security (CCLS, Paris – France). Since 2000, he has taught courses on terrorism and antiterrorism; political violence, political movements and social change; international relations and security studies for undergraduate and postgraduate students at Sciences-Po Paris, Université de Montréal, Université Libre de Bruxelles and the University of Manchester. He has published extensively on issues of defence and security, conflict and violence, terrorism and radicalisation, and he is co-editor of the Manchester University Press book series *New Approaches to Conflict and Security Analysis* and *International Political Sociology* Routledge book series.

Emmy Eklundh is a teaching fellow in Spanish and international politics in the Department of European and International Studies at King's College, London. She completed her PhD in politics at the University of Manchester. Emmy's research is mainly centred on the post-crisis eruptions of protest in Southern Europe and in particular the Indignados movement in Spain. She is especially interested in how this ties in with questions of democratic theory as well as social theory at large. Current research projects include analysis of social media usage within social movements, as well as the rise (or return) of left- and right-wing populist movements and parties in Europe.

Fabienne Brion is Professor in Critical Criminology at the Université Catholique de Louvain (Louvain, Belgium). She is the co-editor of *Michel Foucault. Wrong-Doing, Truth-Telling. The Function of Avowal in Justice* (2014), and has also published extensively on radicalisation, criminology and extremism.

Henrique Tavares Furtado is Senior Lecturer in Politics and International Relations at the University of the West of England. His research analyses the politics behind different representations of violence (state-led or subversive forms of terrorism) in post-conflict or post-authoritarian scenarios. His work also focuses on human rights and transitional justice, with a particular focus on South America. He has published in *Critical Studies on Terrorism* and written for openDemocracy.

Japhy Wilson is Lecturer in International Political Economy at the University of Manchester. His research addresses the entanglement of space, power and ideology in the politics of development. He is the author of *Jeffrey Sachs: The Strange Case of Dr Shock and Mr Aid*, and co-editor (with Erik Swyngedouw) of *The Post-Political and Its Discontents: Spaces of Depoliticization, Spectres of Radical Politics*.

Mark Neocleous is Professor of the Critique of Political Economy, Brunel University, a member of the Editorial Collective of Radical Philosophy, and the author of eight books, the most recent of which is *The Universal Adversary: Security, Capital and the 'Enemies of All Mankind'* (2016). His work revolves around the mechanisms for managing capitalist modernity through the logic of 'police', 'security' and 'war', and the relationship between this logic and reactionary shifts in political order. His work also focuses on the nature of the political imaginary: how the state has been imagined through categories associated with human subjectivity, how enemies have been imagined as monstrous and how we imagine our political relationship with the dead. He is currently working on the idea of security as an autoimmune disease.

Michael Dillon is Emeritus Professor of Politics at Lancaster University. He has published widely in philosophy and political theory as well as security studies. In addition to the chapter published here, his latest essay, 'Political Spirituality: *Parrhesia*, Truth and Factical Finitude', will be published in Philippe Bonditti, Didier Bigo and Frédéric Gros (Eds.) *Foucault and the Modern International – Silences* (2017). His last book was *Biopolitics of Security: A Political Analytic of Finitude* (2015). His current interests lie at the performative intersection of politics, philosophy and religion. He is working on a new book project provisionally entitled *Baroque Politics: Finitude, Infinity and the Event*.

Norma Rossi is Senior Lecturer in the Department of Defence and International Affairs, at the Royal Military Academy Sandhurst. Her research centres on the relations between states and violent non-state actors, with a specific interest in organised crime. Her doctoral thesis from the University of Reading examined the way the identities of the Italian state and the Sicilian Mafia are mutually and relationally constituted.

Paolo Cossarini holds a PhD in Political Science from the Autonomous University of Madrid. His research focuses on modern and contemporary political thought, democratic theory and populism, the role of emotions in politics, as well as border and migration studies. He has published in *Global Discourse*, *European Political Science*, and *Revista de Estudios Políticos*, among other journals.

J. Peter Burgess is a philosopher and political scientist, Professor and Chair of Geopolitics of Risk at the Ecole Normale Supérieure, Paris, and Adjunct Professor at the Center for Advanced Security Theory, University of Copenhagen. He is series editor of the *Routledge New Security Studies* collection. His research and writing focus mainly on the theory and ethics of security and insecurity. He has contributed to research and foreign policy in Europe, and developed and directed a number of comprehensive collaborative research projects with Norwegian and European partners. He has published eleven books and over seventy articles in the fields of philosophy, political science, gender studies, cultural history, security studies and cultural theory.

CPSIA information can be obtained
at www.ICGtesting.com
Printed in the USA
BVOW03*1156180417
480984BV00006B/12/P